THE BEST OF
CORWIN

INCLUSIVE PRACTICES

T0368824

The Best of Corwin Series

Classroom Management
Jane Bluestein, Editor

Differentiated Instruction
Gayle H. Gregory, Editor

Differentiated Instruction in Literacy, Math, and Science
Leslie Laud, Editor

Educational Neuroscience
David A. Sousa, Editor

Educational Technology for School Leaders
Lynne M. Schrum, Editor

Equity
Randall B. Lindsey, Editor

Inclusive Practices
Toby J. Karten, Editor

Response to Intervention
Cara F. Shores, Editor

INCLUSIVE PRACTICES

TOBY J. KARTEN
Editor

With contributions by

Toby J. Karten · Mara Sapon-Shevin · Victor Nolet

Margaret J. McLaughlin · M. C. Gore

Richard A. Villa · Jacqueline S. Thousand · Ann I. Nevin

June E. Downing · Spencer J. Salend

Bob Algozzine · Ann P. Daunic · Stephen W. Smith

CORWIN
A SAGE Company

CORWIN
A SAGE Company

FOR INFORMATION:

Corwin
A SAGE Company
2455 Teller Road
Thousand Oaks, California 91320
(800) 233-9936
Fax: (800) 417-2466
www.corwin.com

SAGE Ltd.
1 Oliver's Yard
55 City Road
London EC1Y 1SP
United Kingdom

SAGE India Pvt. Ltd.
B 1/I 1 Mohan Cooperative
Industrial Area
Mathura Road, New Delhi 110 044
India

SAGE Asia-Pacific Pte. Ltd.
33 Pekin Street #02-01
Far East Square
Singapore 048763

Acquisitions Editor: Jessica Allan
Associate Editor: Allison Scott
Editorial Assistant: Lisa Whitney
Production Editor: Melanie Birdsall
Typesetter: C&M Digitals (P) Ltd.
Cover Designer: Rose Storey
Graphic Designer: Nicole Franck
Permissions Editor: Karen Ehrmann

Printed in the United States of America

Library of Congress Cataloging-in-Publication Data

A catalog record of this book is available from the Library of Congress.

978-1-4522-1737-6

This book is printed on acid-free paper.

11 12 13 14 15 10 9 8 7 6 5 4 3 2 1

Contents

Preface

Toby J. Karten

Residential settings, separate schools, self-contained classes, mainstreamed into the *regular* class, integration, pull-out, push-in, replacement classes, in-class support services, co-teaching models, consultation, and inclusion. These name some types and combinations of services students with special needs have encountered over the past few decades. When I first began my teaching career, *those kids*—the ones who looked, acted, or learned differently—were either not in the same school as the students who lived on their block, or were in a classroom that was far removed in location and curriculum from their grade-level peers. Inclusion was not an option at that time. As the years marched on, so did society's view of disabilities and inclusive education.

Today, both public and private sectors have changed and become inviting for students with differences, not disabilities. The educational pendulum continually swings back and forth, but now 21st-century learners with special needs are increasingly learning side-by-side with their age- and grade-level peers. Thankfully, inclusion extends beyond classroom stages and enters all aspects of society, from airports and supermarkets to gainful employment. Inclusion of students with different abilities has given birth to a generation that invites and embraces differences.

Drumroll . . . and the winner is . . . EVERYONE! This winning scenario occurs because more and more schools are now setting up inclusion programs that welcome and accept students with disabilities as integral learners who are worthy of receiving high quality educations. Administrators and educators are the inclusion protagonists who collaborate with students and families with award winning standards-based lessons to make inclusion successes everyday realities. Legislators, administrators, educators, and families have high expectations for all learners. Inclusion classrooms, in turn, offer opportunities for increased academic and social participation and an array of successful postsecondary outcomes. Inclusion is more than an educational concept; it's a way of thinking that says students of all abilities belong in the general education setting when the appropriate structures, services, strategies, scaffolding and supports are in place. Today's classrooms are educating students to achieve the knowledge and skills that they need to be effective contributors in a global community. Each and every student's inclusion and contribution is valued.

Since high expectations are no longer optional, inclusion implementation in schools today requires that evidence-based strategies ensure that students are not only afforded the opportunity to be educated in the least restrictive environment of the general education classroom, but the opportunity to achieve curriculum successes there as well. Educators are most often willing to include students, but they are now hungry for additional resources and supports to accomplish that task. Achieving social, emotional, behavioral, communication, and academic acumens require that there is intensive classroom planning; direct skill instruction; whole-class, small-group, and individualized tiered interventions; and consistent monitoring to ensure meaningful inclusion applications and outcomes across school, home, and community settings. Beyond access are the inclusion roadmaps, or strategies, which allow educators to view the general education classroom as a viable path to achieve these goals.

This compilation from a selection of Corwin inclusion-focused books offers the best of the best inclusion strategies and practices, housed in one resource. It is a conduit that seamlessly transfers the research practices into pragmatic classroom applications for general and special education staff. It includes ideas from the primary to secondary grades and across the disciplines that highlight and capitalize upon the strengths and abilities of the collaborative inclusion partners in schools and homes. Inclusion is more than a possibility when professionals possess the inclusion knowledge and skills, positive attitudes, and ongoing professional resources and planning opportunities.

Chapter 1 begins with the foundation of inclusion by examining the legislation, research, and attitudes about inclusion. As the book progresses, we respectively are invited to change the world, write effective individualized education programs (IEPs), and unlock the inclusion doors with good teaching practices for K–12 learners who possess a spectrum of social, behavioral, emotional, intellectual, learning, physical, communication, sensory, and perceptual levels. This book offers expert advice about organizing the inclusion classroom, applying the curriculum strategies and interventions, writing and implementing IEPs, raising academic core curriculum achievements, valuing the integrity and application of inclusion strategies, sharing classrooms as co-teachers, reaching students with moderate to severe intellectual disabilities within the general education setting, achieving valid assessments without enabling accommodations, and establishing effective and crucial school-home partnerships.

Although there are no inclusion solutions, templates, or definitive answers that fit the mold for every student, this inviting book offers a worthy read that whets inclusion appetites to view inclusion as not only a doable, but also a palatable way to capitalize upon the strengths and skills of staff, students, and families. Examine its content to create, evaluate, analyze, apply, and understand, and remember the good teaching practices, reasons for inclusion, and lessons on establishing and determining effective inclusion programs, resources, and services from the planning to instruction and assessments.

The best part of this compilation is its proactive and collaborative nature. These separate chapters have joined together to inform readers of the major inclusion dynamics. The educational experience of each of these contributing experts averages more than 25 years and spans over 50 countries. It is boggling to fathom that these seasoned authors have a combined total years of experience that yields a sum of approximately 400 years! Their inclusion knowledge is an eternal flame that brightens and enlightens. Instead of saying out of the *mouths of babes*, in this case, it is out of the *mouths of the sages*. View these citations from each chapter to gain insightful snapshots of the rich and inviting content that follows:

Chapter 1: "Legislation and research support inclusion, but educators are the ones who must support the child by turning the rhetoric into successful classroom practice."

Chapter 2: "Courage, inclusion, integrity, cooperation, and safety are all essential components of a healthy classroom community in which all students and their teachers can grow in an atmosphere of support and mutual help."

Chapter 3: "With this new emphasis on results, every teacher needs to fully understand what it means to provide access to the general education curriculum in a way that leads to increasing levels of achievement and ultimately better school outcomes."

Chapter 4: "Learning problem locks make life and learning difficult for students with exceptional learning needs. Reading about them could discourage us. But that is counterproductive. What we must do is learn how to use keys to help our students open the locks."

Chapter 5: "Next, here's a huge benefit of inclusion. Instead of singling out students within the room for specialized instruction, drill, redrill, or just about any needs governed by the *paper IEP* or the *commonsense IEP* (it's educationally prudent), why not teach the skill or strategy to the whole class?"

Chapter 6: "Partners must establish trust, develop and work on communication, share the chores, celebrate, work together creatively to overcome the inevitable challenges and problems, and anticipate conflict and handle it in a constructive way."

Chapter 7: "Careful thought and planning are needed to ensure that the adapted lesson clearly reflects what the class in general is learning and the link to the required standards for that class and grade level is strong."

Chapter 8: "In terms of your students, it is important to make sure that testing accommodations are fair and do not adversely affect your students who receive them or their classmates."

Chapter 9: "A belief in sharing the responsibility for educating children is a characteristic of home-school partnerships, which emphasize collaborative problem solving and shared decision-making strategies to provide students with consistent, congruent messages about learning and behavior."

Overall, this book offers tangible ways to exemplify that inclusion is not just a service or setting, but it is a way of life. Its content honors and demonstrates how the integral inclusion principles reap infinitesimal benefits for students, educators, administrators, and families. Inclusion stagnation is never an option, but a continuum of collective knowledge is destined to yield excellent inclusion outcomes for many generations to come. Advocate for inclusion as the first option of service. Enjoy the read and then, of course, the implementation.

Introduction

Toby J. Karten

This volume is an overview of the concept of inclusive practices, featuring excerpts from nine works by recognized experts. The following is a synopsis of what you will find in each chapter.

Chapter 1. Examining the Research Base and Legal Considerations in Special Education

Toby J. Karten

Toby J. Karten untangles the inclusion web with an outline of the legislation, research, and reasons for inclusion beyond compliance. Chapter 1 delves into how inclusion principles set the stage for successful lifelong academic and social outcomes.

Chapter 2. CIVICS: An Agenda for Our Schools

Mara Sapon–Shevin

Through numerous musical, personal, pragmatic, and inclusive analogies and examples, Mara Sapon-Shevin insightfully invites us to translate inclusive theory into classroom practices. Chapter 2 offers tangible ways to embrace and appreciate differences by highlighting the principles of courage, inclusion, value, integrity, cooperation, and safety. Shapon-Shevin presents these inclusion civics connections as a nonnegotiable agenda.

Chapter 3. A Decision-Making Process for Creating IEPs That Lead to Curriculum Access

Victor Nolet and Margaret J. McLaughlin

As Victor Nolet and Margaret J. McLaughlin purport, the individualized education program (IEP) outlines the relationship between goals to instruction and ultimately student proficiency with access to the curriculum standards. State standards are mentioned, and now, with the core standards adopted, this chapter informs its readers how to collectively perform *educational triage* to bypass a child's disability via that roadmap known as the IEP.

Chapter 4. The Locks on the Doors to Learning

M. C. Gore

Through pedagogical metaphors, M. C. Gore outlines the characteristics and struggles of students with exceptional learning needs (ELNs). Chapter 4 offers educators the inclusive metacognition to continually design keys to unlock otherwise closed learning opportunities for middle and high school students.

Chapter 5. How Teachers Teach: Good Practices for All

Toby J. Karten

Karten emphasizes the valuable and applicable things to do in all classrooms on a daily basis, outlining the essential ways to deliver content-driven, standards-based, and challenging K–12 lessons that benefit all learners. Reflections on classroom structure, collaboration, communication, metacognition, spiraling objectives, vertical and horizontal alignments, and interdisciplinary lessons are explored.

Chapter 6. What Is Co-Teaching?

Richard A. Villa, Jacqueline S. Thousand, and Ann I. Nevin

As Richard A. Villa, Jacqueline S. Thousand, and Ann I. Nevin point out, thoughtful and committed co-teachers are effective when each one shares his or her knowledge, skills, and classroom responsibilities. These inclusion experts outline how to achieve effective co-teaching with the ingredients of ongoing face-to-face interactions, positive interdependence, interpersonal activities, monitoring, individual accountability, and administrative support.

Chapter 7. Teaching Core Curriculum to Students With Moderate to Severe Intellectual Disabilities

June E. Downing

June E. Downing offers an array of classroom scenarios across the grades and subjects to delineate ways for students of all ability levels to successfully receive quality curriculum. Accessibility occurs when educators prepare, adapt, and adjust their instruction accordingly whether, as Downing purports they are learning about the Boston Tea Party or solving algebraic equations. Overall, Chapter 7 outlines how complexities are reduced for both educators and students.

Chapter 8. Determining and Implementing Valid and Appropriate Testing Accommodations

Spencer J. Salend

This comprehensive chapter examines the elements and challenges educators face to match valid testing accommodations to individual student characteristics. Assessment expert Spencer J. Salend explores the range of testing accommodations that fall under the headings of presentation, response, timing, scheduling, setting, and linguistically based.

Chapter 9. Effective Home-School Partnerships

Bob Algozzine, Ann P. Daunic, and Stephen W. Smith

Collaborative home-school partnerships yield excellent dividends for all students. Bob Algozzine, Ann P. Daunic, and Stephen W. Smith advocate that schools take responsible steps to build equity, respect, trust, and competent partnering communications and relationships with homes.

About the Editor

Toby J. Karten is an experienced educator who has worked in the field of special education since 1976. She has an undergraduate degree in Special Education from Brooklyn College, a master's degree from the College of Staten Island, and a supervisory degree from Georgian Court University. Being involved in the field of special education for the past three decades has afforded Ms. Karten an opportunity to help many children and adults from elementary through graduate levels around the world. Along with being a resource teacher in New Jersey, Ms. Karten has designed a graduate course titled *Skills and Strategies for Inclusion and Disability Awareness.* She has presented at local, state, national, and international workshops and conferences. Ms. Karten has been recognized by both the Council for Exceptional Children and the New Jersey Department of Education as an exemplary educator, receiving two "Teacher of the Year" awards.

Ms. Karten is married and has a son, as well as a few dogs. She enjoys teaching, reading, writing, artwork, and—most of all—learning. As the editor of this book, she believes that inclusion does not begin and end in the classroom, but is a philosophy that continues throughout life. Hence, inclusion is not only research-based, but life-based as well!

About the Contributors

Bob Algozzine is a professor in the Department of Educational Leadership at the University of North Carolina, Charlotte, and project codirector of the U.S. Department of Education-Supported Behavior and Reading Improvement Center. With twenty-five years of research experience and extensive, firsthand knowledge of teaching students classified as seriously emotionally disturbed, he is a uniquely qualified staff developer, conference speaker, and teacher of behavior management and effective teaching. He is active in special education practice as a partner and collaborator with professionals in the Charlotte-Mecklenburg schools in North Carolina and as an editor of several journals focused on special education. He has written more than 250 manuscripts on special education topics, including many books and textbooks on how to manage emotional- and social-behavior problems.

Ann P. Daunic is an Associate Scholar in the Department of Special Education, School Psychology, and Early Childhood Studies at the University of Florida. For the past 12 years, she has directed applied research projects focused on the prevention of problem behaviors through school- and classroom-based interventions, including conflict resolution, peer mediation, and instruction in social problem solving. Her interest in preventive interventions for students at risk for school failure reflects an academic background in psychology and her experience as a college counselor for economically and educationally disadvantaged students from the New York City metropolitan area. She has also served as a private high school administrator and guidance counselor, collaborating with teachers and parents to address the social and instructional needs of students with behavioral and academic difficulties. She is currently Director of the Prevention Research Project, a four-year study funded by the Institute of Education Sciences to evaluate the efficacy of a social problem-solving curriculum for fourth- and fifth-grade students. Associated research interests include merging social-emotional and academic learning and the role of social cognition in the self-regulation of emotions and behavior.

June E. Downing, PhD, is Professor Emerita of Special Education at California State University, Northridge, and prior to that was at the University of Arizona in Tucson, where she did research and prepared teachers to work in the area of moderate, severe, and multiple disabilities. She is a national leader in the field of special education that targets the needs of students with severe disabilities, especially with regard to inclusive education. She has published numerous articles, chapters, monographs, and seven books on students having severe and multiple disabilities. She served for six years on the Executive Board of TASH, an international advocacy organization for individuals with severe disabilities, and was a past president of the California Chapter of this organization—CalTASH as well as AZTASH. She has served as an associate editor of *Research and Practices for Persons With Severe Disabilities* and currently serves on this board as well as several other professional editorial boards. She is presently serving as an educational consultant, traveling extensively in the United States and abroad to do presentations on various subjects.

M. C. (Millie) Gore, EdD, is Hardin Distinguished Professor in the Special Education Program of the Department of Counseling, Kinesiology, and Special Education at the Gordon T. and Ellen West College of Education at Midwestern State University in Wichita Falls, Texas. She is the author or coauthor of several books, including the Corwin title (with Dr. John F. Dowd) *Taming the Time Stealers: Tricks of the Trade From Organized Teachers.*

Dr. Gore received undergraduate and master's degrees from Eastern New Mexico University and a doctorate from the University of Arkansas. She and her husband, Don, spend their spare time with three adopted dogs: Sir, a Sheltie rescued from a puppy mill; Miss Winnie, an emotionally fragile Australian Shepherd cross; and Miss Ebbie Lou, three and a half pounds of fierce Chihuahua-Papillion independence.

Margaret J. McLaughlin is professor of special education in the Department of Special Education and associate director of the Institute for the Study of Exceptional Children and Youth at the University of Maryland, College Park.

She has been involved in special education all of her professional career, beginning as a teacher of students with emotional and behavior disorders and learning disabilities. She conducts research investigating educational reform and students with disabilities, including how students with disabilities are accessing standards and the impact of high stakes accountability on students with disabilities. She has consulted with numerous national, state, and local agencies and organizations on issues related to students with disabilities and the impact of standards-driven reform policies. She teaches graduate courses in disability policy and has written extensively in the area of school reform and students with disabilities.

Ann I. Nevin, PhD, Professor Emerita at Arizona State University and faculty affiliate of Chapman University in Orange, California, has a proven track record of collaborating with K–12 students and college students in ways that allow their voices to be heard. The author of books, research articles, and numerous chapters, Ann is recognized for her scholarship and dedication to providing meaningful, practice-oriented, research-based strategies for teachers to integrate students with special learning needs. Since the 1970s, she has co-developed various innovative teacher education programs, including the Vermont Consulting Teacher Program, Council for Exceptional Children Collaborative Consultation Project Re-Tool, the Arizona State University program for special educators to infuse self-determination skills throughout the curriculum, and the Urban SEALS (Special Education Academic Leaders) doctoral program at Florida International University. Her advocacy, research, and teaching spans more than 35 years of working with a diverse array of people to help students with disabilities succeed in normalized school environments.

Victor Nolet is Director of Assessment and Evaluation for the Woodring College of Education at Western Washington University. He received his PhD from the University of Oregon. He has been a special educator for over 30 years. He began his career on a project to help individuals with mental retardation move from a state institution in Columbus, Ohio, into community settings. He has worked as a community-based mental retardation case worker and as a program coordinator in adult residential facilities. He has also worked extensively in public school settings, as a speech-language therapist, a high school resource room teacher, and as director of a regional program for high school students with intensive service needs. Nolet was on the faculty of the Department of Special Education at the University of Maryland for three years prior to joining the faculty at Western Washington University. His current interests focus on the impact of teacher education programs on preK–12 student outcomes and the impact of accountability systems on students with disabilities. He is currently investigating the characteristics of indicator systems that link the pre-service preparation of teachers to learning outcomes for public school students. He also is currently involved in an analysis of the validity of teacher work samples as measures of classroom-based practice for science and mathematics teachers. Nolet has served as Senior Consultant for the Educational Policy Reform Research Institute and has written and presented extensively on topics related to classroom-based assessment, assessment systems, and access to the general curriculum. In his spare time, Nolet plays old time and contra dance music on the fiddle, mandolin, and stand-up bass.

A former teacher in the New York City school system, **Spencer J. Salend** is a professor at State University of New York at New Paltz, where he teaches courses on educational assessment and serves as the coordinator of the special education program. He is the author of the best-selling, easy-to-read, and practical book, *Creating Inclusive Classrooms: Effective and Reflective Practices* (2008). Widely known for his work in translating research into practice, he has published and presented on such topics as educational assessment, inclusive educational practices, and students from culturally and linguistically diverse backgrounds. In recognition of the significance of his research and its benefits to others, he was selected as a recipient of the State University of New York's Faculty Scholar Award and the Chancellor's Research Recognition Award. He has also served as a project director and program evaluator for numerous federal and state projects and has shared his work by engaging in a variety of professional development and activities.

Mara Sapon-Shevin is Professor of Inclusive Education in the Teaching and Leadership Department of the School of Education at Syracuse University. She teaches in the university's Inclusive Elementary and Special Education Teacher Education Program that prepares teachers for inclusive, heterogeneous classrooms. She frequently consults with districts that are attempting to move toward more-inclusive schools and to respond more positively to student diversity, providing workshops and support for teachers, students, parents, and administrators. Mara presents frequently on inclusive education, cooperative learning, social justice education, differentiated instruction, friendship, community building, school reform, and teaching for diversity. She works with other educators and community members to design workshops and learning experiences to help participants build relationships across ethnic and racial groups and collaborate for friendship and peaceful coexistence. Mara can often be found leading conference groups in community building, singing, and dancing.

The author of over 150 books, book chapters, and articles, Mara is also the coauthor of a seven-session curriculum titled *Endracism/Endinjustice: Challenging Oppression, Building Allies* (with C. J. Smith, available from Syracuse University, 2004) designed for high school and college students. She is the coproducer of a DVD titled *And Nobody Said Anything: Uncomfortable Conversations About Diversity* (with R. Breyer, Syracuse University, 2005) that explores critical teaching incidents on social justice for faculty in colleges and universities.

Active in the community, Mara sings with the Syracuse Community Choir and is involved in the Children's Music Network. Her most recent book is *Widening the Circle: The Power of Inclusive Classrooms* (Beacon Press, 2007). Her other passions include dancing, quilting, scuba diving, and chocolate—some of which she tries to do at the same time!

Stephen W. Smith is a Professor in the Department of Special Education at the University of Florida (UF). Prior to receiving his PhD in Special

Education from the University of Kansas, he was a teacher of special education students for eight years. Dr. Smith teaches graduate courses in the area of emotional and behavioral disorders and research in special education at UF and has conducted multiple federally funded investigations of effective behavior management techniques, including the study of social conflict and the effects of schoolwide peer mediation programs. As the Principal Investigator of a large-scale prevention science research grant funded by the U.S. Department of Education, Institute of Education Sciences (IES), Dr. Smith is investigating the effects of a universal cognitive-behavioral intervention in the form of a social problem-solving curriculum to reduce student aggression and chronic classroom disruption. He has presented his findings and recommendations at numerous state, regional, national, and international professional conferences. While at UF, Dr. Smith has received three teaching awards and a University Research Award, and he has served twice as a UF Research Foundation Professor. He is a member of the IES Social and Behavioral Education Scientific Research Review Panel and is a member of the Executive Board of the Division for Research, Council for Exceptional Children.

Jacqueline S. Thousand, PhD, is a Professor in the College of Education at California State University San Marcos, where she co-coordinates the special education professional preparation and master's programs. Prior to coming to California, she directed Inclusion Facilitator and Early Childhood Special Education graduate and postgraduate professional preparation programs at the University of Vermont. Here she also coordinated several federal grants, all concerned with providing professional development for educators to facilitate the inclusion of students with disabilities in local schools. Jacqueline is a nationally known teacher, author, systems change consultant, and advocate for disability rights and inclusive education. She has authored numerous books, research articles, and chapters on issues related to inclusive schooling, organizational change, differentiated instruction and universal design, cooperative group learning, creative problem solving, and co-teaching and collaborative planning. She is actively involved in international teacher education endeavors and serves on the editorial boards of several national and international journals. Jacqueline is a versatile communicator who is known for her creative, fun-filled, action-oriented teaching style.

Richard A. Villa, EdD, has worked with thousands of teachers and administrators throughout North America. In addition, Rich has provided technical assistance to the U.S., Canadian, Vietnamese, Laotian, British, and Honduran Departments of Education. His primary field of expertise is the development of administrative and instructional support systems for educating all students within general education settings. Rich has been a middle and high school classroom teacher, special educator, special education coordinator, pupil personal services director, and director of instructional services. He has authored over a hundred articles and book chapters regarding inclusive education, differentiated instruction, collaborative planning and teaching, and school restructuring. Known for his enthusiastic, knowledgeable, and humorous style of teaching, Rich is a gifted communicator who has the conceptual, technical, and interpersonal skills to facilitate change in education. His professional development activities have covered a range including keynote addresses and papers presented at national and international conferences, two-day guided practice workshops for school teams, three-to-five day programs, three-week intensive workshops, and semester-long (15 weeks) programs offered through universities.

Examining the Research Base and Legal Considerations in Special Education

Toby J. Karten

DISABILITY LEGISLATION

Legislation has changed the way society thinks about disabilities and has also driven research to find better ways for schools to deliver appropriate services to children in the least restrictive environment. Basically, students have rights to a free, appropriate public education that addresses their diverse needs. Teachers must understand what legislation and research say about students with differing abilities in regard to the curriculum, instruction, assessment, and daily living skills. In addition, there is thankfully now a huge emphasis upon improving both the academic and functional outcomes of students with disabilities with research-based interventions. Legislative information, standards-based reforms, and strategic research about disabilities are detailed in this chapter, along with the reasons why we need to do inclusion.

INTRODUCTION: WHY DO INCLUSION?

Affective Comparison

Directions: Think of a time when you were excluded from an academic or social activity as a child or an adult. List the emotions you experienced as a result of this exclusion. Contrast this experience with a time when you were included or allowed to participate with others, and list those emotions as well under the appropriate heading.

Inclusion Versus Exclusion	
Inclusion	**Exclusion**

The primary reason for inclusion is the list of positive inclusive emotions. The Latin root of inclusion is *includo,* meaning to embrace, while the Latin root of exclusion is *excludo,* meaning to separate or shut out. Unfortunately, in the beginning haste to include students, administrators in some school districts created the impression that inclusion is just a way to save money, with the unintended outcome that it only burdens teachers. All educational players now realize that inclusion will not succeed without the proper scaffolding. Most teachers are skeptical because there is no script or template to follow for inclusion. Even though inclusion has been in the forefront for a while, it is still in its infancy and will continually evolve. Simply stated, inclusion is a way of life and a preparation for adulthood. It supports the civil rights of all learners. Inclusion may not be the most appropriate placement to meet all students' needs, yet it should be considered as the first viable option. Now think of teaching a student who has similar exclusionary emotions to the ones you listed under the Exclusion column, and how he or she would feel about school. How could you learn, if you were experiencing these exclusionary emotions?

> Any moral here???

ESTABLISHING LEGISLATIVE KNOWLEDGE

Courting Issues

Laws were designed to protect people with disabilities by giving them access to the same societal opportunities as those accessible to people without disabilities. Segueing to a more detailed examination of the special education laws and research, answer the following "true or false" questions.

True or False?

_____ 1. Eighteen percent of the school-age population has a disability.

_____ 2. Cooperative learning is a competitive teaching strategy.

_____ 3. Right angles of learning refers to measuring the classroom.

_____ 4. About 5–6% of the school-age population has a learning disability (LD).

____ 5. Section 504 of the Rehabilitation Act has been in effect since 1983.

____ 6. FAPE stands for Federally Approved Programs for Education.

____ 7. IDEA is an educational program that protects children ages 5 to 21.

____ 8. Teachers can call for a new IEP meeting anytime they need additional support.

____ 9. A student who is not classified can be considered for Section 504 protection.

____ 10. There are 13 specific disability categories under IDEA for students from ages 3 to 21.

____ 11. ADA protects individuals with physical or mental impairments that may limit a major life activity.

____ 12. People with mental retardation, e.g., developmental or cognitive disabilities, or intellectual impairments, are more likely to have children who are also cognitively impaired. (The term *mental retardation* has a negative connotation and should be avoided, even though it is still a formal classification under IDEA.)

Inclusion Web

Special education laws demand that the general education classroom be looked at as the first placement option and the least restrictive environment for students with disabilities. The web below outlines more inclusive particulars about inclusion.

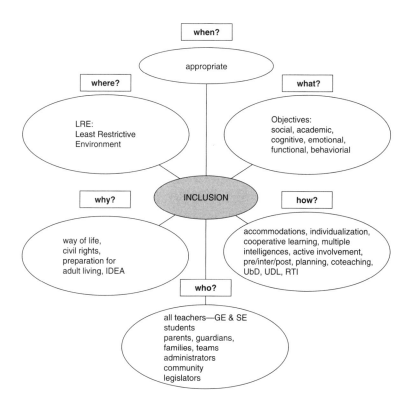

> The "true or false" activity might have been frustrating if you did not have background knowledge about special education or the laws. Compare it to the spelling pretest given to students who have no prior knowledge of the words. Teachers sometimes begin a content area, assuming children have prior knowledge.
>
> Moral: All students do not have the same background knowledge or experience. Learning should be at an optimum, while frustrations are kept at a minimum since they only interfere with and thwart the learning process. Ascertaining what students know before the lesson proceeds then helps to guide instruction. (See page 5 for answers to the true or false statements.)

Research about cooperative learning affirms that it confers both social and academic advantages (Jenkins, Antil, Wayne, & Vadasy, 2003; D. Johnson & Johnson, 1975; Kagan, 1994; Slavin, 1990). Socially, positive interactions increase as students work collaboratively toward a common goal. Academically, students are willing to spend more time learning from each other rather than from the teacher, resulting in better products with often challenging curricula. Cooperative communication also bridges schools to adulthood, since it is a prerequisite for future employment relationships. Getting along with others is a skill that schools can foster through cooperative learning. Team skills, increased self-esteem, improved peer interaction, and higher task completion with learning assignments are some of the benefits that are yielded when structured cooperative groups heterogeneously work together in classrooms. Overall, cooperation is a functional skill for educators and peers in inclusive classrooms to repeatedly foster and model.

Special education (SE) services are provided without cost to the students and families under all three laws of IDEA, ADA, and Section 504, with the least restrictive environment being the first option unless the severity of the disability prohibits that placement. The intention of this next legislative review is to increase the knowledge of SE laws and to *walk the cooperative talk.*

Jigsawing Reading

To review the basic terminology and legislation in the field of special education, cooperative groups equitably divide the legislative readings on the following pages to collectively share knowledge and then answer 6 out of 10 listed questions under the heading Cooperative Legislative Review. This jigsaw technique is a cooperative learning strategy, where teachers direct students to learn and share content with each other. Having choices of which questions to answer empowers the student under the teacher's auspices. Teachers monitor learners and drift to different groups, clarifying questions and concerns, while addressing individual and group thought processes. The following readings summarize pertinent facts about legislation, along with past/present/future concerns about special education and the rights of people with disabilities.

Cooperative Division

1. Everyone reads the IEP/ADA/504 comparison.

Then, equitably divide the following:

2. Details about the least restrictive environment

3. Description of 13 disability categories under IDEA

4. History of the ADA

5. Civil rights for people with disabilities

6. Past, present, and future concerns

Answers to true/false

1. F—Approximately 9% of all children and youth ages 3–21

2. F—Noncompetitive

3. F—It's a hierarchy of learning objectives.

4. T—Students falling under the LD category vary from state to state, e.g., low of 2.2% in Kentucky, 7.7% in Iowa and Oklahoma.

5. F—1973

6. F—Free and Appropriate Public Education

7. F—Ages 3 to 21 (students with developmental delays from birth to age 3 are eligible for services under IDEA Part C, e.g., physical development, cognitive development, communication, social or emotional development, or adaptive [behavioral] development)

8. T

9. T—Examples include a child with asthma (staff trained to administer EpiPen), diabetes (glucose monitoring with trained personnel, access to water, bathroom), food allergies (safe snacks available), juvenile arthritis (word processor, scribe), AD/HD (modified schedule, homework decreased, reduced or minimized distractions). Review this site for more 504 ideas: http://specialchildren.about.com/od/504s/qt/sample504.htm.

10. T

11. T—Life activities include walking, speaking, working, learning, caring for oneself, eating, sleeping, standing, lifting, bending, reading, concentrating, thinking, and communicating.

12. F—Children can be affected by the limitations, but their mother's illnesses during pregnancy and use of drugs and alcohol are major contributors.

Sources:

About.com: Special Needs Children, http://specialchildren.about.com/od/504s/qt/sample504.htm.

Holler, R., & Zirkel, P. (2008). Section 504 and public schools: A national survey concerning "Section 504-only" students. *NASSP Bulletin*, 92(1), 19–43.

IES National Center for Education Statistics: Participation in Education. (n.d.). *Indicator 8: Children and youth with disabilities.* Retrieved May 3, 2009, from http://nces.ed.gov/programs/coe/2009/section1/indicator09.asp.

National Center for Educational Statistics (2003), Institute of Education Sciences, U.S. Dept. of Education. 1990 K Street, NW, Washington, DC 20006, (202) 502–7300, http://www.nces.ed.gov.

National Center for Learning Disabilities, http://www.ncld.org, as cited in http:www.ideadata.org.

National Dissemination Center for Children with Disabilities, http://www.nichcy.org/Laws/IDEA/Pages/BuildingTheLegacy.aspx.

IDEA 1990 & Individuals with Disabilities Education Improvement Act (IDEIA 2004)	American with Disabilities Act of 1990 (ADA) Americans with Disabilities Act Amendments Act of 2008 (ADAAA)	Section 504 of the Rehabilitation Act of 1973/ Impact of ADAAA 2008
Children ages 3 to 21 with disabilities listed below are eligible for a free and appropriate public education in the least restrictive environment (LRE). IDEA is a statute that funds special education programs under the following categories: • Autism • Deafness • Deafness–Blindness • Hearing Impairments • Mental Retardation • Multiple Disabilities • Orthopedic Impairments • Other Health Impairments • Emotional Disturbance • Specific Learning Disabilities • Speech or Language Impairments • Traumatic Brain Injury • Visual Impairments States may choose to add a 14th category of developmental delay for students ages 3–9 who exhibit significant physical, cognitive, behavioral, emotional, or social differences in development, in comparison with children of the same age and for students from birth to age 3, under IDEA Part C. The IDEA defines an Individualized Education Program (IEP), which lists written statements of current academic and functional levels. Long-term and short-term objectives are required	Civil rights antidiscriminatory law that protects people with disabilities from discrimination in public services, if reasonable accommodations can be provided there by state and local governments Physical or mental impairment has to substantially limit one or more life activities (walking, breathing, seeing, hearing, speaking, learning, working, caring for oneself, eating, sleeping, standing, lifting, bending, reading, concentrating, thinking, and communicating) A word such as *concentrating* qualifies a student with attention issues such as a child who may have a diagnosis of AD/HD. Disability determinations are made without regard to mitigating measures, e.g., medication, appliances, medical supplies, low-vision devices (not eyeglasses or contacts), prosthetics, hearing aids, and mobility devices. Person must have a record and be regarded as having such an impairment. This does not include transitory or minor disabilities that have a duration of 6 months or less. Prevents employment discrimination against individuals with disabilities who meet other job qualifications	Civil rights law that stops discrimination against people with disabilities in public and private programs/activities that receive financial assistance Services under 504 protection include special education and general education with appropriate related services, accommodations, and aids. ADAAA extended more eligibility for K–12 students under Section 504. Before ADAAA, students with 504 plans comprised about 1.2% of national school-age children. That number is expected to increase, e.g., to incorporate those with AD/HD, diabetes, food allergies (Holler & Zirkel, 2008). Similar to IDEA, but can include students and staff of all ages who may not be covered under IDEA classifications Disability has to limit student's ability to learn or perform other major life activities Students who use illegal drugs are not eligible for 504 plans. Lists mitigating measures, e.g., low vision (except contact lenses or eyeglasses), hearing aids, cochlear implants, assistive technology Includes reasonable accommodations and modifications

IDEA 1990 & Individuals with Disabilities Education Improvement Act (IDEIA 2004)	American with Disabilities Act of 1990 (ADA) Americans with Disabilities Act Amendments Act of 2008 (ADAAA)	Section 504 of the Rehabilitation Act of 1973/ Impact of ADAAA 2008
for students who take alternate assessments. Accommodations, modifications, and evaluation criteria are listed for each child.

Present levels of academic achievement and functional performance are written in students' IEPs as snapshots of each child's current status and progress achieved. The word *functional* refers to routines of everyday living that are nonacademic, to better prepare students with disabilities for postschool adjustments.

Implementation of early intervening services by LEAs (Local Education Agencies) to include professional development for educators and for related staff to deliver scientifically based academic and behavioral interventions, e.g., literacy, services, supports

Limitation of related services for devices that are surgically implanted, e.g., cochlear implants

Supplementary aids and services are provided in general education classes as well as extracurricular and nonacademic settings.

IEPs are based on each child's individual and unique needs. | Helps to ensure public access to transportation and communication

Can include special education students who are involved in community jobs or those people with disabilities visiting schools

Can refer to private, nonsectarian schools

OCR (Office of Civil Rights) enforces Title II of the ADA, which extends the prohibition against discrimination to public schools, whether or not they receive public funding.

Expanded definition of *substantially limited* rather than mandating a *severe* or *significant* restriction

The definition of *major life activities* says that the impairment only needs to limit one major activity in order to be considered as an ADA disability, although it may limit more as well.

Amendments of ADA affect 504 plans in forms and procedures, increasing the eligibility of students in K–12 grades protected under Section 504. | Limited amount of money a school district can spend if the services are too costly, since unlike IDEA, there are no provisions that districts are reimbursed

State and local jurisdictions are responsible.

Requires a plan with a group that is knowledgeable about the unique needs of the student

Specification of educational benefits, aids, services, class, and assessment modifications, e.g., reading test questions aloud, behavior intervention plans, preferential seating

Periodic reevaluations

Like IDEA, local education agencies must provide impartial hearings for parents who disagree with the identification, placement, or evaluation.

Do not need both an IEP and a Section 504 plan, if student qualifies for services under both, since one way to meet 504 requirements is to comply with IDEA

General education teachers must implement provisions of Section 504; their refusal would mean district can be found to be noncompliant. |

Least Restrictive Environments

According to IDEA, FAPE (free appropriate public education) must be provided in the least restrictive environment (LRE), which considers the general education classroom setting as the first option for academic and nonacademic benefits along with the effects of that placement on other children. Special education services are then linked to both academic and functional goals in what is then deemed as the LRE. The assumption under the law is that every child with a disability is educated in the general education classroom; if this is not the case, then the school district must provide documentation for why this should not occur.

A continuum of some alternative placements is determined on an individual basis with planning, interventions, and documentation of effectiveness merited in all environments. The LRE includes the following:

Least Restrictive Environment Options

- *General education classroom* with moderate support, e.g., consultation periods, in-class support by a special education teacher or other trained personnel for part of the day; or perhaps two teachers, general education (GE) and special education (SE), coteaching and coplanning lessons for all children in the classroom. The two teachers (GE+SE) may work together in an inclusion setting to help students with response to the curricula through strategic planning, specified interventions, and data that monitors ongoing benchmark assessments.
- *Pull-out programs* to support or replace some subjects that may be taught in a resource room. Academic subjects such as reading, language, science, social studies, or mathematics may be taught or supported in another setting within the school. The student fully participates in all other classroom content areas and activities with peers and follows the rest of the class schedule, with maximum social integration. This combination of services allows for periods of direct skill instruction, along with social and academic inclusion with peers.
- *Special education classroom* in a neighborhood school with the possibility of mainstreaming for certain subjects with academic and social goals delineated and adequate supports provided in the general education classroom and all settings. Special class placement can also be self-contained.
- *Special school* if education cannot be provided in the neighborhood school.
- *Home instruction* if the student's needs cannot be met in the school due to social, academic, physical, or medical issues.
- *Residential placement* that is provided in a setting other than the neighborhood school or home, which can include instruction in hospitals or residential institutions. Even though a placement such as a hospital is considered one of the most restricted environments, it may actually be the least restrictive setting for someone who may have a mental illness, if it is deemed the most appropriate one to service that individual's needs.

IDEA has four parts, with these inclusive elements:

Part A: General Provisions. This part includes purpose of special education law, definitions of terms, and congressional findings.

Part B: Assistance for Education of All Children with Disabilities. This part includes state formula grant program, eligibility, evaluations, IEP, funding, procedural safeguards, and preschool grants.

Part C: Infants and Toddlers with Disabilities. This part delineates early intervention programs for infants and toddlers with disabilities, along with findings and policies.

Part D: National Activities to Improve Education of Children with Disabilities. Included here are discretionary programs, state improvement grants, supporting and applying research, personnel preparation, parent training and information centers, technical assistance, technology development, and disseminating information.

When IDEA was reauthorized in 2004 as IDEIA, Individuals with Disabilities Education Improvement Act, major reauthorization points involved a focus on linking goals with academic and functional outcomes connected to research-based response to interventions (RTI). There was also an allowance to remove benchmarks and short-term objectives from a student's IEP unless that student is participating in an alternate assessment, e.g., usually a student with a severe cognitive impairment who responds markedly differently to stimuli, cannot solve problems, or has overall difficulties in communicating or providing a response. States may include benchmarks, but it is not federally mandated. Some states include benchmarks for subjects for which students are receiving replacement instruction, rather than the subjects where students have full inclusion, since the curriculum standards and objectives in the general education curriculum are then looked at as those students' goals. Overall, as with IDEA, parents, guardians, families, school personnel, and students are integral collaborative players in this process who must always consider and focus on matching all students' strengths with appropriate IEP services.

Some examples of appropriate services can include the following:

- Braille for a student with blindness or visual impairment
- Positive supports and intervention plans for a student with behavioral issues
- Communication and language supports for a student with deafness or hearing impairment; a student who is nonverbal; or a student who may have articulation, receptive, or expressive language needs
- Appropriate assistive technology services and devices *needed* by the student, though not always required by the district; e.g., a portable word processor or an instructional assistant serving as a scribe for a student with dysgraphia, although beneficial, may not be part of every school district's standard procedure
- Occupational or physical therapy for students with gross or fine motor needs, e.g., improvement with gait, balance, handwriting

As always, the present level of performance reflects how a child's disability impacts both his or her participation and progress in the general education curriculum. To qualify for services, a child's educational performance must be adversely affected as a result of the disability. The levels of academic achievement and functional performance are the crucial foundations for the development of the IEP, since they drive the appropriate services needed to address, improve, and remediate the impact of a disability on a student's performance. Families are notified of student progress through periodic reports, e.g., quarterly intervals. Most important, IDEA 2004 directs IEP teams to implement instructional programs that have proven track records based on peer-reviewed research that gives merit to a program's effectiveness in both academic and behavioral domains. That means that schools are not arbitrarily using a program, but rather there is a research-based reason for that choice.

Appropriate accommodations for standardized assessments should not modify or alter test results, but provide valid assessments that truly yield information on what the test is intended to measure. Thus, appropriate testing accommodations may include but are not limited to extra time, smaller testing group, different format, or familiar examiner. If a child has an alternate assessment based upon academic achievement standards (AA-AAS), it most likely indicates that the grade-level curriculum is not appropriate, e.g., if the student has a severe cognitive disability. An alternate assessment based upon modified achievement standards (AA-MAS) is still aligned with grade level standards with some modifications such as simpler language, fewer choices, or even less clutter. The frequency, location, and duration of all services are stated in the IEP, indicating how often, where, and for how long the services should be given.

Supporting high-quality, intensive professional development for personnel who work with children with disabilities, including training related services personnel and paraprofessionals or instructional assistants, is essential. The use of technology to maximize accessibility for children with disabilities, e.g., NIMAS (National Instructional Material Accessibility Standards; see http://nimas.cast.org) provides accessible instructional materials such as digital textbooks. Braille or text-to-speech formats are mandated for those students who would require such services. Use of transition services within a results-oriented process to the maximum extent possible to facilitate movement from school to post-secondary activities includes further recommendations for continuing education, independent living, and community participation. Transitional plans are federally required at age 16, and offered earlier if warranted.

The overall philosophy is to help students with disabilities meet challenging state academic achievement standards and at the same time yield high functional achievements. Services for the homeless, foster children, children with disabilities in the military, and the needs of English language learners (ELLs) are also addressed. Reducing misidentification of children with disabilities by encouraging direct skill instruction is something that IDEA 2004 strongly advocates.

Highlights of IDEA 2004 include the following:

- Awarding attorney fees to local education agencies if parent's case is determined frivolous or improper based on legal precedents. Law is written in such a way as to put most of the liability on the parent's attorney for pursuing a frivolous suit. There is also a 2-year time limit to file, starting from the date the local educational agency (LEA) knew of the issue in question, with information kept confidential.
- With reference to learning disabilities, IDEA says discrepancy between achievement and intellectual ability is not the sole indicator for LD classification. It allows for a process that determines if the child is responding to classroom interventions (RTIs). This targets students who are functioning below classroom standards to receive help, even though no discernible discrepancy may be

revealed between tested intelligence and school performance. It focuses on early identification with assistance for early intervention services, without the specific determination of a learning disability. It includes monitoring, assessing, modifying classroom programs, and intervening, instead of referring students for automatic LD identification, giving merit to the provision of appropriate early intervention services in natural environments to meet the needs of individual children. RTI is implemented differently in many states, with a problem-solving approach that includes these overall three tiers of interventions:

1. Core (whole class) receives instruction and monitoring to determine needs and effectiveness of instruction

2. Targeted (small groups) with students who need more strategic interventions identified

3. Intensive (small groups, 1:1) for students with more chronic needs who require frequent monitoring of rigorous interventions

- Excusing IEP team members from attending meetings if all agree attendance is deemed unnecessary beforehand, with IEP team obtaining that member's input prior to the meeting, e.g., parent or guardian signs off with LEA agreement that the member's area of the curriculum or related services are not being modified or discussed in the meeting
- Trying to consolidate meetings, such as combining reevaluations with IEP team meetings
- Federal timeline of 60 days allowed for evaluation, unless states have enacted other timelines or parent or guardian enrolls the student in another school district, or does not produce the student for evaluation
- Changes to a child's IEP do not require another meeting if the LEA and parent or guardian of the child agree.
- IEP can be amended or modified without redrafting the entire IEP.
- Alternative means of meeting participation and communication, such as video conferences, conference calls, and email; e.g., parent(s) and guardian(s) must give informed consent prior to an initial evaluation, with email as an acceptable mode.
- Families have the right to obtain one free independent evaluation for each school evaluation (or reevaluation) if they believe that the evaluation conducted by qualified school personnel was inappropriate. If a school district does not agree to pay for an independent evaluation, then a hearing officer is obtained to determine whether or not another evaluation is warranted. If a private evaluation is conducted, the school district considers the findings, but does not necessarily have to agree with or implement the recommendations.
- Reducing paperwork burdens on teachers by conducting reviews of processes, forms, and expanding use of technology in IEP process
- Reducing number of times copy of procedural safeguards is given to parents or guardians, now only required once a year, unless parents request them again
- Use of positive discipline and other behavioral assessments and classroom approaches to prevent emotional and behavioral violations from reoccurring
- Change in discipline code on a case-by-case basis to ensure the safety and appropriate educational atmosphere in the schools under the jurisdiction of

the local educational agency, allowing schools to expel students without first determining whether the behavior was linked to the child's disability. Students can be removed for up to 45 school days with instruction in another setting (IAES, interim alternative educational setting).

- Recording the incidence, duration, and type of disciplinary actions, and determining if misbehaviors were the result of a failure of the IEP
- Setting up procedures that require the state educational agency (SEA) to develop a model form to assist parents in filing a complaint, and a due process complaint notice
- Delaying due process hearing while all parties attempt to meet to resolve problems, and not allowing parties to raise issues at due process hearings that were not raised in original complaint
- LEA conducts a Child Find to ensure and provide equitable services to children with disabilities who attend private schools within the LEA, without regard to where the children may reside (Office of Special Education Programs, 2005). Part C of IDEA refers to children from birth to age 3.
- Strengthening the role and responsibility of parents, and ensuring that families have meaningful opportunities to participate in the education of their children at school and at home

Resources for Further Updates

Council for Exceptional Children—www.cec.sped.org

Legislative information from the Library of Congress—http://thomas.loc.gov

U.S. Department of Education, No Child Left Behind—http://www.ed .gov/nclb/landing.jhtml

Wrightslaw, information about special education laws—www.wrights law.com

American Recovery and Reinvestment Act of 2009—www.ed.gov/policy/ gen/leg/recovery/factsheet/idea.html

U.S. Department of Education, Building the Legacy: IDEA 2004—http:// idea.ed.gov

Response to Intervention (RTI) and Literacy Collaborative—www.lcosu .org/documents/PDFs/RtI_in_Literacy_Collaborative_Schools.pdf

PACER Center: Champions for Children With Disabilities—www.pacer.org/ about/index.asp

DISABILITY CATEGORIES UNDER INDIVIDUALS WITH DISABILITIES EDUCATION ACT (IDEA)

In order to receive funds under Part B of IDEA, states must assure that a free and appropriate public education (FAPE) is provided to children within 13 disability categories, at no cost to the parents, guardians, and families, in conformity with the individualized education program.

Exact classification language of each state is decided after it looks at federal regulations and does its alignment. As the United States Department of Education points out, the federal role in education is limited as per the 10th Amendment. Education policy is determined at state and local levels. School districts across the United States have many interpretations and implementations of federal disability laws. Sometimes states use different terms, but it is not the label that is important; it is matching the criteria under that disability category. Labels are just for eligibility. There is an enormous disadvantage for students when certain words and a condition title are needed to describe and convey a *disability*, rather than a person. Again, some states use different terms, as words develop negative connotations, but criteria remain the same and are aligned with federal regulations, with varying state interpretations and school applications.

IDEA Categories

Autism

A developmental disability significantly affecting verbal and nonverbal communication and social interaction, generally evident before age 3, that adversely affects educational performance. Added to IDEA in 1990.

Deafness

A hearing impairment so severe that a child is impaired in processing linguistic information through hearing, with or without amplification, resulting in adverse effects on educational performance.

Deaf-Blindness

Simultaneous hearing and visual impairments, the combination of which causes such severe communication and other developmental and educational problems that a child cannot be accommodated in special education programs solely for children with deafness or blindness.

Hearing Impairment

An impairment in hearing, whether permanent or fluctuating, which adversely affects a child's educational performance but is not included under the definition of "deafness."

Mental Retardation

Significantly sub-average general intellectual functioning, existing concurrently with deficits in adaptive behavior, manifested during the developmental period, which adversely affect a child's educational performance. Mental retardation is still listed as a category under the federal law, but some states have chosen other titles due to the associated negative connotation, e.g., intellectual, developmental, cognitive disability.

Multiple Disabilities

Simultaneous impairments (such as mental retardation/blindness or mental retardation/orthopedic impairment), the combination of which causes such severe educational problems that the child cannot be accommodated in a special education program solely for one of the impairments. The term does not include children with deaf-blindness.

Orthopedic Impairment

A severe orthopedic impairment that adversely affects a child's educational performance. The term includes impairments caused by a congenital anomaly such as clubfoot, or absence of a limb. Impairments caused by disease include poliomyelitis or bone tuberculosis, and impairments from other causes such as cerebral palsy, amputations, and fractures or burns that might cause contractures (loss of joint motion).

Other Health Impairment

Having limited strength, vitality, or alertness, due to chronic or acute health problems such as attention deficit hyperactivity disorder, heart condition, tuberculosis, rheumatic fever, nephritis, asthma, sickle cell anemia, hemophilia, epilepsy, lead poisoning, leukemia, diabetes, and Tourette syndrome (listed as a chronic or acute health problem under IDEA 2004), which adversely affects a child's educational performance.

Emotional Disturbance

A condition exhibiting one or more of the following characteristics over a *long period* of time and to a marked degree, which adversely affects educational performance:

a. An inability to learn that cannot be explained by intellectual, sensory, or health factors

b. An inability to build or maintain satisfactory interpersonal relationships with peers and teachers

c. Inappropriate types of behavior or feelings under normal circumstances

d. A general or pervasive mood of unhappiness or depression

e. A tendency to develop physical symptoms or fears associated with personal or school problems

The term includes children who have schizophrenia. The term does *not* include children who are socially maladjusted, unless it is determined that they have a serious emotional disturbance.

Specific Learning Disability

A disorder in one or more of the basic psychological processes involved in understanding or using spoken or written language, which may manifest itself in an imperfect ability to listen, think, speak, read, write, spell, or do mathematical calculations. The term includes such conditions as perceptual disabilities, brain injury, minimal brain dysfunction, dyslexia, and developmental aphasia. The term does *not* include children who have learning problems that are primarily the result of visual, hearing, or motor disabilities; mental retardation; emotional disturbance; or environmental, cultural, or economic disadvantage.

Speech or Language Impairment

A communication disorder such as stuttering, impaired articulation, a language impairment, or a voice impairment that adversely affects a child's educational performance.

Traumatic Brain Injury

An acquired injury to the brain caused by an external physical force, resulting in total or partial functional disability or psychosocial impairment, or both, which adversely affects educational performance. The term does *not* include brain injuries that are congenital or degenerative, or brain injuries induced by birth trauma. Added to IDEA as a category in 1990.

Visual Impairment, Including Blindness

A visual impairment includes both partial sight and total blindness, which even with correction adversely affects a child's educational performance.

Source: National Dissemination Center for People With Disabilities, http://www.nichcy.org.

The following is a mnemonic to help you remember all 13 IDEA disabilities:

All very determined students deserve many more opportunities than school has ever offered.

All (autism)

very (visually impairment)

determined (deafness)

students (speech and language impairment)

deserve (deaf-blindness)

many (mental retardation)

more (multiple disabilities)

opportunities (orthopedic impairment)

than (traumatic brain injury)

school (specific learning disability)

has (hearing impairment)

ever (emotional disturbance)

offered (other health impairments).

HISTORY OF THE AMERICANS WITH DISABILITIES ACT (ADA)

The Americans with Disabilities Act (Public Law 101–336), passed in 1990, was designed to prohibit discrimination against people with disabilities by state and local governments and provide equal opportunities in the following areas:

- Public accommodations
- Employment
- Transportation
- Telecommunications
- State and local governments

ADA's intent was to afford people with disabilities the same opportunities as everyone else to lead full and productive lives. Its goal was to break down barriers for people with disabilities that stop them from achieving emotional and social independence. As a civil rights act, its enforcement enables our society to benefit from the skills and talents that people with disabilities have always possessed, but have been thwarted from demonstrating. The overall goal in schools is to offer reasonable accommodations for students with disabilities to achieve the same results and be given the same benefits as students without disabilities.

The ADA Amendments Act (ADAAA) of 2008 defines *disability* as an impairment that substantially limits major life activities such as breathing, seeing, hearing, speaking, learning, caring for oneself, working, eating, sleeping, bending, lifting, communicating, thinking, reading, and concentrating. Included here are examples of major bodily dysfunctions that directly impact major life activities, related to the circulatory, respiratory, digestive, and reproductive systems, along with the functions of neurology, brain, cell growth, immune system, bowel, and bladder. If the impairment is temporary, such as a non-chronic condition of a short duration, then that person is not covered under ADA. For example, someone with a broken leg would not qualify. Disabilities that are 6 months or less in duration do not qualify. In addition, ADA states that a person must have a record of an impairment, thereby including someone recovering from a chronic or long-term impairment such as mental illness or cancer. The definition expands further by including someone who is regarded as having such an impairment. This involves how others regard or look at someone with a disability. ADA would protect someone who might have a facial disfigurement such as cleft palate from being denied employment because of workers' reactions. It would also allow an individual who has motor impairments due to cerebral palsy to perform a job that someone might incorrectly assume he or she cannot cognitively perform due to the person's discriminatory perception of the individual. The U.S. Equal Employment Opportunity Commission (EEOC) and the Supreme Court had made many decisions that are reversed by the ADAAA in terms of how to define "substantially limits," with ADAAA being less rigorous. In addition, the conditions are looked at without regard to the ameliorative effects of medication, medical supplies or equipment, prosthetics, assistive technology, reasonable accommodations or auxiliary aids, or behavioral or adaptive neurological modifications. This means that the underlying impairment is looked at without considering the effects of the extra devices; just the disability itself is addressed.

An individual is deemed "qualified" for a job position if he or she possesses the skills, education, or other job requirements of the position, with or without reasonable accommodation. This basically prohibits discrimination against individuals with disabilities in the private sector. Court systems are currently interpreting this law on an individual basis.

Examples of reasonable accommodations include the following:

- Modifying a work schedule
- Providing menus in Braille, or a waiter reading the menu to a customer who is blind (the former allows for more independence)
- Installing numbers in Braille in office or hotel elevators and outside rooms
- Allowing seeing-eye dogs in public facilities
- Providing a sign interpreter at theater performances, if the theater is given sufficient notice by someone with a hearing impairment
- Providing assistive listening devices
- Training personnel to administer insulin to people with diabetes
- Removal of existing barriers, if it is readily achievable and can be done without much difficulty or expense. For instance, if a ramp or elevator could not be built because the business is not profitable enough, curbside service could be provided to people with disabilities. However, not every building or each part of every building needs to be accessible.
- Accommodations could be as simple as lowering a paper towel dispenser, widening a doorway, or providing special parking spots.

Courts levy penalties against a business if it shows bad faith in complying with ADA. Acts of bad faith might include deliberately ignoring a person's request, hostile acts, or refusing voluntary compliance. The Justice Department considers the size and resources of individual businesses before civil penalties are issued. Complaints must be valid. For example, refusing employment to someone because he or she suffers from depression, has AIDS, or has a history of alcoholism would be discrimination based upon societal stereotypes, not the person's ability to perform a job. However, someone with myopia or hypertension is not covered by ADA because the condition is correctable (e.g., with eyeglasses and medication). If a person needs to use a seeing-eye dog, the owner of a restaurant cannot arbitrarily deny admittance to the dog and the patron who is blind. Similarly, if the venue is given ample notice, sign language interpreters must be provided at theaters and other public gatherings for people who cannot hear.

Court cases continually wrestle with the meaning of the word *disability*. In 1998, a golfer with a birth defect in his right leg, Casey Martin, was allowed to ride a golf cart instead of walking the course in tournament play. At the time, the PGA thought that Mr. Martin would have an unfair advantage over other golfers, but the Supreme Court determined that a golf cart was a reasonable accommodation, since Casey Martin suffered from fatigue, and walking the course would have been an additional burden for him. In May 2004, the Supreme Court allowed a man in a wheelchair—George Lane, who was a defendant ordered to testify—and Beverly Jones, a court reporter with a mobility impairment, to sue the state of Tennessee for monetary damages since they needed to appear in a second-floor courtroom in a building without elevators. In this ruling, it was determined that there was a failure to provide people with disabilities access to the courts. Other cases concern seniority issues being honored (e.g., person with a disability cannot take the job of a worker without a disability who has higher seniority), whether someone's health might be impacted by a certain job (e.g., working with chemicals if you have a preexisting medical condition), being granted testing accommodations on a graduate level, claiming too much noise interfered with passing a nursing exam for someone with a mental impairment, or whether someone who has chronic fatigue syndrome can adequately perform a job. Topics also include the possibility of granting indefinite periods of leave or open-ended schedules.

Reasonable accommodations mean that with the accommodation in place, the person is otherwise able to perform all of the job requirements. Safety is sometimes a mitigating factor; for example, someone who is blind cannot successfully claim discrimination because he or she is not hired as an airline pilot. ADA enters school settings by guaranteeing that staff, parents, families, and students with disabilities have access to school plays, conferences, graduation ceremonies, and more. It translates to guaranteeing the same access to students with disabilities as peers without disabilities have, e.g., a librarian assisting a student in a wheelchair so he or she has access to books on higher shelves or allowing a student who has cerebral palsy to be a cheerleader. There are no special education rules in ADA; however, it does have an impact on education as well. Overall, as a civil rights act, ADA protects persons with disabilities in the private sector and school settings by guaranteeing reasonable accommodations, services, aids, and policies, as it works in alignment with other state and federal laws.

CIVIL RIGHTS FOR STUDENTS WITH DISABILITIES UNDER SECTION 504

Section 504 of the Rehabilitation Act of 1973 generally refers to adjustments in the general education classroom, but can include other educational services as well. It states the following:

> No otherwise qualified individual with a disability in the United States . . . shall, solely by reason of her or his disability, be excluded from the participation in, be denied the benefits of, or be subjected to discrimination under any program or activity receiving Federal financial assistance. (http://www.ed.gov/about/offices/list/ocr/docs/placpub.html. The regulation implementing Section 504 in the context of educational institutions appears at 34 C.F.R. Part 104.)

Public school districts, institutions of higher education, and other state and local education agencies are required to provide the protections found in Section 504. Both ADA and Section 504 are enforced by the Office for Civil Rights (OCR), while IDEA is enforced by the Office of Special Education and Rehabilitative Services (OSERS), which are both components of the U.S. Department of Education. ADA does not limit the rights or remedies available under Section 504. Students with IEPs may also have 504 plans, while students with 504 plans do not necessarily have IEPs.

For a person to be classified as having a disability, he or she must have a record of a physical or mental impairment that limits one or more major life activities, and be regarded as having such an impairment. A life activity includes functions such as caring for oneself, performing manual tasks, walking, seeing, hearing, speaking, breathing, learning, and working, along with the amended additions from ADAAA 2008, which include eating, standing, sleeping, lifting, bending, reading, communicating, thinking, and concentrating. In addition, other life activities not included in 504 can also be protected. Trained personnel who have particular knowledge of the strengths, abilities, and unique needs of the students conduct the evaluation of students with disabilities to determine placements. The information is not solely based upon one assessment, and must assess the student's need, not the impairment. For example, a student with blindness cannot be asked to count the number of hands raised, but would need to be given an alternate kinesthetic accommodation to test the child's ability to actually count, not his or her ability to see the hands. Placement decisions come from varying sources, including teacher recommendations along with aptitude and achievement tests, and they must take into account cultural, social, physical, and adaptive needs.

Like IDEA, Section 504 states that every effort must be made to educate students with their nondisabled peers, if the academic and social needs can be met there. Appropriate education for a student with a disability might include placement in a general or special education class with or without supplementary services or related services. Specific recommendations must include strategies and delineate accommodations. Disability documentation needs to be provided, and necessary accommodations must be requested. Individuals who qualify for Section 504 protection can fall under any of the 13 IDEA classifications or others such as the following examples; this is not an exhaustive list:

AD/HD	Diabetes
AIDS	Emotional/Psychiatric Disability
Arthritis	Epilepsy
Asthma	Hearing Impairment/Deafness
Cancer	Learning Disability
Cerebral Palsy	Visual Impairment/Blindness

Strategies, names of implementers, monitoring dates, and general comments are examples of elements included in 504 plans. If a student qualifies for services under IDEA, that student does not need both an IEP and a Section 504 plan. The reason is that one way to meet 504 requirements is to comply with IDEA. General education teachers must implement provisions of Section 504, or that district may be found to be noncompliant with the federal law. Again, the general education teacher needs to review the 504 plans of students to effectively implement appropriate educational services. School districts must properly identify and evaluate students with disabilities who need services, supplying an educational plan under Section 504, which is then protected by procedural safeguards. In this scenario, teachers also need proper instruction and preparation to meet an individual child's needs if that child has a 504 plan. Parents and guardians, building administrators, teachers, support staff, and the Section 504 coordinator are involved in developing the plan. The coordinator may be a principal, guidance counselor, special education director, supervisor, or another appointed qualified staff member. A 504 plan can be as simple as including strategies that break down long-term projects into smaller sequential steps, sending home a duplicate set of texts, or maybe sitting a child nearer to the center of instruction— e.g., chalkboards or interactive whiteboards. It may also include training staff how to use an EpiPen (to inject emergency allergy medication) or allowing a child with diabetes more frequent breaks or access to unlimited water. Overall, health and learning plans are determined and outlined in 504 plans.

Section 504 laws apply to elementary, secondary, and post-secondary schools. Trained personnel who assess the needs, not the impairments, must conduct evaluative procedures in order to determine placement. Placement decisions consider the maximum extent to which the student can be educated with his or her peers without disabilities. This may be accomplished with and without supplementary and related services, but must be subject to periodic reevaluations. Parents and guardians are informed about all placement and evaluation actions, and may examine their child's records. Students may not be denied access to any nonacademic activities, such as clubs, transportation, athletics, and counseling, based upon their disability.

PAST, PRESENT, AND FUTURE CONCERNS

Special education was not always accepted in the larger school community. Before the passage of Public Law 94-142 (Education of the Handicapped Act) in 1975, students with disabilities did not receive the most appropriate services. After the act was passed, students were entitled to receive a free and appropriate public education, designed to meet their unique needs. The result of this law was the development of specialized programs and services. However, nowhere does the law explain what *appropriate* means, or use the word *inclusion.* Approximately 20 years later, it was discovered that these separate programs were actually excluding students with disabilities from exposure to the general education curriculum and not preparing them for successful community integration. IDEA 1997 advocated people-first language— looking at the student first, and then the disability. After all, students should not be defined by what they cannot do, but rather their strengths should be highlighted. IDEIA 2004 now mentions RTI as a part of the evaluation for identification of a student with a specific learning disability. RTI is not mandated, but offered as an option, instead of solely using the discrepancy model, which involves a discernible discrepancy revealed between tested intelligence and school performance. Therefore, more accountability is now placed upon the types of instruction, programs, and interventions offered. Yes, students have differences, but now classrooms must proactively offer appropriate interventions before automatic student labeling. Sometimes it's the instruction, not the disability, that's the culprit of lower performances.

Today's thrust is upon inclusion and improving student outcomes with appropriate interventions, but new concerns are already becoming evident. Debates between teachers and administrators include topics such as time for planning and collaboration, types of supports and assessments given, modifications of curriculum, how to divide instructional time to equally provide learning for all groups of learners, behavioral concerns, and accountability issues. Often teachers are so overwhelmed by their busy days that they are unable to preplan, evaluate, and assess lessons with cooperating teachers. In the ideal world, common planning time should be allotted in both general and special education teachers' schedules, giving them the time to design and evaluate lessons. Consistent constructive review of both successful and unsuccessful teaching methodology is an integral inclusionary factor. Response to interventions has entered classrooms, but just who determines what constitutes an effective intervention and assessment is still an issue in its infancy, morphing with each new report and study. Reliability and validity of programs require further determination.

Teachers are seldom unwilling to include students, but some lack the training or experience regarding what strategies, programs, or academic or behavioral scaffolding need to be provided, without sacrificing any one group of learners. State and national curricula further complicate these issues and cause concern about taking time away from instruction of much-needed skills, as well as concerns about individuality of instruction. Accountability of student performance raises the following question among teachers, students, parents, administrators, and learners:

"Does fair mean equal?"

Outcomes and delineated standards for all students have become our nation's goal. Standards have now been applied to all students, with no one taken out of the accountability loop as with past SE practices. Several studies (Mostert & Crockett, 2000; Norris & Schumacker, 1998; Skiba et al., 2008) have revealed that in the past, schools have disappointed former special education students with ineffective interventions. Now, research highlights that aligning the content standards with assessments and appropriate instruction results in higher learning outcomes for all students, those with and without disabilities (Browder, 2006; Thurlow, 2003; Wiener, 2005).

Special education teachers face further challenges as they try to balance and align the standards with students' IEPs and the assigned curriculum. Educators feverishly think of ways that students with disabilities can achieve mastery or progress toward those standards. The curriculum is not diluted for any group of students, but taught in sub-skills that reflect the standards in smaller, more palatable bites. Individual strategies, materials, and accommodations are geared toward achieving higher outcomes for all students. As the years progress, hopefully assessments and accountability systems will highlight weaknesses in school systems, not in students.

This will require both GE and SE teachers to have a greater knowledge of the curriculum, content standards, and the strengths of students with dis*abilities* who are now expected to achieve those standards. Educators of students with more severe cognitive disabilities also take steps to help their students achieve strides toward the curriculum standards. Ignoring improvements toward achievements is simply not an option for any group of students. Inclusion is marching onward, with everyone honoring abilities and ways to increase academic, behavioral, social, emotional, and functional levels in all domains. Overall, the SE trend is now moving from access to accountability (Chambers, 2008). Thankfully so!

Unfortunately, at times, an abundance of paperwork has scared away many teachers from continuing in the field, since quite often their time is deducted from much-needed student instruction in order to comply with writing IEPs and data reports, attending meetings, and keeping on top of changes in legislation. In the attempt to "get it right," families, general and special education teachers, and all students can be frustrated by the sometimes confusing system, which makes it harder to focus on helping students with disabilities achieve academic and social successes. Some of the revisions in IDEA 2004 address that—e.g., reducing the number of meetings, allowing revision consent by email, combining meetings.

Inclusion is a fabulous concept, but the pragmatics involved do not always result in its proper implementation. Inclusion has sometimes actually resulted in *ex*clusion. Students with disabilities who are included in a general classroom are at times overwhelmed by the pace, complexity, and amount of work they are expected to do, and prior knowledge they are assumed to have. Special educators should be integral members of the larger school community, but this is often not the case. Special educators and students possess the ability to make integral, productive contributions to the classroom. All students and teachers need to be treated as equals both in the general classroom and across the whole school district. As delineated in Chapter 6 on collaboration, special education and general education teachers can work as partners to instruct all students in shared classrooms with ability levels ranging from nonverbal with autism to gifted.

The educational goals of students with disabilities are just as valid as those of other students. High expectations need to be developed for all students in the classroom, but without proper supports, children and teachers can become lost and frustrated by the system. Sometimes, wonderfully conducted research offering promising techniques seems difficult or impossible to pragmatically translate into classrooms composed of students with mixed abilities.

General education teachers want all students to succeed, but they need more direction and training on how to differentiate instruction without sacrificing any one group of students. Inclusion has sometimes dangerously erased direct skill instruction that was formerly given in separate classrooms. Public Law 94-142, the grandmother of IDEA, originally called the Education of All Handicapped Children Act, which was passed by Congress back in 1975, was designed to provide services to students whose academic needs were not being met in the general education classroom. Today, unless the dynamics of the general education classroom are changed, these academic, social, cognitive, and emotional needs will still not be met. RTI can and should be used to monitor progress and adjust interventions accordingly, yielding benefits for all learners who are struggling with the curricula, not just those learners who receive special education (Chambers, 2008). Interventions are offered in general education classrooms first, before students are assumed to require special education services. The thinking here is that perhaps it is the instruction that is the issue, rather than the student who is disabled. Many families, administrators, educators, related staff, and students have concerns and sometimes diverse desires, interpretations, and ways to think about both general and special education deliveries, services, and interventions.

Somewhere in *edutopia,* a happy balance needs to be achieved with interventions to determine what kind, what extent, how, where, and who will deliver the interventions.

Special education is headed in the right direction. With more fine-tuning, this transitional stage will effectively ride the current turbulent waves. Education never worked well with a one-size-fits-all philosophy. Inclusion is a great idea, if it is properly implemented, but should not be considered the only option if the child's academic and social needs are not being met by placement in the general classroom. Accountability, along with appropriate identifications and interventions, is essential. Special education is an *evolutionary,* not a *revolutionary,* process. Significantly reducing the bureaucracy, paperwork, and litigiousness that too often springs from disagreements over implementation of the law; settling school discipline issues; and figuring out how to continually and appropriately fund IDEA and just which academic and behavioral interventions are appropriate ones are not simple issues. Education is a complex issue for parents, guardians, teachers, administrators, all staff members, and children of all abilities. However, always keep in mind that the ultimate goal is successful outcomes for all!

COOPERATIVE LEGISLATIVE REVIEW

Directions: As a review of these readings, choose either Option 1 or Option 2.

Option 1: Cooperatively answer 6 of the following 10 questions on a separate piece of paper. Circle the question numbers you will be answering. Each person should write down the answers (true cooperative learning).

Option 2: If your group has access to multiple computers, cooperatively divide, complete, and then share questions and answers to the Legislative Web Quest (Questions 1–5) instead.

Rationale for collaborative options: Choosing questions or assignments to answer or complete empowers learners. Questions are teacher-guided, but students gain some control and responsibility as self-regulated learners. Within your classrooms, these types of choices can be offered from early grades onward to continually develop and foster independent learning and increased student responsibility. In addition, completing assignments collaboratively fosters interpersonal and team skills.

Option 1:

1. Describe three laws that protect persons with disabilities.
2. List the 13 IDEA categories.
3. Who can benefit from a 504 plan?
4. Think of a disability scenario that the ADA is protecting.
5. Compare and contrast the benefits and pitfalls of inclusion.
6. If you could amend any of the laws, what changes would you make?
7. Where do you see special education going in the next 10 years?
8. Tell how children with disabilities can benefit from inclusion.
9. How can general education teachers influence a child's classroom success?
10. Do you think special education is going in the right direction?

Option 2   **Legislative Web Quest**
1. Identify and briefly describe three major disability laws that affect students in school settings.
2. Name the elements of an IEP.
3. Briefly describe two court cases and their implications for inclusive environments. (Possible choices from 18 below)
4. Identify the elements listed in a student's transitional plan.
5. What rights do families have in formulating IEP documents?
Use these Web sites for your responses: www.wrightslaw.com, www.cec.sped.org, www.nichcy.org, http://IDEA.ed.gov

Court Cases	Main Concepts
1. *Pennsylvania Association for Retarded Children v. Commonwealth of Pennsylvania*, 1972	Students with disabilities are not excluded from appropriate educational opportunities
2. *Mills v. Board of Education of the District of Columbia*, 1972	Need to provide whatever specialized instruction will benefit the child, with due process and periodic review (precursor of IDEA)
3. *Board of Education of the Hendrick Hudson Central School District v. Rowley*, 1982	FAPE (Free Appropriate Public Education)
4. *Brookhart v. Illinois State Board of Education*, 1983	Passing state tests to receive HS diplomas
5. *School Board of Nassau County, Florida v. Arline*, 1987	Defenses under 504—reasonable accommodations
6. *Honig v. Doe*, 1988	Suspension & expulsion
7. *Timothy W. v. Rochester, New Hampshire School District*, 1989	Proof of benefit not required, there is zero reject

Court Cases	Main Concepts
8. *Sacramento City Unified School District, Board of Education v. Rachel H.*, 1994	LRE (Least Restrictive Environment)—educational & nonacademic benefits weigh in as well, e.g., social, communication
9. *Gadsby v. Grasmick*, 1997	States to ensure compliance with IDEA
10. *Sutton v. United Airlines, Inc.*, 1999	Disability defined with corrective devices
11. *Cedar Rapids v. Garret F.*, 1999	Related services
12. *Toyota Motor Manufacturing, Kentucky, Inc. v. Williams*, 2002	Substantial limitation in major life activity under ADA
13. *AW ex rel. Wilson v. Fairfax County School Board*, 2004	Manifestation determination—*Did the disability impact the student's ability to control the behavior?*
14. *Schaffer ex rel. Schaffer v. Weast*, 2005	Burden of proof in a due process hearing on party seeking relief
15. *Arlington Central Sch. Dist. Bd of Ed v. Murphy*, 2006	Entitlement to parents to recover fees paid to expert witnesses if they prevail
16. *Winkelman v. Parma City School District*, 2007	Parents who act as their child's lawyer in IDEA actions, if they are not licensed attorneys
17. *Board of Ed of City of New York v. Tom F.*, 2007	Reimbursement for private education if student was not enrolled in public school
18. *Forest Grove School District v. T. A.*, 2009	Reimbursement for private special-education services when a public school fails to provide FAPE, free appropriate public education

IMPLICATIONS OF THE ELEMENTARY AND SECONDARY EDUCATION ACT (ESEA)

Let me begin this section with a few questions before we delve into the *meaty* implications of ESEA. When George W. Bush reauthorized ESEA as NCLB, No Child Left Behind, at the turn of the millennium, panic permeated throughout school districts, with teachers asking a question such as

> *If my students fail the standardized tests, will I be fired?*

A decade later, teachers asked a question such as

> *How many times do I have to administer this benchmark test?*

In the future, teachers may ask,

> *Whatever happened to the good old days when we had time for things other than tests, such as fun learning activities?*

Now let's review the history of NCLB before we return to those three questions. In its legislative infancy, NCLB was ESEA, the Elementary and Secondary Education Act of 1965. In the years 2001 to 2002, ESEA was updated and signed into law by President George W. Bush, with the intention that it would provide a better education for all children. Schools are now held more accountable for results, while families are given additional school selection options. In addition, methods of teaching and teacher qualifications are more heavily scrutinized. NCLB focuses on improving the academic achievement of all students, allowing everyone access to future progress and lifelong achievements, including those from the highest- to the lowest-income schools. The expanded definition includes the application of rigorous, systematic, and objective procedures to obtain reliable and valid knowledge relevant to education activities and programs (in the amended Section 9101-37 of ESEA). This includes rigorous data analysis with multiple measurements, observations, controls, and designs. Peer-reviewed academic journals are valued over educator magazines or practitioner journals. Instead of snapshot approaches with short-term results, assessments now involved longitudinal data that reveal and advocate more accountability, which impacts the selection of instructional programs. The data and results are viewed as valuable information and tools that yield improvements. Annual reading and math assessments are in place, with achievements made in *adequate yearly progress* (AYP). Children with disabilities are included in district testing, allowing for a small percentage of students with more significant cognitive impairments to receive *alternate assessments based on modified academic achievement standards* (AA-MAS). The Department of Education designates a status label for assessment systems in its effort to both enforce the act and realize the intricacies involved with the development, compliance, and implementation of valid standards and assessments. Under ESEA, school report cards are provided, indicating annual progress from state, district, and individual schools. Federal money is available to recruit more qualified teachers and be put toward targeted needs. Teachers are encouraged to look at *what* is taught, and *how* it is taught, using research-based and scientifically proven methods. Choices are given to parents and students with access to supplemental educational services for those students attending failing schools, along with sanctions levied for schools that do not comply with the legislation.

As this book is going to press, the ESEA act, which is also known as NCLB, will again be reauthorized, with talk of not only content changes but a name change as well. The goal is to strengthen the act with more overall accountability and pragmatic school connections. The following represents some recommendations for improvements in the act from educational organizations:

Sample of American Association of School Administrators (AASA) recommendations:

- Establishing evaluation scales to measure success/failure in working toward performance standards
- Use of accountability systems with either growth or status models to judge school successes
- Targeting assistance to students with highest needs with tailored accountability systems, e.g., students with disabilities, English language learners (ELLs)

- Ongoing improvement and alignment of state standards to match knowledge and skills schools expect students to master
- Focus on helping improve achievements among highest-poverty students

American Federation of Teachers (AFT) recommendations include the following:

- Allowing credit for system's progress or proficiency, e.g., school not solely judged upon strict percentages in each labeled subgroup if it already starts with a larger number of students who are academically behind
- Not sacrificing other subject areas outside those being tested, but the integration of content areas with other subjects, e.g., reading, math, science involved across disciplines, including continual focus on lessons that involve art, music, social studies, world cultures, physical education, alongside the reading, math, science, and more
- Data accumulated should be disseminated in a timely fashion, e.g., before the onset of the next school year, to be appropriately applied to classrooms
- Modified tests and appropriate guidelines for students with disabilities and English language learners, allowing students appropriate assessments and accommodations, e.g., guided by IEPs, linguistically modified
- Allowing schools to receive interventions and continued financial support to foster and maintain improvements
- Establishing a learning environment index that relates to students' achievements, e.g., gauging professional supports available, materials, safe conditions

Sources: http://www.ed.gov/policy/elsec/leg/esea02/index.html, http://www.ed.gov/nclb/landing.jhtml, http://www.thefreelibrary.com/AASA+responds+to+NCLB+commission+report-a0162242259, http://www.aft.org/topics/nclb/downloads/NCLBRecommend060606.pdf

Now, back to those original questions and some answers:

If my students fail the standardized tests, will I be fired?

No, but the types of programs, instructional strategies, accommodations, frequency, duration, and location of interventions, assessments, and evaluations will be reviewed and revised to determine just why the learning gaps exist. The focus needs to address how to better deliver targeted curriculum standards—not pointing fingers, but promoting remediation.

How many times do I have to administer this benchmark test?

It's not about how many times a benchmark test is given, but what that benchmark test reveals in terms of instruction and curricular focus. It's better to have more formative assessments, rather than being surprised by one giant summative evaluation! Benchmark tests hopefully reveal the effectiveness of strategies and interventions, with students' responses telling administration and staff what standards need to be addressed or what deliveries require fine-tuning.

*Whatever happened to the good old days when we had time for
things other than tests, such as fun learning activities?*

With creativity, perseverance, and diligence regarding the curriculum standards, teachers will realize that assessments do not replace *fun*, but accompany tangible learning results. The distribution of time to concentrate on learning does not translate to the deletion of other activities, but must correlate with the standards and all subjects. Then the message is transmitted to students that learning is fun and not just about the test! Accountability is crucial, but can only be accomplished if it accompanies higher student motivation.

Accountability Questions to Ponder

- How is increased accountability for students with disabilities a step in the right direction?
- What is the impact of reauthorization of NCLB in individual students from different ability groups?
- Can a revised ESEA/NCLB eventually replace IDEA?
- What impact will sanctions have on schools with students with disabilities?
- Will teachers teach to the test, or can all subjects be equally balanced?
- What will the educational picture look like in the next few decades?

(Answers can and will vary.)

TRANSLATING RESEARCH INTO LEARNING STRATEGIES THAT WORK

Researchers and Professional Literature Say the Following:

- Structured, well-delivered, research-based interventions positively influence student performance within inclusive environments, honoring high expectations and best practices for all students (Beattie, Jordan, & Algozzine, 2006; Damasio, 2003; Karten, 2007b; LeDoux, 2002; McNary, Glasgow, & Hicks, 2005; Sousa, 2007).
- Successful quality inclusion programs involve team approaches with collaborative efforts from schools and families, allowing for flexibility to perceive when something works well and adaptation to change it when it does not work (Willis, 2009).
- Social skills do not come naturally to students with autism and must be directly taught if they are going to be mastered, e.g., what to explicitly do and say in each situation (Baker, 2005).
- The stages of backward design—or *understanding by design* (UbD)—involve identifying the desired results first, determining acceptable evidence, and then planning experiences and instruction accordingly. This includes the acquisition of important information and skills, making meaning of the content, and then effectively transferring that learning beyond the school (Wiggins & McTighe, 2005).

- Teachers must understand the role of culture in human development and schooling in order to make good decisions about classroom management and organization (Rothstein-Fisch & Trumbull, 2008).
- "A teacher can be ten times more effective by incorporating visual information into a classroom discussion. . . . Our brains have more receptors to process the images coming in than the words we hear" (Burmark, quoted in Association for Supervision and Curriculum Development [ASCD], 2002, n.p.).
- Teachers need to present new information in smaller chunks and offer strategic stopping points for demonstration, descriptions, summarization, discussion, and predictions. Teachers also need to take steps to establish and communicate learning goals and track student progress as they interact with that new knowledge (Marzano, 2007).
- "Students need to know that they're accepted. I had one student with a learning disability; everyone told him what was wrong with him, but no one tried to help him realize what was good in him" (Tomlinson, quoted in ASCD, 2002, n.p.).
- "Students need multiple opportunities to meet standards, and those opportunities should include differentiated instruction, accommodations and modifications, and opportunities for advanced learners" (Harris, quoted in ASCD, 2002, n.p.).
- Teacher efficacy (thinking that you will influence students' successes), collaborative relationships, mentoring/advocacy, and community building are essential components of inclusive classrooms (Cramer, 2006).
- The people who work in the school building, e.g., principal, assistant principals, educators, instructional assistants, and all staff, along with their families, are the actual *inclusive experts* who know the students the best (Hammeken, 2007).
- "Traditionally special education legislation has focused on compliance with the procedure for providing special services described in the federal and state laws. However, the philosophy and the mandates contained in the 1997 Individuals with Disabilities Act (IDEA) shifted that accountability to focus on how students are meeting the new standards, thus increasing expectations for students with disabilities" (U.S. Department of Education, 1998, n.p.).
- IDEIA 2004 includes RTI, response to interventions, a different way to identify students with disabilities and intervene with instruction and assessments for students who may be struggling (www.nasponline.org/advocacy/rtifact sheets.aspx).
- Schools who do not have forward-thinking programs for students with special needs are usually the ones with families who do not advocate for their children (Tramer, 2007).
- The absence of interventions in the early school years has a negative impact on academic, emotional, social, and behavioral growth of students with reading and behavior disorders (Cybele, 2003; Levy & Chard, 2001; Trout, Epstein, Nelson, Synhorst, & Hurley, 2006).
- Universal design of curriculum and instruction offers learning alternatives to students with and without disabilities and provides a framework to both create and implement lessons that value flexible goals, methods, and assessments (Pisha & Stahl, 2005; www.cast.org).

- Discussions, communications, connections, and learning in context help learners in inclusive classrooms develop better literacy and numeracy competencies along with higher cognitive skills (Chorzempa & Lapidua, 2009; Graham & Harris, 2005; Hyde, 2007; Karten, 2009; Steen, 2007).

- "The public wants schools to hold kids accountable, but they also want schools to recognize that kids are kids" (J. Johnson, 2003, p. 37).

- "Teachers who were involved in inclusive school programs felt that the students with disabilities could benefit from the curriculum of the general education classroom if two basic changes in classroom practice were made . . . modifying the curriculum to enhance the relevancy for each student and modifying instructional techniques. . . . Teachers' interviews felt that the curricular and instructional changes were made possible by collaborative relationships developed, as teachers worked together to determine methods that could be used to best meet the needs of all learners. . . . Specific difficulties that impeded effective teaming included problems with scheduling and uncooperative teachers. The teachers commented that having enough time for planning is a critical aspect of effective teaming" (McLesky & Waldron, 2002, p. 53).

- Coteachers who work together in inclusive classrooms collaboratively improve student outcomes with the mastery of the curriculum standards and emotional growth (Friend & Cook, 2003; Karten, 2007b; Nevin, Cramer, Voigt, & Salazar, 2008).

- "The way to ensure that alternate assessment provides a vehicle for learning new skills is to include students in the construction, monitoring, and evaluation of their own portfolio work. Not only will this process reduce the burden on teachers, but students will have greater ownership of their own learning as they develop important component skills to the essential, long-term outcome of self-determination" (Kleinert, Green, Hurte, Clayton, & Oetinger, 2002, p. 41).

- Learning that is associated with students' interests and experiences is more likely to be retrieved from students' prior knowledge (Allsopp et al., 2008a; Karten, 2007b, 2008a, 2009).

- "Having opportunities to make choices in academic tasks can provide the environmental predictability needed to minimize inappropriate behaviors of students, while strengthening appropriate responses and increased levels of engagement. . . . For students with EBD [emotional behavioral disability], predictability and control may be critical concepts and skills that are necessary for appropriately coping with the environment" (Jolivette, Stichter, & McCormick, 2002, p. 24).

- Research-based instruction yields information on how children learn and how teachers need to teach with continual screening of essential skills, early interventions, progress monitoring, and data-driven decisions (Russo, Tiegerman, & Radziewicz, 2009).

- "We must still go a long way toward defining what curricular access means for *all* students. *We must also become more strategic* and more committed to designing professional development for general and special educators that promotes mutual understanding of standards and curricula and of how diverse students learn. Instructional planning must result in more than a sequence of lesson plans: it must become a road map for bringing a group of students on *different routes to some common destinations*" (McLaughlin, 2000, p. 31, emphasis added).

- Students with special needs require academic and social support with effective accommodations, modifications, and guidance to achieve educational and emotional gains in inclusive settings, e.g., differentiation of instruction, honoring individual student strengths, needs, and potentials (Beattie et al., 2006; Karten, 2008a, 2009; Littky, 2004; McKinley & Stormont, 2008; Salend, 2005; Tomlinson, 2008).

My Pragmatic Research Investigation

My research says . . .

Source:

INCLUSION AND THE STUDENT WITH DIS*ABILITIES*

When *inclusion* replaced the word *mainstreaming*, many teachers and professionals embraced the idea while others thought if they resisted it enough, it might go away. Mainstreaming had students included in classrooms for subjects they were more prepared for. Inclusion says, let's include the students and make it work. There are no guidelines, but listed on the next page are several ways students, teachers, and peers can fit in. As the book progresses, all of these will be delineated further, with specific curriculum classroom applications.

Activity: Each person puts his or her name on an index card or Popsicle stick that is then randomly pulled from a hat, can, or jar to read the numbered inclusion ideas listed below. Each number on the list can also be clapped to focus attention, thereby adding a musical/rhythmic component. This procedure establishes equity in the classroom and stops the *ooh-ooh child* from volunteering to read everything or answering all of the questions. It also wakes up sleepers. In the classroom, sensitivity and variation can be used to help students with reading difficulties; e.g., have students with and without reading difficulties select the Popsicle sticks to be part of the activity, instead of to determine who reads, or intermittently ask some students to paraphrase statements instead so they are not embarrassed by reading words that are too difficult in front of the class. Always mix it up by also asking the best readers in the class to do non-reading activities as well.

Eighteen Inclusive Principles

1. Ask for help.

2. Differentiate content (what you are teaching) from process (how you teach—delivery and strategies).

3. Work with specialists as a team to modify and adapt the curriculum to meet the special needs of students while allowing for flexibility in scheduling.

4. Teach students how to learn by offering lessons in study skills along with the curriculum.

5. Get the whole class involved so that everyone is working together to help each other by establishing a team mentality.

6. Use cooperative learning and let peers work together to develop friendships.

7. Know when to change course.

8. Increase your own dis*ability* awareness.

9. Be aware of the physical classroom setup.

10. Provide directions in written form for children with auditory problems and in verbal form for those with visual difficulties.

11. Teach to strengths while avoiding weaknesses to minimize frustrations; e.g., honor students' favored intelligences after informal inventories.

12. Help students with methods to organize their written work.

13. Collect files containing additional higher-level materials and activities for students who require more challenges.

14. Allow students to work on various assigned tasks.

15. Be aware of multiple intelligences.

16. Value opinions of families and community.

17. Model appropriate behavior.

18. *Believe in yourself and your students!*

INCLUSION IS . . .

> *Directions for Inclusion Acrostic Activity:* Write a word that describes inclusion next to each letter below. You can use whatever words you desire, but a suggestion for one of the Ns is the word *naturally.* Hopefully, including others can become something automatic and "natural" — a way of life.

Acrostic writing is sometimes used to focus thoughts and enhance creativity.

I

N

C

L

U

S

I

O

N . . . aturally

Success Stories

Whatever happened to that kid? Remember the one who wouldn't sit still in class and kept jumping around from activity to activity, without completing the specified requirements? Well, that child grew up and became the dancer who loves to express herself through body movements. Or that child might be the CEO who supervises others, multitasking and delegating the details to subordinates. Whatever happened to that child who doodled all day in class? Well, that child may now be the renowned architect or engineer who just designed that incredible building or new prototype for that ingenious car. Maybe the fidgety child who could never sit still learned to work with his hands, create sculpture, be a chef, or even work as a sign language interpreter. Maybe the child who had trouble making friends is now a guidance counselor or child psychologist. Maybe the child who has Down syndrome is now gainfully employed and has learned to live independently. Maybe the child who couldn't stop talking is now a lawyer or a journalist. What about the child who could barely read at grade level? Well, that child now loves audio books and has figured out how to decipher the written word by using different learning strategies. That child also went on to college. Sure, the child might have needed a remedial reading and writing course, but with strong perseverance and support from friends, educators, and family, that child never gave up on her goals. That child graduated with a college diploma and is now gainfully employed. Maybe that child never went to college, but is now taking adult education courses to learn more. Maybe that child learned a trade and is now a whiz with computers, or maybe that child is an electrician or a plumber. Maybe that child learned to focus on her strengths and abilities. Maybe that child was helped by a teacher who successfully found a way to include her in the classroom. Maybe that child was included in society, not because it was the law, but because it was the right thing to do. Legislation and research support inclusion, but educators are the ones who must support the *child* by turning the rhetoric into successful classroom practice.

2

CIVICS

An Agenda for Our Schools

Mara Sapon-Shevin

What does it mean for a school or a classroom to be a community? What are the characteristics that define community, and what are the values that might be central organizing forces in those communities? And perhaps most significantly, why does it matter whether schools look like and feel like communities?

There is a growing recognition of the importance of developing respect for human dignity, for teaching students to be active participants—both in their education and in the community—and for beginning this important work at a young age. Creating classroom communities where students feel accepted and feel like they belong is not just about a feel-good curriculum. Rather, there are clear correlations between students' sense of belonging and their academic and social achievement.

In a review of the research on "Students' Need for Belonging in the School Community," Osterman (2000) found that the experience of belongingness is critical in an educational setting and that students' experience of acceptance influences multiple dimensions of their behavior and achievement in school. She also cautions that some schools adopt organizational practices that not only neglect but may actually undermine students' experiences of membership in a supportive community.

A study by Battistich, Schaps, and Wilson (2004), who are associated with the Child Development Project (CDP), found that students who had been part of their comprehensive elementary school intervention designed to reduce risk and increase resilience performed far better when they reached middle school. Students who had been part of the CDP were more engaged in and committed to school, were more prosocial, and engaged in fewer problem behaviors than comparison students during middle school. They also had higher academic performance.

Social studies education has come to mean not only teaching history and geography but also teaching about social justice in the broader context and interpersonal behavior at a direct level. In her book *Social Studies for Social Justice*, Rahima Wade (2007) argues that

> Starting in kindergarten we must educate youth to care about humanity and to begin to understand the immensity of the challenges that will face them as adults. We must embark upon teaching them the skills and knowledge that

will ultimately enable them not only to live productive and empowered lives but also to work alongside like-minded others for the betterment of those who suffer from oppression and other inequities. (pp. 1–2)

Educators are realizing that we need not dichotomize or choose between *teaching skills* and *teaching students to be caring and responsible human beings*. We need not sacrifice reading to teach sharing or abandon math goals in favor of teaching mutual support and help. Rather, the classroom community can be structured so that students learn reading *through* sharing and work on math goals *with* teacher and peer support.

And the growing focus on culturally relevant pedagogy and multicultural education also makes it clear that our sense of community must be expansive, inclusive rather than exclusive. We must teach our students to be members of multiple communities, fluent at moving between communities, and knowledgeable about a wide range of people and cultures.

I would like to revive an old word, a word that has fallen into disuse and ill repair. The word is *civics*. What is civics? Civics can be defined as those skills, attitudes, and beliefs needed to be a member of a community. Civics was a course that many people in previous generations took—it was a course about learning to become a useful citizen. Few schools offer courses in civics these days; for some, the word civics may even have negative connotations—as indoctrination into unquestioning obedience or mindless parroting of official rules and regulations. For many, the phrase "citizenship education" is equally narrow and limiting, implying that becoming a U.S. citizen, for example, means embracing particular values of Christianity or the dominant culture in ways that diminish or even destroy the histories and cultures of other groups. But what if we saw our task as preparing world citizens?

I would like to propose here that we adopt a new kind of civics curriculum, a civics curriculum that would help us to shape classrooms, schools, and a society that values community. Learning to be a part of that community is an essential, perhaps *the* essential, goal we should set for our students and ourselves.

In an article titled "Educating Global Citizens in a Diverse World," James Banks (2003a) argues that

> Cultural, ethnic, racial, language, and religious diversity exist in most nations in the world. One of the challenges to diverse democratic nation-states is to provide opportunities for different groups to maintain aspects of their community cultures while at the same time building a nation in which these groups are structurally included and to which they feel allegiance. A delicate balance of diversity and unity should be an essential goal of democratic nation-states and of teaching and learning in a democratic society. (para. 1)

Banks (2003a) sees the goal as achieving a balance between unity and diversity and refuses to see these two objectives as antagonistic or incompatible. He feels strongly that

> Because of growing ethnic, cultural, racial, language and religious diversity throughout the world, citizenship education needs to be changed in substantial ways to prepare students to function effectively in the 21st century. Citizens in this century need the knowledge, attitudes, and skills required to function in their cultural communities and beyond their cultural borders. . . . Students also need to acquire the knowledge and skills required to become effective citizens in the global community. (para. 4)

Because my focus is on teaching children to be part of community at many levels—the classroom, the school, the neighborhood, the nation, and the world—my civics curriculum looks different from previous civics courses that emphasized laws, governmental structures, and regulations. This civics curriculum is founded on six values that could inform our teaching, our curriculum, and our interactions with others. These values might run through the entire school community and beyond, guiding the behaviors of students, parents, teachers, and administrators. Each value is as important for the adults in a school as it is for the students; it is hard, for example, to ask students to be courageous if they do not see that behavior modeled by adults. It is not enough to make schools safe for students to learn if we cannot also make schools safe places for teachers to learn, to grow, to take risks, and to challenge themselves. The proliferation of programs on character education shows the growing recognition that teachers (and parents) teach values all the time by everything they do, regardless of their awareness of that agenda. Our goal is not to be value neutral. The relevant discussion is not about whether to teach values but which values to teach, how thoughtful we are about what we are teaching, and how these values should be selected and operationalized.

Within this new civics curriculum, civics can be represented as follows:

C ourage

I nclusion

V alue

I ntegrity

C ooperation

S afety

What would each of these principles look like if it were used as an organizing principle for our teaching and classroom communities?

COURAGE

Courage is one of those "soft" words we don't use much in education. To state that courage should be one of the defining values of our educational system is to push hard against a system that is more comfortable talking about accountability, effectiveness, and quality management systems. But if we are going to change our schools so that they serve *all* children within respectful, nurturing communities, then courage is what it will take.

A song by folksinger Linda Allen (2001) says, "Courage is the letting go of things familiar." Courage is what it takes when we leave behind something we know well and embrace (even tentatively) something unknown or frightening. Courage is what we need when we decide to do things differently. Perhaps we have always done ability grouping, but now, decide to leave it behind and embrace more heterogeneous ways of grouping students. Perhaps we have always segregated students with significant behavioral and learning challenges, and now, we decide to work toward more inclusive, integrated models of education. These changes required preparation, training, and support—yes—but they also require courage. Courage is recognizing that things familiar are not necessarily things that are right or inevitable. We mustn't mistake what is comfortable with what is possible.

An Australian teacher, Rosemary Williams (personal communication, 1995), describes what she does as "bungee teaching." She explains, "First you take the training, then you check the ropes, then you assemble your support team on the ground—but at some point, you have to jump." You can't wait to feel fully ready or prepared because you never will. We might identify our commitment to changing the ways schools respond to diverse learners as "bungee inclusion." We must, of course, make a plan, prepare ourselves, and gather information and resources. But at some point, we must decide that we will go ahead and do it, even though we don't feel ready, even though we are scared, insecure, and being asked to do something we have never done before.

What gets in the way of our acting courageously? The first obstacle is often fear. We are all scared of the unknown, of looking bad, and of failure or humiliation. Many of us have felt punished in the past for taking risks, making it difficult to break out of our molds and do things differently.

But there is much at stake. When we act in solidarity with others to change patterns of exclusion and isolation, we take a strong stand that goes far beyond our schools. The song "Courage" by Bob Blue (1990) makes this point eloquently.

Courage

A small thing once happened at school that brought up a question for me
And somehow it forced me to see the price that I pay to be cool
Diane is a girl that I know; she's strange like she doesn't belong
I don't mean to say that it's wrong, we don't like to be with her though
And so when we all made a plan, to have a big party at Sue's
Most kids at our school got the news, but no one invited Diane
The thing about Taft Junior High is secrets don't last very long
I acted like nothing was wrong when I saw Diane start to cry
I know you may think that I'm cruel, it doesn't make me very proud
I just went along with the crowd, it's sad, but you have to in school
You can't pick the friends you prefer, you fit in as well as you can
I couldn't be friends with Diane, or soon they would treat me like her
In one class at Taft Junior High we study what people have done
With gas chambers, bombers and guns in Auschwitz, Japan and My Lai
I don't understand all I learn; sometimes I just sit there and cry
The whole world stood idly by to watch as the innocent burned
Like robots obeying some rule, atrocities done by the mob
All innocents doing their job, and what was it for, was it cool?
The world was aware of this hell, but how many cried out in shame?
What heroes and who was to blame, a story that no one dared tell
I promise to do what I can to not let it happen again
To care for all women and men; I'll start by inviting Diane

Lyrics available at www.matchups.com/blue/courage.html

Many people can relate to this song because they were Diane, are the parent of Diane, have taught Diane, or remember the Diane from their school days. At an early childhood conference, I shared this song with a large audience. After my presentation, a woman approached me and said, "I just want you to know—I was Diane." And she burst into tears. The woman, now in her 40s, described how she had grown up rural and poor and had gone to school in clothes that did not meet the standards of her classmates. Her teacher, in an attempt to create community, had sat the children in a circle. But no one wanted to sit next to this "raggedy, country girl," and so the teacher had placed her in the center. This woman's pain, more than 30 years later, was still real and tangible. The hurts of rejection and of being left out, teased, or humiliated— unfortunately—are familiar to many people.

But there is another pain as well; the pain experienced by those of us who saw Diane, who saw another child rejected and teased, and didn't know what to do. This is the same pain we experience when we see a homeless person in the street or witness some other travesty of justice or fair play—the sense that something is wrong here, that something should be done, and, often, that we don't know what that something is. When we see another person rejected, isolated, or turned away, we can recognize that a blow to any member of the community is, in a way, a blow to the entire community. If we are a solid unit, a cohesive group, then we cannot tolerate mistreatment of any individual.

The song also allows us to see that it is within schools that most children first experi- ence grouping, labeling, and the valuing and devaluing of individuals. It is in school that we learn who is of worth and value and who is beneath contempt. It is in school that we learn how to befriend and how to turn away. And those lessons, once learned, have tremendous implications for all aspects of our lives. But there is also good news: it is within schools that we can teach children to act in solidarity; we can teach children to have the courage to step away from the crowd or challenge the bullies if that crowd is hurting someone; we can allow children opportunities to take risks and to act courageously. It is within schools that we can teach children to have the courage to make a difference.

INCLUSION

What does *inclusion* mean? Inclusion means we all belong. Inclusion means not having to fight for a chance to be part of a classroom or school community. Inclusion means that all children are accepted. Although the concept of "all children" should be fairly self-evident, it is still difficult for many to grasp. "But, of course, you don't mean a child like Matthew?" someone will ask. Although children will require different levels of support and resources, the concept of inclusion means all children—all children, not just those who are clean or who have agreeable parents or who come to school ready to learn. *All* means all. Or to paraphrase a country-and-western song, "What part of all don't you understand?" (Perry & Smith, 1992).

Inclusion can be distinguished from earlier terms such as *mainstreaming* or *inte- gration* by understanding what it means that there is a "presumption of inclusion." In other words, you don't have to earn your right to be included or struggle to maintain it. It is up to the teachers and administrators involved to make inclusion a viable pos- sibility, not the responsibility of the children to prove that they are entitled to be edu- cated with their peers.

What gets in the way of our acting inclusively? Unfortunately, many of us have been systematically taught patterns of exclusion, and some of us have even come to accept exclusion as inevitable or undesirable. Growing up, many of us were told that there simply wasn't enough time, success, room, or love for everyone and that some people had to be excluded. Those messages, once internalized, can be difficult to counteract (Sapon-Shevin, 2007).

The dangers of embracing a philosophy of exclusion go beyond the day-to-day hurts of not being invited to birthday parties or chosen from the team. In their most extreme forms, a philosophy of exclusion leads to the destruction of our communities.

An experience I had with exclusion was illuminating. In the summer of 1993, the Nazi Party announced that they would hold a march and rally near Syracuse, where I live. They announced that they had scheduled their march for Yom Kippur (the most sacred of Jewish holidays) and that the march would go from the Auburn town hall to Harriet Tubman Square (a landmark to the famous African-American abolitionist). For weeks, a small group of us met, trying to discern the appropriate response to such a demonstration of hatred and prejudice. There were some that favored doing nothing, arguing that the best way to discourage such behavior was to have it met by silence and lack of attention. But unfortunately, media attention had already created a situation in which the chances of nothing happening were small. It seemed inevitable that the event would be well attended (if only by onlookers) and that there would be considerable press and media coverage. The decision, finally, was to assemble a group, as a "visible presence" (as we called ourselves) and to hold signs that said, simply, "No." Another group of people appointed themselves peacekeepers and committed to maintaining the peace and keeping things from becoming violent. The period of planning for the march was a tense time for me. I was upset by the fact that there were Nazis marching, and as a Jewish woman, I felt particularly vulnerable and frightened. But my feelings were stirred even further by the fact that my then-14-year-old daughter, Dalia, wanted to be part of the demonstration. Part of me, as a parent, was proud that I had raised a child who was willing to take a stand, a child who went to 30 hours of meetings as well as 10 hours of nonviolence training over two weekends. And another part of me, of course, was terrified, frightened that I was somehow agreeing to let my precious child be somewhere she could get badly hurt. I wrestled with this through many sleepless nights and was only somewhat reassured by the many people who made personal pledges to look after her and keep her safe throughout the march.

But my biggest lesson came from my younger daughter Leora. Leora, at 11, was not coming to the march. We had decided that she would spend the day with Robin Smith, a friend of the family, attending synagogue with her in the morning. Because Leora worries a lot about the people she loves, we hadn't shared every detail of the march with her. Riding in the car two days before the march, I said to Leora, "I just want to tell you what's happening on Saturday: Papa, Dalia, and I are going to go to Auburn to march, and you are going to spend the day with Robin." Leora immediately began to cry. "Why are you crying?" I asked. "Because I'm scared," she responded. "What are you scared of?" I pushed. "I'm scared you'll get hurt," she replied.

I reassured her, as well as I could, that we were committed to nonviolence, that we would take every precaution, and that we would leave if the march became violent or difficult. Leora began to cry again. "Now what?" I asked. She looked at me plaintively. "Why are they doing this?" I took a deep breath. My experience has always been that when children ask a question, they want a real answer. They don't want research or statistics or an article to read; they want an immediate, simple answer. "Well," I ventured to say, "I think they are confused people who think that only white people should live and that anyone who is black or Jewish or gay or lesbian or disabled or an immigrant shouldn't be allowed to live." She looked at me, paused for a moment, and then, shaking her head, offered, "Picky, aren't they!"

Leora's characterization of race hatred and a politics of violence and exclusion as "picky" is both laughable and yet completely on-target. When and where did those folks learn who was "in" and who was "out," who was acceptable and who was unacceptable? What were the school experiences of the young Nazis, and what did they learn? What are the risks of failing to teach children an inclusive response to difference?

Schools can become the places where we teach children to be inclusive, teach them to embrace differences as typical and acceptable, and encourage them to reach across categories and lines and labels to form friendships and strong relationships. Whatever lessons we teach young people, whether in kindergarten or third grade, shape their understandings beyond the walls of school.

Jowonio School in Syracuse, New York, recently celebrated its 40th anniversary. Jowonio (an Onondagan word that means "to set free") was the first school in the country to systematically include children who were labeled as "autistic" within regular classrooms with "typical" children. The administrators, teachers, parents, and students at Jowonio are solidly supportive of inclusive communities and of the importance of many kinds of children learning to play and work together. At the event organized to celebrate Jowonio's 25th anniversary, I offered this poem as a celebration of the gifts that Jowonio has given to the community and as my appreciation of the meaning of inclusive schooling.

What the Children of Jowonio Know

The children of Jowonio know—not because they have been told—but because they have lived it

That there is always room for everyone—in the circle and at snack time and on the playground—and even if they have to wiggle a little to get another body in and even if they have to find a new way to do it, they can figure it out—and so it might be reasonable to assume that there's enough room for everyone in the world

The children of Jowonio know—not because they have been told—but because they have lived it

That children come in an dazzling assortment of sizes, colors and shapes, big and little and all shades of brown and beige and pink, and some walk and some use wheelchairs but everyone gets around and that same is boring—and so it might be reasonable to assume that everyone in the world could be accepted for who they are

The children of Jowonio know—not because they have been told—but because they have lived it

That there are people who talk with their mouths and people who talk with their hands and people who talk by pointing and people who tell us all we need to know with their bodies if we only listen well—and so it might be reasonable to assume that all the people of the world could learn to talk to and listen to each other

The children of Jowonio know—not because they have been told—but because they have lived it

That we don't send people away because they're different or even because they're difficult, and that all people need support and that if people are hurting, we take the time to notice, and that words can build bridges and hugs can heal—and so it might be reasonable to assume that all the people on the planet could reach out to each other and heal the wounds and make a world fit for us all

VALUE

The third central organizing characteristic of our communities can be defined as value. What would it mean to not only believe but also act on the belief that all people are of value and everyone counts? What would it take to organize our schools so that we could really value every individual, for himself, without reference to the value of other individuals?

Two of the biggest obstacles to this kind of valuing are our predisposition to devalue people and our systematic instruction in ranking people according to set criterion. Many of us were raised with sometimes explicit and sometimes very subtle messages about who was good and who wasn't. From outright racist, homophobic, or anti-Semitic statements such as "You can't trust a Jew," or "Faggots are dangerous," or "Blacks aren't as good as whites," to more subtle messages about who we should or shouldn't play with, invite to our parties, or interact with, many of us were kept from seeing the value in all human beings.

At the same time, many of us were not allowed to value ourselves fully either. Ironically, when a four-year-old is thrilled with the picture she has drawn, pointing out the details of color and shading, we label that child as having "good self-esteem," but when a 44-year-old is pleased with what she has accomplished, we label that pride as "arrogance," "showing off," "snobbishness," or being "full of oneself." And if it is hard to be pleased with ourselves, our accomplishments, and our triumphs, it becomes increasingly hard to appreciate others. A child who has been told he or she is no good, lazy, and stupid is unlikely to be able to reach out to another child with warmth and acceptance.

Often, comparison with others also keeps us from taking pride in who we are. No matter how accomplished I am at something, someone has achieved more. I am thrilled with how I've decorated my new house, but surely there are people with nicer homes; I am now able to run 2 miles without stopping, but there are people (younger and older than I am) who run 10 miles a day effortlessly. We find ourselves making constant comparisons: "Well, I have a better job, but she has a better car; I have a bigger house, but her children are doing better." Constant devaluing and ranking and constantly looking at how we compare to others keeps any of us from feeling really pleased or accepting of ourselves or of others.

Unfortunately, our schools are structured so that we often focus most of our attention on what children cannot do, on their weaknesses or areas of need. This keeps us from seeing the whole child and narrows our lens of appreciation. A mother once told me about her daughter, who I'll call Jackie. Jackie was adopted as a young person and experienced a difficult early life. Now, at 10, reading was still elusive for her. But Jackie's gift was gymnastics. She excelled on the balance beam, did graceful backflips, and flowed on the parallel bars. This was where Jackie was affirmed and experienced a sense of success and belonging. The school, however, concerned about Jackie's failure to progress in reading, suggested to her mother that Jackie should quit gymnastics so she would have more time to work on her reading. Luckily for Jackie, her mother was a strong advocate for her child and gently told the well-meaning teachers that it made no sense to deprive Jackie of the one thing that made her feel good about herself to work on her weakness. And somewhat predictably, after several years during which Jackie felt better and better about herself as a person and a learner, she was better able to profit from reading instruction and learned to read. If her life had come to revolve around the one thing she was not good at, one wonders what might have happened, not only for her reading but also for her self-esteem and sense of herself as a valued and valuable human being.

How can we create classrooms where children learn to value and appreciate one another? At a recent workshop, I asked participants to bring in and share with a small group an object that was important to them. People brought and shared a variety of things: a shell, an old photograph, a childhood book, a stuffed animal, a plaque. I then asked each person to talk about one of the other people in their group, telling others not what that person had shared but what they had *learned about that person* from what they had shared. People's responses were profound: "I learned that relationships are very important to Sharon—she cares deeply about her friends"; "I learned that Steve loves nature and that he really notices the beauty around him." And perhaps most touchingly, this about a woman whose outward reserve could have been mistaken (without this exercise) for standoffishness or aloofness, "I learned that there's more to Mary than meets the eye. She really has a deep, spiritual side to her." Many people were quite moved during the sharing experience. The joy of being seen so clearly and so fully by relative strangers was overwhelmingly affirming.

My daughter Dalia invented a Thanksgiving ritual that we participate in each year. She gives each person enough little slips of paper for every other person at the table and asks them to write one thing they like or appreciate about each person. Little people who cannot write are encouraged to draw or dictate their messages. All the slips are put in a box, and the box is then passed around the table. Each person takes a turn drawing out a slip of paper and reading it: "I like Sharon's warmth and the way she reaches out to people." "I like the way Iman cares about his work and is committed to making a difference." "I like the way Lucy giggles when something is funny and makes everyone else giggle too." The slip of paper is then given to the person it is about.

This is a challenging task for some people because in addition to appreciating and valuing people you know very well (siblings, relatives), you must also notice things to appreciate about relative strangers who you may have only met hours before. It is also hard for some people to receive their appreciations—societal messages about not feeling good about oneself can make it difficult to say, "Yes, I do have a great sense of humor. Thanks for noticing." And yet I have never seen anyone who did not take these little slips of paper home, tucked in a purse or a shirt pocket. Many people have reported, years later, that they still have the slips pasted on their mirrors or on their desks.

We need to give all people multiple chances to show themselves fully and be seen by others. And we must give many opportunities for people to see others, notice things about them, and appreciate them. Rather than belittling people for craving approval, we can realize that all people want, need, and deserve appreciation, and we can help students and teachers find appropriate and systematic ways of receiving and giving such appreciation.

INTEGRITY

The second *I* in *civics* stands for integrity. Integrity means wholeness. What would it be like to be able to claim (or reclaim) all parts of yourself? What would our lives be like if there were no lies or secrets about who we really are, if we were able to show ourselves fully, knowing that we would be accepted in our complexity, acceptable even with our seeming contradictions and inevitable inadequacies?

One way of looking at this issue centers on how schools respond to differences. Are differences seen as something to be avoided, ignored, worked around, and minimized? Or as characteristics to be understood, valued, appreciated, supported, and celebrated?

When my daughter Dalia was almost three years old, my childcare situation fell apart suddenly, and I embarked on a quest to find a new day-care center. I visited one center that I really liked. The teachers seemed warm and supportive, and then, at the end of my visit, I sat down with the director. "There's something I haven't mentioned," I said. "Dalia is a vegetarian." "Oh, dear," exclaimed the director, "I don't think we could handle that. I mean we've never had a child like that before. That would mean explaining it to the kids, and their parents and the staff would have to make special accommodations, and I just don't think we could deal with that." Our interview ended rather abruptly. It was clear to me that this was not the place for my daughter. If this was how the director reacted, I could only imagine what discomfort and fear she would communicate to her staff and they to the students. How could my daughter be in such a setting and be comfortable with who she was?

So I went to the last day-care center on my list of possibilities, nervous now about the outcome of my search. This day-care center was lovely: tiny chairs and toilets, lots of parental involvement, and a strong commitment to diversity and inclusion. At the end of my visit, I nervously initiated the same conversation about Dalia and her eating requirements. "Oh, that's no problem," said this director. "We have Mohammed, who doesn't eat pork; and we have Rachel, who keeps kosher; and we have Justin, who is lactose intolerant. We just make it all part of our teaching curriculum with the children."

And so they did. Dalia's vegetarianism was well accepted and well understood by her classmates. She came home one day and told me, "Today, I explained to my friends why I don't eat Jell-O because gelatin is an animal product, and they didn't know that." And Dalia learned about other religions, other dietary requirements and customs, and about respecting differences. The children were not only accepting of one another, but also they were knowledgeable. It was not uncommon to hear children say, "Justin—you can't eat the yogurt because it's a dairy product, but we have some bananas you could eat," or to hear them brainstorming inclusive snacks: what could they make that all of them could eat?

The children, following the wonderful model of their teachers, evidenced not just acceptance of diversity but understanding and celebration. There are those who say that our goal should be teaching children to tolerate differences. Certainly, tolerance is better than hatred, prejudice, and active rejection. But I would like us to set our goals higher than tolerance. After all, how many of us want our friends to simply tolerate us? Don't we want enjoyment, appreciation, and depth of understanding?

Tom Hunter (n.d.), a children's songwriter, writes movingly about a teacher who saw and accepted him fully: Mrs. Squires (see Box 2.1).

BOX 2.1   MRS. SQUIRES

I don't remember a lot about third grade, but I do remember Mrs. Squires, and what I remember are not her lesson plans or unit themes. Nor do I have any recollection of her knowledge of Piaget, or whether she used math manipulatives. What I do remember are moments, and one in particular about two weeks after school started when she asked me to stay after school. I remember being afraid, because staying after school was supposed to mean you were in trouble. Right away, she said, "You're not in any trouble; I just want to talk with you."

To understand what followed, you need to know that I stuttered a lot when I was a child. I used to say, "stuttered badly," until someone helped me to realize I was good at it—better than any other kid in my class. That was small comfort at the time, but I did like the idea—I never stuttered badly; I stuttered a lot, and well.

In our empty classroom that day after school, Mrs. Squires told me, "I know people have ended sentences for you when you've had trouble talking, and I know teachers have said you didn't have to read out loud. In this class, I have a message for you—I will not end sentences for you, and you're going to have to read out loud when it comes your turn." She paused, and then said, "And we'll get through it together."

I don't remember any heavy drama in that moment. No lights flashed. No angel choirs sang— at least none I heard. What I do remember is the feeling that something significant had just happened. For one thing, she had wanted to talk with me alone like that. But there was something more too, some sense that I was learning something new and important.

When it came to my stuttering, every other grown-up I knew had tried to fix me, to make it all better. In a way, of course, that made sense—stuttering is not fun for the stutterer or the listener. It's natural enough to want to decrease the frustrations, understandable that people believe attempts to "make it all better" are kind and helpful. Mrs. Squires had a different message. Rather than "We'll make it all better," she said, "We're in this together."

The conversation that day after school wasn't long. I'm not sure I said anything, but I did get the message. It wasn't a verbal thing, really, though I do remember the words. It was an experience, something like being able to relax a little, maybe like a deep breath. It was a moment when someone paid attention to what was important to me, in a way that others hadn't.

The experience of having the realities of my life noticed deepened through that year with Mrs. Squires. I remember that when someone giggled during one of my longer speech blocks, she said there was no room in her classroom for that. I remember a couple of times when she found me at recess to tell me she was fascinated by what I was doing with my mouth. She never did end sentences for me. I did have to read out loud when it came my turn. And she was always there, sometimes walking across the room to stand quietly beside me when I had trouble reading or talking.

I don't know when it happened, really. It probably wasn't on any particular day I could identify, or at any particular time. But gradually, I became aware that Mrs. Squires stuttered, too. She wasn't as good at it as I was, but she did stutter. She'd pause at odd times to get a word out. Sometimes her mouth would twitch noticeably, or she'd briefly bounce on one sound or another until she said the word. I don't remember it as a big deal. It was just the way she talked, and it's probably why she was so interested in me. We shared something, a world of speech and sounds and fears that most people don't know about. She knew me in ways others didn't.

Not long ago, I was talking with a teacher friend of mine about how rare and difficult it is for teachers (and adults in general) to celebrate their own talents, to acknowledge what they are good at. She mentioned being good at singing, knitting, cooking, and telling stories. Then she said, "I think I'd also have to say I'm good at sadness." When I looked confused, she said she'd known a lot of sadness as a little girl, and more as a young woman. She had worked hard at coming to terms with it, and now, as a teacher, she's aware of how well she connects with children who themselves know sadness. She's good at it. Right away, I thought of children who need her as their teacher—children (in growing numbers) who know sadness well and simply need someone to share it with them.

(Continued)

(Continued)

I believe we all have our own versions of what that teacher said, experiences that make us good at something or other. I'm probably not as good at sadness as she is, nor am I as good at stuttering as I once was. I am good at creating situations in which people are listened to, situations in which children get to stutter out what's in them, or sit there and wonder for a long time, or have feelings and observations that they simply want acknowledged. I love it when we can get through it together. It's in my bones, carried with me from those moments when some one connected with me and what I knew.

Mrs. Squires connected well, and I'll always be grateful. But she's not the only one. It's what any teacher does when he or she understands the human interaction at the heart of good teaching. The lesson plans fade. The latest programs to raise test scores come and go. This "effective strategy" gives way to that one. What lasts are moments of connection. I believe we carry those moments with us forever, sometimes in fuzzy pieces of memory, sometimes in clear and detailed ones. Moments of connection make us feel we belong. Moments of connection open us up to learning.

I'm glad I got to see Mrs. Squires again, and to thank her. She smiled as she listened to me remember her from thirty-nine years ago. "I don't remember all of that," she said, "but I do remember some of it. We shared something pretty special." She stuttered a little as she said it.

How can we create schools in which the Mrs. Squires of the world flourish so that children can be accepted, loved, and taught for who they are?

COOPERATION

What would it be like if our classrooms and our teaching were based around a principle of cooperation, people working together to achieve a common goal, supporting and helping one another along the way? Unfortunately, few of us experienced schools or learning as a cooperative enterprise. More likely, we either worked in isolation from one another or were pitted against one another in competitive situations such as spelling bees, tracked reading groups, and so on. Because of our personal histories, we often think of competition as inevitable or even desirable.

Consider the following scenario, so familiar to many of us. The game is Musical Chairs. An adult is leading a group of children in the game. They are instructed to walk around the chairs to the music and then, when the music stops, to get in the chair nearest to them. The child who is left without a chair is out of the game and must go sit on the sidelines.

The children do as they are told. They move around the chairs to the music, eyeing the chairs and one another with nervous suspicion. When the music stops, they scramble for the chairs, knocking one another over and shoving others out of the way. One child who gets a chair yells to another child, who is approaching, "I was here first." Two children try to sit on the same chair, and the stronger child pushes the weaker child onto the floor.

One of the children who is pushed out of a chair and eliminated from the game goes over to the corner and starts to cry. A well-meaning adult approaches the child and says, "Come on, now it's just a game. You're not being a very good sport." When the game is over, one child is victorious—the last child left with a chair. All the other children have been eliminated. The adult leader smiles and asks the students, "Now wasn't that fun? Would you like to play again?"

What did we learn from playing this game? We learned that there aren't enough chairs to go around. We learned that pushing and shoving in the name of winning was acceptable behavior. We learned that it's all right to shove a child who is smaller, weaker, or who doesn't understand the game to win. We learned that other people are what stand in the way of our winning or being successful. And we learned that only some of us are smart, are capable, are good, are winners.

It is clear how this kind of competition is destructive to community. Our classmates become—not our allies and our support—but our enemies who must be conquered for us to be victorious.

But we could play, instead, Cooperative Musical Chairs. In this version of the game, children walk around the chairs to the music, and although there are fewer chairs than children, the goal is phrased, "Everyone must be on a chair for the group to win." So what happens? Children share chairs; they giggle; they sit on laps; they problem solve. "Someone hold on to LaDonna; she's falling off Michael's chair." "Quick, grab Eli; he can fit in over here." The goal is not to exclude, but to figure out, as a group, how everyone can be accommodated and included. As the number of chairs is reduced, the challenge increases, and children usually engage in extensive problem solving and negotiation to figure things out, certainly a higher-level cognitive skill than pushing classmates off chairs!

But competition isn't the only obstacle to our envisioning cooperation as our normative goal structure. Strong patterns of isolation and an unquestioned stress on *individual achievement* also make cooperation seem elusive or unrealistic as a goal. Often, when we accomplished something as a child—a Lego construction, a puzzle, a drawing—and brought our creation to an adult for comment and approval, there were two comments. First, "Oh, how nice," then followed swiftly by, "And did you do it all by yourself?" The message is clear: things accomplished alone are of higher value and more deserving of praise and appreciation than things accomplished in collaboration or cooperation with others. Teachers who discourage students from helping one another ("I want to know what you can do, not what your neighbor can do") and who see students erecting boundaries around their desks with textbooks are seeing some of the unfortunate but inevitable results of a focus on individualism and competition.

Structuring our schools and our classrooms cooperatively would mean looking closely at not just how we teach but also what we teach as well. Do we encourage students to find out about peaceful, collaborative responses to conflict, or do we study only the battles and the wars and ignore the peace in between? Do we actively teach students the skills they need to work together: listening, sharing materials, negotiating conflict, asking questions, and encouraging one another's participation and involvement?

Teachers are similarly affected by the goal structures set by administrators and other instructional leaders. Are teachers encouraged to share their ideas and materials, or are there prizes for the best teacher of the year, thus discouraging collaboration and interaction? Are teachers provided with opportunities to meet, talk, share, problem solve, and support one another? Are forms of teaching that entail cooperation—team teaching, cross-age groupings—encouraged and supported? The current focus on competitive merit pay for teachers and the publication of each school's test scores hardly encourage collaboration and mutual support.

Embracing cooperation as a guiding principle would mean believing the poster that says, "None of us is as smart as all of us" and enacting that belief in all aspects of our curriculum, pedagogy, and school organizational structures.

SAFETY

Safety is the last characteristic of our school communities. Many kinds of safety are required for children to learn. At the most basic level, there is physical safety. Children (and teachers) must be confident that they will not be hit, hurt, or physically abused in any way. In many schools, ensuring that basic kind of safety is a serious challenge. But physical safety is not enough. Safety also means emotional safety—the safety to be yourself, to be vulnerable, to ask for help, and to be warmly supported. It is physiologically impossible for people to learn when they are afraid. When you are standing on the ski slope, terrified that you will die, it is difficult to listen to and integrate instruction. And if you are terrified of failure or humiliation, you can't learn either.

When my daughter Dalia was in the seventh grade, just months after having started at a new school, she came home one day and announced, "Today at school, I learned to tell time." I was very surprised by her announcement. "But Dalia," I began, "you've known how to tell time since first grade!" "No," Dalia explained, "I never really understood it—didn't you ever realize that's why I have a digital watch? I've really been faking it for all these years." As the story unfolded, it seemed that Dalia had told several of her close friends at lunch that she didn't know how to tell time. Rather than responding with scorn or derision, they simply showed her how. Several things about this story are remarkable. First, they met her revelation with positiveness rather than scorn. Second, they then went on to teach her how. And perhaps important from a different angle, how easily people can learn when they are not expending their energy trying to cover up or get by, afraid that someone will find out about their weakness or deficiency.

Unfortunately, most of us do not feel safe enough to let others in on the places and ways in which we are struggling. In some school settings, it is impossible for the teachers themselves to ask for help and support without being stigmatized and scorned. Several years ago, a local first-grade teacher, Marie, was fired after her first year of teaching. The teachers' union became involved, and there was considerable community interest because firing was unusual in this district. When the full story was shared, one of the points made against this teacher was that four times during the year she had gone to the principal in tears.

Going to the principal in tears is not unusual for first-year teachers or for many other far more senior-level teachers, nor is struggling with your first teaching assignment. This young teacher felt overwhelmed by trying to implement a multilevel, multiple intelligence curriculum in her classroom as a first-year teacher. All such cases, of course, are complex; to fully assess the situation, we would want to know more about Marie's overall performance in the classroom and about her success with students. Certainly, students are entitled to be taught by thoughtful, stable, and effective teachers. But new teachers are also works in progress requiring nurturance and support. The principal's reaction could have taken many forms: "Why don't I take Mrs. Lopez's class for an afternoon—she does a lot of differentiated instruction—and she can come spend time with you," or "Why don't I take your class, and you can spend time in hers," or "Why don't I send you to this differentiated instruction conference that's coming up," or "Maybe we should set up a teacher study group on Wednesday morning before school—we can have coffee and doughnuts and talk about multilevel teaching." Any of these responses would have been helpful, supportive, and might have helped Marie to become a better teacher. But instead, the principal's response was to document Marie's fears and to make careful note of her feelings of inadequacy and lack of adequate preparation.

This is an example of a teacher not having the safety she needed to ask for help. In this case, she actually did ask for the help she needed, but the consequences of showing her vulnerability and needs were devastating. Teachers and students alike need the safety to take risks, the safety to show their vulnerability and the safety to grow. Without this kind of safety, teachers become narrow and defensive of their current practice, and students focus their energy on staying safe and looking good rather than on taking on new projects and stretching themselves.

Courage, inclusion, value, integrity, cooperation, and safety are all essential components of a healthy classroom community in which all students and their teachers can grow in an atmosphere of support and mutual help. The values identified in this chapter are important for teachers as well as for students. The challenge now is to operationalize these values in ways that seem doable—to take a characteristic and translate it into specific practices and procedures for the classroom. We do not want to reduce these values to the word of the week shared in an assembly or over the loudspeaker each month but not represented in any concrete way in classroom practices. Only by translating theory into practice can we reap the benefits of our desire and commitment to creating cooperative, inclusive classrooms.

A Decision-Making Process for Creating IEPs That Lead to Curriculum Access

Victor Nolet and Margaret J. McLaughlin

By now, you should be acquainted with how to find the general education curriculum and how to assess a student's performance within that curriculum. You should also be able to distinguish between a curriculum accommodation and a curriculum modification, as well as an alternate assessment and alternate achievement standards, and how to design instruction that matches the type of content you must teach. Now we need to discuss how to consolidate all of these pieces to create an individualized education program (IEP) for a specific student with a disability.

In Chapter 1, we described the required components of an IEP that directly relate to accessing the general education curriculum and participating in state and district assessments. Those are only some of what is required to be addressed in an IEP.

Now we discuss how to proceed with a planning process that links IEP goals to standards. The process we outline does not address every aspect of what IEP planning should involve, nor should it be confused with an actual IEP document. All school districts have established their own forms and procedures for developing IEPs, which reflect the requirements in the 2004 Individuals with Disabilities Education Improvement Act (New IDEA). Our process gives IEP teams a logical and sequential way to think about an individual student in relation to a standards-based curriculum. First, we will describe the essential decision points in IEP planning, and then we will apply these to some individual students.

Figure 3.1 provides a flow chart to help guide you through the key decisions that the IEP team must make as they think about how to ensure that a student with a disability accesses the general education curriculum. It might be

Figure 3.1   An IEP Decision-Making Process

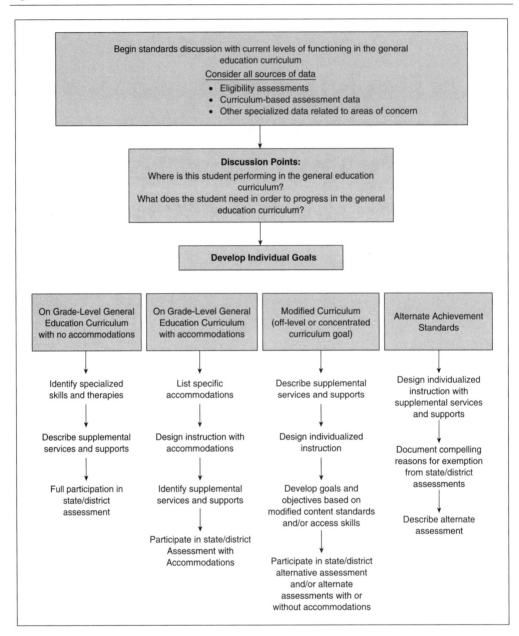

helpful to compare an actual IEP form with which you are familiar to our process as we discuss each step.

STEP 1: INSTRUCTIONAL ASSESSMENT

The IEP process begins with an analysis of a student's present levels of academic achievement and functional performance, including how the disability affects the student's involvement and progress in the general education curriculum. The assessment strategies we discussed in Chapter 4 will be critical in this analysis. Please note, though, that as we consider assessment here, we are assuming that evaluation to determine eligibility already has occurred and that the adverse educational impact of the student's disability has been identified.

This first step toward access requires the IEP planning team to define the student's current level of academic achievement and functional performance in *all* of the curricular areas that may be affected by the disability. Instructional assessment at this stage involves collecting information about levels of performance in each of the subject matter areas addressed in the general education curriculum. Assessment of specific skills and operations is also required. This analysis will have to include more than a simple inventory of skills, such as math computations or a reading comprehension score, obtained from an off-the-shelf assessment instrument. Instructional assessment for IEP planning must be referenced to local general education curriculum goals that are aligned with state content and achievement standards. Assessments must focus on the content and organization of the student's information networks. The team has to understand what underlying knowledge and learning strategies a student has acquired through prior learning and experience and how well the student applies that information to a variety of contexts. Remember: Do not fall into the trap of thinking that because a student has not mastered a basic skill such as reading decoding, he or she is not ready to understand more complex knowledge or operations.

Knowledge of the general education curriculum is essential to the IEP decision-making process and is the primary reason that the IEP team must include someone who has that curricular knowledge. However, special education teachers and other service providers also need to understand the scope of content and sequence of the curriculum. The decision framework for finding the general curriculum, presented at the end of Chapter 2, will help team members identify the knowledge, skills, and processes that will need to be assessed. This will require a three-phase process:

Phase 1: Identify the critical, enduring knowledge associated with the general education curriculum within each subject matter domain that all students at a particular grade level are expected to learn.

Phase 2: Analyze the key knowledge, skills, and processes that a skilled learner must have to be proficient in using that core knowledge. This step is somewhat analogous to the process of task analysis familiar to many special educators, except that it is not hierarchical (e.g., moving downward to the lowest possible level of skill) and it does not involve the kind of fine-grained molecular analysis that often results in irrelevant goals and objectives focused on meaningless subcomponents of basic skills. Remember that the whole is bigger than the sum of the parts when we are talking about the kind of generative thinking and problem solving that is required in the general education curriculum.

Keep in mind the core elements of curriculum that we discussed in Chapter 2: Curriculum has a purpose, it involves a domain, and it involves time. Think about the overall goals that the math, science, or language arts curriculum is intended to accomplish. Examine the goals for a specific grade level or range. Look back to see what these curriculum goals expect students to have already learned, and look ahead to see what the students will be expected to learn in the near and far future. Finally, consider how the various types of facts, concepts, rules, and processes fit together in the curriculum to help the student develop more expert knowledge networks.

Phase 3: Determine the individual student's use of the critical knowledge, skills, and learning processes and strategies. For example, you will want to have information about the student's skill level in areas such as basic reading, more specifically, phonemic analysis, fluency, specific vocabulary, and language structures and concepts. In fact, in each subject matter area, you need to know more than just a student's test results. You need to understand if low performance is due to problems with retention and learning processes or if it may be related to the ways in which a student is expected to demonstrate knowledge. For example, are the student's difficulties with written expression preventing the student from demonstrating the depth of knowledge of a specific topic?

Assessment must also include how the student accesses information to solve problems and learn new things. For example, think about how a student's learning and memory problems might interfere with accessing and using strategic knowledge about reading. If students fail to activate a comprehension strategy such as multipass, is it because (a) they never learned the strategy in the first place, (b) they forgot how to initiate the strategy, or (c) they don't recognize the features in a reading task that would indicate that the strategy would be helpful? The type of specialized instruction indicated on an IEP will be somewhat different under each of these conditions.

Of course, you will also want to know what past instructional strategies have worked to help this student learn. This analysis will involve some of the assessment tools discussed in Chapter 4 as well as a more general analysis of the learning processes involved in acquisition and use of the information to be learned.

The following questions can guide your assessment:

- **What will "typical" students at this child's grade level be expected to know and to do in the subject matter curriculum (math, science, reading, physical education, etc.) during the time frame addressed by the IEP (typically one school year)?**
- **What are the key goals or performance expectations associated with the subject matter knowledge?** Define precisely what a proficient level of student achievement looks like. Examples include being able to (a) read independently specific types of text and answer certain types of questions, (b) accurately estimate size and measures in a variety of daily situations, and (c) write a coherent multiparagraph, persuasive essay that logically develops an idea and conforms to rules of grammar and punctuation.
- **How is the target student currently performing in these areas?** Look at a variety of evidence, including curriculum-based assessments, work samples, and input from parents, teachers, and other IEP team members. The criterion-referenced assessment strategies we discussed in Chapter 4 would be useful here. Also useful is examining work samples

of other students who are considered to be proficient or advanced as well as students at or below basics in the specific grade-level subject matter. Teachers can determine what the performance targets are and also identify the areas in which a specific student needs additional instruction.

- **In what ways are the student's disabilities impacting his or her performance?** In addition to specific skill deficits, such as in reading or math, educational assessments should consider such things as the student's focus on, and attention to, instruction; the student's organizational skills; and other learning processes.

The outcome of Step 1 of the IEP decision-making process is a clearly defined road map that defines a student's starting point with respect to grade-level standards and curriculum goals in various subject areas in addition to the learning that must be developed.

STEP 2: CHOOSING IEP GOALS AND IDENTIFYING SUPPORTS

At this step in the process, you have accumulated a body of evidence that identifies the student's level of performance in the curriculum. Is there evidence that the student requires additional intensive instruction to attain proficiency or make progress in particular areas of the curriculum? If so, what accommodations, modifications, and specialized instruction or other services does the student require within the specific curriculum area? In other words, what does the student need to catch up or keep up?

For example, a sixth-grade student may have a basic understanding of grade-level scientific concepts and terminology, but ability to read the science textbook is below grade level. This student will require more intensive vocabulary drills and reading accommodations in order to keep up in the science area. He may also need direct instruction in reading fluency and basic writing processes *and* require accommodations (such as a writing software program and a spell checker) to help him in the general education curriculum. This student's IEP must include goals to improve academic achievement and functional performance in specific skill areas. It also must address how the student will be supported and accommodated in other areas in order to continue to progress in the grade-level curriculum. The examples in Box 3.1 and Box 3.2 illustrate the process of selecting an IEP goal and identifying appropriate supports.

Boxes 3.1 and 3.2 illustrate two examples of curricular accommodations. In Jason's case, he can be expected to fully access the grade-level standards with accommodations. In Felix's case, he will access grade-level content and achievement expectations, with accommodations, in core areas of the curriculum and will also have curriculum modifications in other areas. In both cases, we would expect these students to be able to fully access and progress in the general education curriculum and make progress toward meeting achievement standards.

Now you are ready to actually create IEP goals, objectives, and benchmarks.

Box 3.1 Jason

Jason is a seventh grader who has been receiving special education services since fourth grade. He is a struggling reader and has difficulty with his writing and spelling. Jason is a very slow reader, and as a result, he struggles to complete assignments and his comprehension suffers. However, he has reasonable understanding of material presented orally and is able to complete in-class work when teachers make effective use of the principles of universal design for learning and when there are additional cues available in the environment, such as diagrams on the overhead projector, step-by step directions on the white board, or graphic organizers and study guide worksheets.

When the teachers examined the requirements for each of the core academic areas, they confirmed that Jason is not a fluent reader and often needs help reading textbooks and other curriculum materials. They also noticed that he has specific gaps in the writing process and has both spelling and vocabulary deficits.

Jason's IEP team determines that there are two areas that need to be addressed. First, the IEP team needs to specify the types of accommodations and instructional supports that will help Jason compensate for his slow reading in the content areas. They will also specify strategies for helping him organize his learning process. The overall goal is to help Jason begin to develop well-organized, accessible knowledge networks in various subject matter domains. This will help him learn more complex information later in the curriculum. What will be most important is that he will need to have information represented in multiple formats. Accommodations could include structured study guides, peer study-buddies, and frequent opportunities to use content information in hands-on activities that require complex problem solving but do not require extensive reading.

Second, Jason needs intensive support in reading and writing. The IEP team determines that the special education teacher and reading specialist will implement a specific reading program to help him develop word attack skills. The teacher will also begin intensive drills to strengthen Jason's vocabulary in specific subject areas. The vocabulary list will be developed in collaboration with Jason's content area teachers and will focus on the essential terminology in each area. The special education teacher also will need to help the student acquire, and access readily, a broad repertoire of comprehension strategies that can be employed to learn content area information. A specific writing program will also be initiated to help Jason strengthen his writing processes. These areas require measurable annual goals.

STEP 3: CREATING IEP ANNUAL GOALS

IEP annual goals are the targets that individual students need to reach by the end of an instructional year. Note that the 2004 amendments to IDEA did not

Box 3.2   Felix

Felix, a third grader, has been identified as having both attention deficit hyperactivity disorder and a communication disorder. Felix is not yet reading independently, although he does know his alphabet and most of the letter-sound relationships. While he does not have difficulty speaking, his verbal and written language is developmentally far below that of his peers. Felix also has difficulty paying attention through a typical lesson, and teachers report that "he seems to drift off during class and is very forgetful."

An evaluation of Felix indicates that he has a slightly below average IQ but has some areas (e.g., general knowledge and spatial reasoning) where he is at or above age-level norms.

Felix needs to be given access to the fourth-grade standards and curriculum. He must also be given specific reading instruction as well as instruction in spelling, writing, and language development. This is a tall order, and Felix's special and general education teachers must make some hard decisions that will require a good understanding of the general education standards.

First, it is clear that Felix's IEP goals must address basic reading literacy as well as language development skills (e.g., increase vocabulary and develop more complex sentence structures). His teachers know that Felix needs accommodations and supports to help him learn the fourth-grade content, but given his attention difficulties and his poor language functioning, they know that learning will be slower for him and that he will not be able to keep pace with the entire fourth-grade curriculum.

In math, his teachers determine that Felix needs remediation in the area of computation, but that he will use a calculator and a writing software program during lessons involving problem solving and math applications. They also agree to focus only on the most important or essential curriculum objectives within math.

For example, the fourth-grade math standards for expressions, equations, and inequalities address the following objectives:

(a) Write and identify expressions.
(b) Represent numeric quantities using operational symbols (+, −, ×, ÷ with no remainders).
(c) Determine equivalent expressions and identify, write, solve, and apply equations and inequalities.
(d) Represent relationships using relational symbols (>, <, =) and operational symbols (+, −, ×, ÷) on either side.
(e) Use operational symbols (+, −, ×) and whole numbers (0–200).
(f) Find the unknown in an equation with one operation.

Felix's math and special education teachers collaboratively determine that Felix needs to know the concept of equivalent values and also the basic procedures for creating equivalency. He also needs to understand the operational symbols, so they identify a core set of 20 terms that they consider

(Continued)

Box 3.2 (Continued)

crucial to meet this standard. They discuss the materials that might be used to teach the concepts and agree that they will focus first on one- and two-digit whole numbers.

Similar decisions are made for science and social studies; Felix will have access to computer-based curriculum materials to help him acquire science and social studies information. In addition, the special education teacher designs some simple strategies to help Felix focus on the main idea and develop a sequence for how to approach new learning tasks.

In the reading and language arts area, Felix will devote most of his time to increasing basic word attack skills and fluency. However, he will also keep abreast of other key curriculum standards, such as developing and applying vocabulary through exposure to a variety of texts including listening to, independently reading, and discussing a variety of literary and informational texts. Some specific support strategies his teachers will employ include:

- Discussing words and word meanings daily as they are encountered in texts, instruction, and conversation
- Identifying 12 to 20 new words for deeper study each week and developing a conceptual understanding of new words
- Selecting a number of grade-level books on tape as well as other literature at Felix's reading level
- Selecting vocabulary words from subject matter content and allowing him to select words from books at his reading level.

---

include the requirement that IEPs state objectives or benchmarks, except in the case of those very few students who will take alternate assessments aligned to alternate achievement standards. For these students, the IEP team must specify annual goals and objectives or benchmarks. IEP goals should be clear enough to focus instruction and be able to be measured and reported on periodically. At the same time, goals should not be so microscopic that they limit what is taught. Goals should clearly reflect the general education content and achievement standards and curriculum.

For those students whose IEPs require either instructional objectives or benchmarks, these are simply more discrete stops toward the eventual target or annual goal, perhaps linked to grading periods or other natural breaks in an academic calendar. The parts of an instructional objective are described in Box 3.3. If you need more information about how to develop effective instructional objectives, a tried and true reference is Robert F. Mager's (1997) *Preparing Instructional Objectives: A Critical Tool in the Development of Effective Instruction.*

Box 3.3   Anatomy of an Instructional Objective

The terms "goal" and "objective" often are used interchangeably. Goals indicate the long-term outcomes expected to result from instruction, and objectives are the interim steps along the way. In the IEP, goals usually have an annual focus, and objectives generally reflect what is expected to occur in the next quarter. Content and performance standards in state and district curriculum frameworks can be thought of as goals that have a 1- to 3-year focus. Regardless of their time focus, all goals and objectives answer the following questions:

Who?	Will do?	What?	How well?	Under what conditions?

Who?	Specifies who will be expected to accomplish the goal.
Will do?	An action verb that can be observed when executed.
What?	Tells *specifically* what the student will do.
How well?	Specifies the minimum standard you establish for accomplishing the goal. If this standard is not met, the goal has not been accomplished.
Under what conditions?	Indicates the context in which the goal will be observed. This is an indication of the "level of difficulty." For example, "in 3 minutes on a test" represents a very different set of conditions than "overnight for homework."

Here is an example of a quarterly objective you might develop for a student learning to incorporate peer feedback into a final essay draft:

Who?	*Will do?*	*What?*	*How well?*	*Under what conditions?*
Roger	will write	a final version of a creative essay	with no spelling or punctuation errors	after his writing partner has proofread his first draft.

Instructional objectives originally were championed by educators working in the behaviorist tradition. This has led some teachers to believe that instructional objectives are not appropriate for dimensions such as student

(Continued)

Box 3.3 (Continued)

attitudes or thinking skills that cannot be readily observed. While it is true that not all important educational outcomes can be measured directly, objectives *can* be written for affective or covert cognitive operations. To do so, think about how you would know your instruction has been effective and the desired change in thinking has occurred. For example, suppose you want your student to develop an appreciation for various genres of writing (e.g., essay, biography, science fiction, romance, etc.). Here is a quarterly objective you might write:

During the next two months . . .

Who?	Will do?	What?	How well?	Under what conditions?
Diane	will select	at least three different types	of reading	when given a choice during free time.

When developing IEPs that are referenced to the general education curriculum, teachers should think about setting annual goals that incorporate what students in general education are expected to learn during a particular time period (e.g., during a semester, an academic year, an instructional unit, a grading period, or a multi-year span of time (e.g., Grades K–3, 6–8, etc.) that represents a major transition point in the curriculum.

Thinking about the multiyear goals is important for several reasons. First, special education teachers must keep their eye on what all students are expected to know and demonstrate on the key state and local assessments each year; these assessments reflect accumulated knowledge. This is particularly important when the results of those assessments have consequences for individual students, such as determining whether they are promoted to another grade or receive a high school diploma. Individual students' IEPs should represent stepping stones toward more advanced levels of the curriculum. Teachers cannot afford to set goals that reflect very fragmented or discrete learner expectations for a limited time period, such as one year. While these have traditionally been the types of goals written for IEPs, they will not move the student forward toward the larger sets of knowledge, skills, and processes defined by state standards and measured by state and district assessments.

The Challenge

Past practices in IEP development frequently have focused on measuring the discrete skill deficits of a student with a disability and then task analyzing the skills to identify the smallest teachable units. The specific skill deficits frequently became the annual IEP goals, and the smallest teachable units were translated into IEP objectives. These practices were based on assumptions that learning was hierarchical and that learning more complex skills could not occur until a student mastered all of the small units. This approach will not work for the type of learning we now expect of students. Nor will this approach to defining IEP goals (and objectives or benchmarks) match the type of instruction that is expected of teachers if students are to access the general education curriculum. The following questions will help you translate the knowledge about where a student is functioning in the curriculum into actual IEP goals.

Do We Need a Goal?

In our IEP decision-making process, annual goals and objectives or benchmarks are defined only in those subject matter or educational need areas where a general education curricular goal or content standard is modified or an alternate achievement standard is specified for a student. That is, if a student is expected to demonstrate the same level of achievement of the same knowledge and skills as the student's general education grade-level peers, with or without accommodations, no IEP goals should be required. However, the curricular and instructional supports and accommodations, and the individuals responsible for providing those supports, must be clearly described in the IEP.

Individualized IEP goals should be specified for related services as well as in areas of educational need that may be outside of the general curriculum where the student may be receiving specialized instruction. For example, goals related to speech and language, occupational therapy, or physical therapy may be specified. In addition, social and behavioral goals and supports, specific learning strategies that may be taught, or other skills that are outside of the general curriculum need to be addressed in IEP goals.

The other important questions you will need to answer are:

- **What do we expect the student to be able to do at the end of this instructional year in the areas we identified?**
- **Do we expect the student to be able to demonstrate the same level of achievement or performance in the same manner as a typical student?**
- **Will the student need accommodations? If so, which ones and in which subjects? Will these accommodations also be required during assessments?**

Review the discussion of accommodations in Chapter 5 regarding their purpose as well as the potential types of activities or supports that may be considered accommodations. For example, additional instruction may be provided, or special instruction may substitute for classroom instruction. A student may receive reading instruction through an approach more explicit than that used with other students in the class. There may also be additional opportunities for re-teaching, using more representations, and for practice.

Before considering modifying specific general education curriculum goals, the IEP team should consider if all possible accommodations to the general education curriculum have been made.

Setting IEP Goals for Curriculum Modifications and Alternate Achievement Standards

If the IEP team determines that some part of the general education curriculum must be modified or alternate achievement standards established for a student, the first step is to review whether the student has had access to all possible instructional accommodations and to specifically identify the discrete areas of specific subject matter, knowledge, skills, and processes that may require modifications. IEP goals need to be specified in those areas, and both general and special educators and parents must consult and collaborate on decisions to modify the general education curriculum. Decisions to modify should not be made lightly, because once a student is moved away from the general education curriculum, it is unlikely to expect the student to return to grade-level performance. All members of the IEP team must carefully consider how the changes in content reduce the student's opportunity to learn important knowledge and how that lack of opportunity may impact later achievement and educational outcomes.

Developing annual IEP goals that reflect a modified curriculum require what we earlier referred to as "educational triage" wherein the teachers must decide on the key or critical knowledge within a specific content domain. Questions important to making this determination include:

Will We Teach the Same Content but Define an Alternate Achievement Expectation?

Here, the decision is to expose the student to all of the same knowledge and basic concepts that are provided to the typical student but reduce or alter the expectations of what the student will have to achieve or be able to demonstrate. This decision is very much related to teaching less content; it assumes that although the student will receive instruction in all of what is taught, the student is expected to learn less or at a lower level than the typical same-age peer.

This is a very tricky modification because it assumes that instructional time and other resources will be devoted to fitting the student into all of the classroom instruction, even though the student will have alternate expectations. However, IEP teams are at risk of making ad hoc decisions about what to leave in and what to omit in the general education curriculum that could result in the student losing opportunities to learn important material or specific skills that address other critical educational needs beyond the general education curriculum.

Will We Teach Less Content?

Reducing the overall amount of subject matter content that a student will be explicitly taught is different from teaching the same content but changing the performance expectations. There are a variety of ways to make this modification: The student achieves fewer objectives or curricular benchmarks, the student completes shorter units or parts of a unit, the student reads fewer pages or paragraphs, or the student participates in shorter lessons or parts of lessons.

Key considerations in reducing content are similar to our earlier question in that the IEP team must determine and focus on the most important knowledge within the broad curriculum goals specified for a given grade level. The role of state content and achievement standards in this process cannot be underestimated. The purpose of content standards is to define that critical set of knowledge. It is important to understand that teachers may include in their units of instruction and lesson plans instructional objectives and activities that go beyond the core standards. If the IEP team must limit the amount of content a student learns, the team must know the essential knowledge specified in the standards and not just pick skills from the curriculum that might be easiest to teach or easiest for the student to learn.

Box 3.4 shows an example of how goals and standards should be related.

The modified goals in the example in Box 3.4 are only 2 of perhaps as many as 10 or 12 that define the general education curriculum goals of one fourth-grade math standard related to spatial sense, measurement, and geometry. It is obvious from this example that the process of goal setting can become enormously complex and time consuming if teachers approach the IEP development as parallel activity that tries to restate standards or general education curriculum goals.

Instead, special education teachers need to be familiar with the underlying intended achievement that one would expect to see if the student is making progress toward proficiency in the essential areas of the curriculum. Once the IEP team clearly understands what they want to "see" the student do, the team has a better understanding of how to develop annual goals that reflect the desired student performance intended in the standard.

The IEP team will also need to consider whether the student needs instructional accommodations related to the curriculum modifications as well as other

---

Box 3.4   Relationship of Goals to Standards

Standard: The learner will demonstrate an understanding of, and be able to apply, the properties and relationships in geometry and standard units of measurement.

General Education Curricular Goal: Use manipulatives, pictorial representations, and appropriate vocabulary to identify properties of polyhedra; identify polyhedra in the environment.

Modified Goal: Use a variety of manipulatives, pictures, and real-life objects to demonstrate properties and shapes of familiar objects in the student's home and school environments.

General Education Curricular Goal: Estimate and measure length, capacity, and mass using these units: inches, yards, miles, centimeters, meters, kilometers; milliliters, cups, and pints; kilograms and tons.

Modified Goal: Estimate and measure length, area, and capacity of familiar objects and places in the student's home and school environments using inches, cups, and pints.

areas of the curriculum, and if so, which ones? Is there an accommodation that can augment existing skills and abilities? Can an accommodation compensate for, or bypass, the student's disability without altering the learning task itself?

What Specialized Interventions Will Be Required?

Not only will the IEP team need to determine how the modified curriculum IEP goals will be addressed, but they will also need to consider additional educational needs of the students in areas beyond the general curriculum. The team must address these in the IEP and specify annual goals.

Will We Set Alternate Achievement Standards?

Alternate achievement standards apply to a few students, typically those with significant cognitive disabilities, who may have highly individualized annual IEP goals and objectives or benchmarks. The annual goals are to be based within the same content areas reflected in the state standards but will reflect very different knowledge and skill requirements.

During the time a class is working on a unit on electricity and magnetism, a student who has goals based on alternate standards might complete a unit on personal safety with electricity. The student might use a different set of instructional materials than is used by the rest of the class. For example, a student with reading problems might use books or simple reading materials during a literature class or may only be able to use an assistive technology device to access and respond to information.

Annual IEP goals should clearly specify the expectations and outcomes in terms of what knowledge is to be gained and what the student is to do with that knowledge. IEP goals based on alternate achievement standards should be developed with the same long-term multiyear perspective. That is, the IEP team needs to be clear about why certain knowledge or skills have been selected and what impact these skills will have on long-term educational outcomes. The goals should also be measurable and attainable within the constraints of the instructional time and the instructional environments available to the student. Teachers should be less concerned about how elegantly the goals are stated and focus more on their accuracy as instructional targets. The elements of immediacy and specificity discussed in Chapter 2 should be considered here.

The IEP goals should also be aligned with the alternate assessments required by the state. Finally, IEP goals based on alternate achievement standards should reflect challenging expectations for the student. Goals should not be mired in low-level skills. However, at the same time, they should reflect the critical academic and functional skills essential to a student's future.

IEP OBJECTIVES AND BENCHMARKS

The 2004 IDEA amendments removed the requirement that IEPs have goals as well as objectives and benchmarks, except, as we noted earlier, for those students who will be held to alternate achievement standards. Changing the requirement to develop objectives is seen as reducing paperwork associated with the IEP and also intended to lead to IEPs that are more challenging and better aligned with state standards and the general education curriculum.

Yet, objectives and benchmarks can provide important information to parents, students, and teachers about the specifics of what is to be taught. Objectives are the smaller steps on the map to the ultimate performance targets specified by IEP goals. However, recall that in Chapter 2, we discussed the balance that must be struck between establishing highly observable and measurable objectives and larger, more general statements of curriculum goals. Use of benchmarks is one way to strike this balance.

If objectives define specific steps, benchmarks are the stops along the way to the IEP goals. Benchmarks are the exemplars of performance expected at key points during the school year. For general educators, these frequently translate into instructional units or blocks of instruction delivered during a grading period or semester. In the example in Box 3.4, the goals also would have critical benchmarks and indicators. For example, the student might be expected to use the linear measures to compute length, width, and distance of a variety of real objects at the beginning of the school year, but by the end of the first grading period, the student might be expected to use linear measures to solve word problems. These early benchmarks would be followed by others, addressing other measurement skills for the next period and so forth. If a teacher wanted more specificity, objectives could be written in conjunction with the benchmarks.

Again, thinking of a road map, if you are starting in New York and driving to Los Angeles, you would need to project where you will be each night. The route you take or the speed you choose to travel may be determined based on your own needs or plans, much as you set objectives. However, each day you must monitor your progress and adjust your plans if necessary. So, too, must the IEP provide the map from which teachers, parents, and students design their journey of learning. A word of caution is in order here. The traditional way of writing IEP objectives, with some reference to percentage of mastery, will not be useful for creating objectives pertaining to complex thinking and problem solving. For example, what would it mean to say that a student is able to "write a descriptive paragraph with 85% accuracy"? Instead, IEP teams must think about objectives as a way of locating a student on some continuum of performance. Over time, the student would be expected to move along the continuum in the direction of expertise.

MAKING THE LINK BETWEEN IEP GOALS AND STATE ASSESSMENTS

The link between IEP goals and state and district assessments is critical in this era of high-stakes accountability. The key idea to remember in setting IEP goals is that they should state clear performance targets based on grade-level achievement standards and curriculum that clearly define expected student performance across multiple years. Decisions about goals impact a student's opportunity to learn and also affect how prepared a student will be when the time comes for that student to be assessed.

If the assessments are used to make high-stakes decisions (such as promotion, retention, or graduation), then decisions about goals have serious implications for a student. IEP goals that do not clearly link to the general education curriculum might not address important subject matter that will be assessed. This may mean that a student does not receive a diploma or a school may be subject to consequences. IEP teams must think about the link between goals and assessment.

First, the assessment process used to develop IEP goals should generate multiple types of evidence of the student's level of performance. This body of evidence should consist primarily (if not entirely) of classroom- and curriculum-based measures rather than formal tests. Minimally, before writing a goal, the team will want to collect multiple samples of the student's work or performance in a variety of relevant and meaningful contexts. For example, before developing a written expression goal, various samples of writing on worksheets, journals, and letters might be collected pertaining to social studies, math, and language arts. The team also would want to obtain information pertaining to the student's use of the targeted knowledge or skill from the student's parents (e.g., observations and expectations regarding writing) and teachers (e.g., current and past teachers).

Second, the continuum of competence against which the student's performance will be judged should be included in the IEP. When a goal refers to a scoring rubric that is not part of a published assessment system (e.g., a state performance assessment program), that rubric should be attached directly to the IEP. When a scoring rubric associated with established state or district assessments is used, this rubric can simply be referenced. For example, an IEP goal in mathematics for a middle school student might look like this:

Expected Outcome

Willa will use variables in simple equations, inequalities, and formulas to solve two-step math problems.

Present Level of Performance

On five separate occasions, when presented with two-step math problems requiring use of variables, either developed by her teacher or sampled from the State Assessment Resource Kit, Willa's performance was scored by three different teachers at either "0" or "1" on the state's 5-point scoring rubric for mathematics problem solving.

Annual Goal

By May 12, 2006, Willa's performance in solving two-step math problems requiring use of variables will earn scores of "3" or "4" from at least three separate teachers using the state's 5-point scoring rubric for mathematics problem solving.

From IEP Goals to Instruction

The idea behind setting IEP goals that are referenced to state standards and the general education curriculum is that they will drive changes in where and how the student is instructed. However, this is neither easy nor automatic. Changing how we teach students is an important aspect of guaranteeing access to the general education curriculum. We already have discussed aspects of designing instruction that matches the demands of new standards-based curriculum. We also have addressed the important distinctions between accommodations and modifications. We have noted how IEP goals must be based on a comprehensive assessment of a student's current status in the general education curriculum.

Furthermore, before an IEP team modifies or changes the performance expectations for a student, the team must ensure that the overall conditions of instruction that exist in a classroom will enable the student to achieve the goals. Therefore, teachers need to examine current classroom practices and materials to determine the type and amount of accommodations needed by a particular student. Remember, just because a student may be entitled to accommodations, they should be considered only when the instruction in the general classrooms is unlikely to allow the student to access or progress in the curriculum. To the maximum extent possible, the instructional environment in the classroom should eliminate the need for accommodations and modifications. One way to accomplish this goal is through application of the principles of universal design for learning, discussed in Chapter 5.

It should be pretty obvious by now that special and general educators will be jointly responsible for providing students with disabilities access to the general education curriculum. This will require that teachers engage in a variety of collaborative activities, including joint planning, consultation, and co-teaching. In addition, special and general educators need to participate together in professional development designed to help them develop standards-based instruction. They should collaborate, with families, in school improvement planning and similar school-based activities related to raising the achievement of every student in a school. In other words, there must be collective responsibility for providing every student meaningful and effective access to the general education curriculum.

We know that general and special educator collaboration is a key feature of schools that work successfully for students with and without disabilities (Caron & McLaughlin, 2003). These schools are defined by a common set of characteristics including:

- A clearly defined core curriculum and set of performance standards that *every* teacher understands and can articulate. At the high school level, this is specific to subject matter areas, whereas at the elementary and middle school levels, faculty share an interest in the total curriculum.

- Clear annual school improvement targets, based on student data that include student performance on assessments; parent/community perceptions of the school; student attendance, suspensions, expulsions; and school climate.

• Expectations that every teacher contributes to achieving the school improvement goals and must be involved in the overall school improvement planning process. Often, teachers and parents work in small groups to focus on a particular improvement goal or to collect and examine data and develop strategies.

• Time and opportunity through a variety of venues to problem solve and share ideas and strategies—as a faculty, in small groups, and between individual teachers.

• A shared language among special and general education teachers that centers on curriculum goals and assessments. There is no talk of "your student" or "my student," but "our student."

• Clearly articulated expectations that *every* child in the school can achieve at higher levels and that achievement is valued among all students.

• Students are not "blamed" for low achievement, and no teacher abdicates responsibility for teaching the curriculum just because a student is in special education. *All* teachers accept responsibility for helping *all* students progress and achieve. In addition to these important characteristics, schools that focus on providing every student access to the general education curriculum engage in co-teaching, consultation, and collaboration.

Special and General Education Collaboration

There are different approaches to special and general education collaboration that are commonly used in classrooms. Most common are co-teaching and collaborative consultation (see Friend & Cook, 1996). Both approaches are characterized by equality between teachers or individuals in terms of responsibilities and roles. They also involve shared problem solving and planning. Examples of collaboration to provide access to the general curriculum are shown in Boxes 3.5 and 3.6.

Collaboration can take many forms, as the examples illustrate, but for most teachers in most situations, the need for a balance of authority and responsibility works best. Working collaboratively to assess educational progress and design interventions is best. Even better is having ongoing support and feedback as the strategy or intervention is implemented.

Co-Teaching

Co-teaching is an increasingly common instructional collaboration model that general and special education teachers use to help students access the general education curriculum. As the name implies, co-teaching means that at least one general and one special educator together provide instruction to a group of special and general education students in the same classroom. The principles of co-teaching are similar to team teaching, with the exception that the special educator's primary responsibility is to ensure that students with disabilities in the classroom are accessing the curriculum and otherwise working toward the goals of their IEPS. But, the co-teaching model offers opportunities to meet the needs of a diverse group of students.

Box 3.5 An Example of Collaboration: Watertown School District

Watertown school district has a long history of supporting special education students in general education classrooms. Very few students are educated outside of general education classrooms for any period of time. Special and general educators collaborate and team-teach, and para-educators are available in the schools to assist general and special education teachers with special education students.

The district has strong expectations that students with disabilities will participate in the district curriculum and be held accountable for achieving state standards.

Despite the high level of support, both special and general education teachers are concerned about the level of the state standards and the number of concepts and skills they must teach. This has resulted in an accelerated pace of instruction and more and more students needing expanded opportunities for review and reinforcement of skills.

General and special educators have structured co-planning time and work collaboratively. They have had extensive joint professional development and have a great deal of professional discretion in how to best structure their interactions and instructional groups. General and special education teachers work very hard to ensure that students with disabilities have access to the curriculum. They share knowledge of the standards and the general curriculum and engage in discussions about how individual students are performing in the standards and curriculum. They do not focus on day-to-day lesson plans as much as they plan around units or larger segments of instruction that address specific standards. They load up on planning at the beginning of grading periods and before major instructional units, asking the following questions:

- Which standards will be addressed?
- What will students be expected to know and do at the end of the unit?
- Where are students with IEPs currently performing?
- What are the core and essential standards that every student should attain and which are relevant to student with IEPs?

The answers to these questions help determine the aspects of the curriculum that will be the focus of special education interventions provided by either the general or the special education teacher, or both. All teachers, as well as speech and language therapists and other specialists, have a clear idea of the outcomes a student is expected to achieve after instruction in the intended curriculum.

Box 3.6   Providing Access Through Collaboration

In a fifth-grade classroom, the teacher is presenting a lesson on Egypt and the pyramids. In this class of 23 students are 4 students with IEPs. Among the four students, one is functionally a nonreader, and the other three are about 2 to 3 years below grade level. All have poor attention, memory, and organization. One student has significant behavior difficulties and is on and off medication. Each child is seen separately by the special education teacher about 3 or 4 times a week for intensive instruction in reading and learning strategies.

Each student has a worksheet of a passage to read, followed by questions to be answered. The questions have been modified for the students with IEPs. The lesson addresses several of the state standards in history and reading. The teacher leads a lively discussion with the entire class, using guided questioning to explain why pyramids were built and how they related to religious aspects of Egyptian culture. Then, students break into four discussion groups to read the passage and answer the questions as a group. The students with IEPs participate in the whole class instruction, but during independent seatwork, a general education teacher, an aide, and peers support the individual students. Groups are then re-formed for direct skill instruction. The students with IEPs and one other student requiring remediation meet as a group with the special education teacher who does a lesson on pyramids, asking, "Who, What, When, and Where" questions. There is lively discussion about the most important aspects of building the pyramids. Students take turns dictating sentences (using "who," "what," "when," and "where") and critiquing one another's sentences.

What's right with this example?

- The teachers share a common vision of the key concepts and knowledge to be addressed in the lesson.
- There is active sharing of responsibility for instruction.

What needs improvement in this example?

- Perhaps students with disabilities should not be taken out of the discussion, as they could profit from the language and ideas that are being expressed. These ideas could later be expanded or paraphrased through guided question and answer in a small group.

Friend and Cook (1996) describe five co-teaching approaches:

1. One teaching, one supporting

2. Station teaching

3. Parallel teaching

4. Alternative teaching

5. Team teaching

One teaching/one supporting is the most common form of co-teaching and the easiest to implement. In this model, one teacher has the primary role of designing and delivering instruction while the second teacher floats, helping and observing individual students. A major downside to this model is that too often it is based on having all children learn the same content in the same manner. This means that the special educator's role is to help students keep up or catch up rather than to design individualized accommodations or differentiate instruction. In some classrooms, the special educator functions almost like an instructional assistant in the classroom. In other classrooms, the general and special educators take turns leading a lesson. Aside from the inequities in roles that this approach to co-teaching may create, it does not result in genuine access to the general curriculum for the students.

When two teachers station-teach, they divide the content or lesson, and each is individually responsible for planning and teaching part of it to some part of the class. Students move through both teacher-led groups. Each teacher teaches every student but in small groups. In this model, the special educator functions like another teacher in terms of responsibility for the curriculum.

Parallel teaching involves joint planning, and each teacher delivers the same content and instruction to half the class. This type of co-teaching is best for drill exercises or when the content is so specific that the instruction in both groups is similar.

Alternative teaching is probably the second most common form of special and general education co-teaching. In this model, special and general educators jointly plan instruction, but the special educator focuses on re-teaching or reinforcing materials taught, differentiating instruction, and making curricular accommodations and modifications for small groups of students that may need extra assistance. This model can work for any student who may need some additional help. It is important in implementing this model not to stigmatize or otherwise dumb down the curriculum content. Furthermore, special and general education teachers must be clear about the core and essential knowledge that the students are expected to learn.

Finally, team teaching requires equal planning and equal roles in implementing instruction. In fact, in a team-teaching arrangement, individual teams may use all or any of the strategies discussed above. Teachers will trade off roles and groups of students.

Any or all of the above strategies will only be effective if the collaborating teachers have equal status in the classroom and recognize what knowledge and skills each brings to the collaborative effort.

CONCLUSION

In this chapter, we have presented a model framework for developing individual student IEPs that are truly aligned with state content and achievement standards and the general education curriculum. This is not an easy process, nor can it be done quickly or without a sound understanding of the meaning of curriculum, purposes of assessment, and how to match curriculum demands to instruction—all topics that we have addressed in this book. What is more, we have clearly indicated that in today's climate of high-stakes accountability, providing students with disabilities access to the general education curriculum is even more important to schools and to individual students.

When we completed the first edition of this book, the 1997 IDEA amendments were just becoming reality in the schools and the meaning of "access to the general curriculum" was unclear to many; in addition, the No Child Left Behind Act (NCLB) had not yet been passed by Congress. Now as we complete this second edition, we find a New IDEA with even stronger language linking special education to general education, specifically to requirements that all students with disabilities access one set of state content standards and participate in state assessments and accountability. In today's schools, the New IDEA and NCLB are intertwined, and all teachers and practitioners must focus on improving the performance levels of all students. With this new emphasis on results, every teacher needs to fully understand what it means to provide access to the general education curriculum in a way that leads to increasing levels of achievement and ultimately better school outcomes.

4

The Locks on the Doors to Learning

M. C. Gore

We are high school and middle school teachers. We love our disciplines passionately. Unlike people in some other professions, we have not spent our lives chasing material wealth to adorn our bodies in gold and jewels. Instead, we have spent our lives pursuing ideas. The *big ideas* of our disciplines are our priceless jewels: diamonds, rubies, emeralds, and sapphires. Our jewels catch the light and fling it in a thousand directions. The tools that help us fashion the jewels are the fire over which we soften the gold that encases them, the jeweler's loupe, the gauges, and the cutting tools. Those are our scientific methods, our deconstructions, our primary documents, our peer-reviewed journals, and our stacks of reference books.

We want to share the wealth with young people, and we laugh out loud when students are wowed by the colors, and the shapes, and the way the light dances off the facets of our jewels. But some of our students—often those who have learning problems—appear apathetic about entering our stronghold and immersing themselves in the mounds of gems: They shrug their shoulders, roll their eyes, and yawn. They would much rather play videogames.

Sometimes our tempers flare at their cavalier dismissal. Sometimes we tell ourselves that they do not deserve our treasures, our priceless ideas for which the likes of Socrates, Galileo, Darwin, Alice Paul, Gandhi, Martin Luther King, and countless other great thinkers have suffered. Let those unappreciative, undeserving teenagers rot their minds with their vapid videogames.

What we teachers do not see are the invisible locks that bar those students from entering into our treasure rooms. Not one lock, but many, one after the other, bar their way. When they were younger, these students were as eager as their peers to get their hands on the jewels and to sort, cut, polish, and make jewelry of their own—but years of battling the locks reduced them to a fatalism that is apparent in their mantras of "Who cares?" or "Whatever."

We did not realize until relatively recently that they were bereft of the keys to the locks on the doors. Because the locks are invisible, we did not know they existed. Only in the last 30 years have we begun to know more about the keys that help students open the locks. The keys *do* work for our students with learning problems. They work, and they work well. All we have to do is learn which keys fit which locks and then use them to help all of our students access the treasure. This book is designed to help.

Blueprint of the Stronghold

The metaphor of the jewel and the stronghold works well for this purpose. The rooms are the levels of learning in Bloom's Taxonomy. The rooms are Knowledge, Comprehension, Application, Analysis, Synthesis, and Evaluation. In the first room, Knowledge, we collect the rough, uncut stones; in the second room, Comprehension, we study and sort the stones. The third room is Application, and here we cut and polish the gems. The first of the higher-order thinking skills rooms is Analysis, and in this room we study each stone to determine how best to use it. We decide whether the stone should be a solitaire in a ring or one of a dozen stones in a heart-shaped necklace. In the Synthesis room, we take the stone and create a lovely piece of jewelry. Finally, in the Evaluation room, we bring all of our knowledge together to appraise the exquisite adornment and establish its value.

The doors to each of those rooms are Acquisition, Proficiency and Fluency, Maintenance, Generalization, and Adaptation (Smith, 1981), and our students must go through all the doors to enter each room.

Theoretically, our students must *acquire*, become *proficient and fluent, maintain, generalize/ transfer,* and *adapt knowledge* before they are completely ready to move on to the next level of learning.

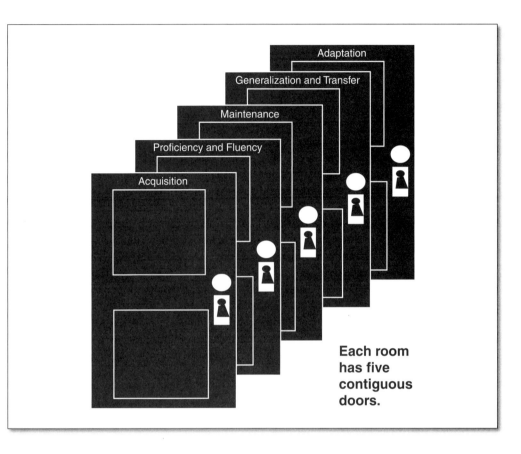

Currently, in pedagogical circles, discounting the importance of knowledge-level learning is de rigueur. We think that is unwise and that the phenomenon comes from a lack of deep understanding of Bloom and colleagues' (1956) Taxonomy of Cognitive Objectives. When we ask teacher friends exactly what the taxonomy means by *knowledge*, they are unable to tell us.

According to the taxonomy, knowledge consists of a discipline's

- Terminology
- Specifics
- Ways and means of dealing with the (1) conventions, (2) trends and sequences, (3) classifications and categories, (4) criteria, and (5) methodology of those specifics
- Universals and abstractions: (1) principles and generalizations and (2) theories and structures

Knowledge is significant, and it is a prerequisite to higher levels of thinking.

Bloom and his colleagues (1956) defined *comprehension* as *being able to translate the data, interpolate it, or extrapolate from a piece of information.* We cannot translate, interpolate, or extrapolate until we have the requisite knowledge, so our students must have full access to the first room before we can enter into the second room. If knowledge is, for example, mastery of the classification that 3, 7, and 9 are odd numbers, comprehension, then, would be interpolating 5 and extrapolating that 1, 11, and 223 are odd numbers.

Comprehension would also include telling someone else that an odd number is one indivisible by 2.

Like Knowledge, Comprehension has five doors. We must acquire comprehension, become proficient and fluent at comprehending, maintain our comprehension, generalize/ transfer, and adapt it. That is requisite to further manipulation of the data.

So it is with Application. We cannot authoritatively apply a concept or skill until we have mastery of its Knowledge and Comprehension. Without knowing that an odd number is indivisible by 2 and without being able to extrapolate that 23 is an odd number, we cannot apply the knowledge and decide whether we can have our students work in pairs when the class has 23 students enrolled.

When we reach the Higher-Order Thinking Skills of Analysis, Synthesis, and Evaluation, we find that each of them has five doors, too. We have to acquire the skills needed to analyze, become proficient and fluent with them, maintain the skill, generalize/transfer the skill when appropriate, and adapt it when necessary. The same sequence applies to Synthesis and Evaluation.

Although the doors are metaphorically and theoretically opened one at a time, in practice, students usually open multiple doors at once; for example, Knowledge and Comprehension often come hand in hand. Locating the rooms and their doors is the first step. Step 2 is understanding the locks, and we describe them next. In Chapter 3, we will discuss three master keys, and in subsequent chapters, we will describe specific keys for accessing specific rooms.

THE LOCKS ON THE DOORS

Rather than discussing each type of disability category separately, we will use noncategorical but useful terms, such as *students with exceptional learning needs (ELN), students with disabilities*, or *students with learning problems*. Unless we note otherwise, the information refers to this generic group.

For simplicity, we have organized the learning problems into categories drawn from the work of cognitive psychologists (Flavell, 1999) with the addition of an Affective category: Input Locks, Information Processing/Retention Locks, Affective Locks, and Output Locks. The Input Locks are Attention Problems, Perception Problems, Discrimination Problems, and Sequencing Problems. The Information Processing/Retention Locks are Confusion, Organization Problems, Reasoning Problems, Memory Problems, and Metacognition Problems. The Affective Locks are Frustration and Motivation Problems, and they are a direct result of the Input Locks and Information Processing/Retention Locks. The Output Lock is Persistence/Production; persistence/production problems are a result of the Affective Locks. We will discuss the Input Locks first because they contribute to the Information Processing/Retention Locks and the Affective Locks.

THE INPUT LOCKS

The Input Locks are problems with attention, perception, discrimination, and sequencing. They all involve difficulty in getting information from the outside world into the processing centers in the brain.

Attention Problems

Using neuropsychological evidence, Sturm and Zimmermann (cited in Schweitzer, Zimmermann, & Koch, 2000) developed a two-level taxonomy of attention. The upper level consists of two categories of attention: intensity and selectivity. Intensity has three subclassifications: alertness, sustained attention, and vigilance. Selectivity has three subclassifications: selective attention or focus, visual/spatial selective attention or change of visual focus, and divided attention.

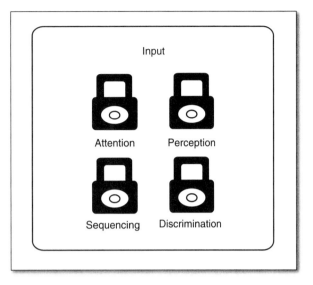

The types of attention that are most important to the teaching and learning process are sustained attention and the selective attention that refers to focus. Klorman (1991) noted that selective attention refers to intentionally focusing on relevant information while ignoring irrelevant information. She also noted that sustained attention refers to processes that are involved in maintaining attention over an extended period of time. If problems in sustained attention occur, they happen when an individual has been engaged in selective attention over a period of time. This is known to scientists and laypeople alike as *mindwandering*.

Unfortunately, many students with ELN exhibit both sustained attention and selective attention problems. For example, students with Attention Deficit Disorder have poorer comprehension on longer reading passages than on shorter reading passages. They also exhibit lower reading comprehension on longer passages than do their peers without attention problems. In addition, students with attention problems tend to be deficient in mathematics achievement, and their mathematics deficits appear to become more pronounced with age (Cherkes-Julkowski & Stolzenberg, 1991; Marshall & Hynd, 1997; Schweitzer et al., 2000).

Research on attention demonstrates that genes are in large part responsible for attention difficulties. At least part of the genetic influences involve multiple alleles on a gene that governs dopamine, dopamine receptors, and dopamine transporters (Bellgrove & Mattingley, 2008; Gizer et al., 2008).

However, regardless of the causes of attention difficulties, we have instructional keys that can help students unlock the locks caused by such problems. By using research-supported strategies, we can help them attend (selective attention) and remain (sustained attention) engaged.

Perception Problems

Visual and auditory perception deficits are hallmarks of learning disabilities (see Johnson & Myklebust, 1967), and their study has been voluminous. Our students with visual or auditory perception problems generally have good visual or auditory acuity; that is, they can see the letters on the eye chart or hear the tone on the audiometer. The problem is that the image or sound has a difficult time finding the right place in the brain so that the brain can make sense of it: The image or sound may travel down the wrong neural path and end up in some place in the brain that cannot make sense of it, or it might wander around before it finally finds the right place where the brain can make sense of it. Unfortunately, the perceptual training programs that characterized treatment of learning disabilities in the early days of the field do not help students' academic performance (Rosen, 1968).

Researchers continue to investigate visual and auditory perceptual problems. Boden and Brodeur (1999) found that adolescents who have reading disabilities are not only slower at processing visual information in the form of the written word but are also slower at processing all visual stimuli. For example, when such students see a dog walking down the street, it takes them longer to realize that what they have seen is a dog. While the difference may only be in milliseconds, the delay translates into significant difficulty in decoding text and other activities that require fluency. Other researchers have noted that students with severe reading disability can be identified by their deficiency in rapid naming ability when they are presented with items visually. Their eyes can see the object, but their brains cannot quickly make sense of what their eyes are seeing. As processing demands increase, the visual perceptual performance of students with ELN slows disproportionately, while the performance of nondisabled students remains strong.

But visual perceptual problems are not the only kind of perceptual problem that students with ELN may experience. Kruger, Kruger, Hugo, and Campbell (2001) found that the majority of the students with learning disabilities they examined had both visual and auditory perceptual disabilities. Not only did the students have difficulty processing visual input, they also had difficulty processing auditory input. Teachers, however, may be puzzled by the varying performance of students with sensory problems: New research with students with dyslexia revealed that while 30% of these students demonstrated visual and auditory processing problems, their performance on visual and auditory tasks was not stable across time (Wright & Conlon, 2009). When a student succeeds at a task one day and then does not perform well on a similar task the next day, we tend to think that the student is simply being lazy, rather than that he or she has a learning problem that waxes and wanes.

Perceptual problems create difficulties for our students outside as well as inside of the classroom. Most and Greenbank (2000) found that eighth graders with learning disabilities in visual and auditory perception were less able than their peers to discriminate the emotions of others, whether the stimulus was auditory, visual, or combined; this resulted in social difficulties. Itier and Batty (2009) noted that impaired visual processing of social partners' eyes and gaze may present a core deficiency in social relationship difficulties, and every secondary teacher recognizes the importance of social relationships in adolescence. Unfortunately, perceptual difficulties tend to remain stable throughout a person's life, so a teenager with perceptual problems that cause social difficulties will become an adult who has those same difficulties.

While we cannot fix their perceptual deficits, we can use teaching strategies that will help our students with ELN compensate for their difficulties. The strategies are easy to use, and research demonstrates that they are effective in helping students with ELN succeed.

Discrimination Problems

Discrimination, in this context, refers to the ability to differentiate between two or more entities. A high school student may have difficulty discriminating between communism and socialism, paramecium and bacterium, sine and cosine, or essential and nonessential information in writing a critical essay. Errors in discrimination often result in overgeneralization and undergeneralization; *overgeneralization* refers to incorrectly identifying an entity as a member of a class when it is not, and conversely, *undergeneralization* refers to failing to identify an entity as a member of a class when it does belong to a class.

In 1970, writing in the *Journal of Learning Disabilities,* Kidd noted that the discriminatory repertoire is the basis of all learning: Understanding an object or a concept consists of class inclusion and class differentiation. First, we must be able to determine to what class a thing belongs—such as a lemon belongs to the class of citrus fruit—and then we must be able to differentiate the thing from other members of that class—such as a lemon is yellow, sour, and more oblong, while a tangerine is orange, sweet, and more round. Such discrimination is difficult for students with ELN, and when the content is challenging, the student's difficulty is compounded.

In addition, Richards, Samuels, Ternure, and Ysseldyke (1990) discovered that students with learning disabilities are more likely to notice salient information than the critical information that teachers direct them to observe; they have difficulty discriminating between the critical data we want them to learn and the irrelevant. For example, they are far more likely to remember Franklin Delano Roosevelt's affair with Lucy Mercer than they are to remember his role in the New Deal. They focus on the wrong information, thereby studying for a test, failing the test, and then earnestly telling us, "I flunked because I studied the wrong stuff!"

Auditory discrimination problems affect many of our students. Watson (1991) examined the relationship of auditory discrimination to intelligence in college students. She found moderate correlations between auditory discrimination and intelligence scores. Subsequently, others have found that young readers who have dyslexia may not be able to maintain phonemic information in their short-term memories long enough to discriminate among sounds and that children with a learning impairment have poorer auditory discrimination on a two-tone discrimination task than do typical children.

Auditory discrimination difficulties also present difficulties for students with ELN; Newport and Howarth (2009) noted that an optimal auditory processing window for social interactions exists. Although the time differentials between normal and abnormal auditory discrimination may differ only by milliseconds, the slight delay may create subtle communication difficulties. Adolescents may be referring to such an auditory difficulty in a peer when they say, "I can't tell you what I don't like about him . . . . He's just weird. . . ."

Visual discrimination difficulties also affect many of our students. Students with learning disabilities are less able than typical peers at discriminating between orthographically legitimate and illegitimate pairs of letters, and some children with intellectual disabilities have difficulty with visual discrimination (Kavale, 1982).

Difficulty with discrimination extends to our students' problem-solving and reasoning ability. For example, McLeskey (1977) found that students with ELN have difficulty discriminating between when a response is and is not appropriate. Whereas McLeskey's nondisabled students tried a complex variety of responses in solving a novel problem, his students with disabilities could not discriminate between situations in which a problem-solving strategy was and was not appropriate. Other researchers have found that adolescents with learning disabilities performed worse on discriminant learning tasks that required them to code, recode, and recall information than did their nondisabled peers.

Discrimination problems extend outside the classrooms to our students' personal lives. Moffatt and others (1995) documented the difficulty persons with intellectual disabilities had in discriminating among emotions and expressing empathy—the greater the degree of intellectual disability, the greater the difficulty with discrimination. As noted earlier, eighth graders with learning disabilities were less able than their peers to discriminate between the emotions of others, such as telling fear from anger or anxiety from sadness.

The research consistently demonstrates that the discrimination tasks in which we engage so cavalierly every day are challenging to our students with learning problems. Fortunately, we can use good inclusion strategies to help them.

Sequencing Problems

The difficulty in sequencing that characterizes so many students with ELN has been documented since the early days of research on learning disabilities. Cohen, Spruill, and Herns (1982) found sequencing to be one of the six most problematic areas for students with auditory learning disabilities. (The others were attention, word retrieval, identification of antonyms, passive relationships, and memory.)

Even many gifted students who have learning disabilities experience difficulty with sequencing. Schiff, Kaufman, and Kaufman (1981) studied gifted children with learning disabilities. The children whom they studied had excellent verbal skills and many talents, but they were deficient in sequencing, as well as motor control and emotional development. The sequencing problems of students with learning disabilities do not retreat with high school graduation—they persist. For example, Blabock (1982) found that college students with auditory learning disabilities experienced persistent problems in sequencing. A number of strategies in this book are designed to help us help our students ensure that they can properly sequence ordered material in our disciplines. With our encouragement, they may be able to generalize/transfer the strategies to other classes and to their lives outside of school.

THE INFORMATION PROCESSING/RETENTION LOCKS

Once the information from the external environment enters the brain of a student with ELN, the student must then process and retain that information. Several locks bar the student from processing and remembering that information. Those locks include Confusion, Organization Problems, Reasoning Problems, Memory Problems, and Metacognition Problems.

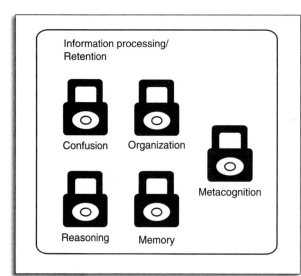

Confusion

Since the early days of learning-disability research, confusion has been documented as a learning problem that is characteristic of children with learning disabilities. Such findings continue to be confirmed and expanded across time. For example, Barkin, Gardner, Kass, and Polo (1981) documented left-right confusion; others have documented confusion in sequencing, sound-ground and figure-ground confusion, linguistic confusion, and cognitive confusion. In contrast to nondisabled peers, even after becoming acquainted with a task, students with learning disabilities continue to be confused about how to execute it.

In 1998, Scott and Nelson reported on the confusion in generalizing social responding experienced by students with learning disabilities, and others have identified their confusion about adult roles. Guyton (1968) even argued that students' confused emotions can compound their cognitive confusion.

A serious facet of confusion is that while nondisabled learners typically realize that they are confused, and can therefore ask for assistance from peers or teachers, students who have disabilities often fail to realize that they are confused. They are confused about their confusion. Because they think that they understand something when they are actually confused, they fail to ask for assistance or clarification. They are both astonished and deeply disappointed when they complete an assignment on which they thought they had performed well, only to find that they failed because they were confused about either the instructions or the content. When they fail an assignment, our students with ELN may document their failure when they tell us, "I was all mixed up about what we were supposed to do!"

The jury is in, and the verdict is not confusing: Our students with learning problems are confused much of the time. But we have the ability to help prevent much of their confusion if we use appropriate instructional strategies.

Organization Problems

Difficulty with organizational skills has long been documented in the literature on learning and emotional disability (Zera & Lucian, 2001). The National Dissemination Center for Children with Disabilities (NICHCY) explained that many students who are learning disabled have difficulty organizing bits of information to consolidate them into concepts, often learning multiple facts that they cannot draw upon to answer related questions. For example, the student may learn that the United States has a legislative branch that makes laws, an executive branch that enforces the laws, and a judicial branch that interprets the laws. However, he or she may not be able to organize this information to answer the question: "Explain the functions of the branches of the U.S. government." NICHCY noted that the entire context of their lives may reflect this disorganization.

Teachers, parents, and adolescent students with disabilities report that their poor organizational skills create problems with completing work, locating materials, and using time wisely. Adolescents with disabilities, and their parents and teachers, identify poor organizational skills as one of their three most problematic areas—the other two being communication and social skills. Such difficulty does not lessen with age; adults with learning disabilities report that poor organizational skills are an important impediment to their career and life success (Malcolm, Polatajko, & Simons, 1990).

Many of the strategies in this book are designed to help students organize information into meaningful wholes. Not only can we use the strategies to their advantage, but our nondisabled students will benefit as well.

Reasoning Problems

Many students with learning problems have trouble with reasoning skills. In fact, the problem is so pronounced that in 1993, Stanovich proposed a new category of learning disability: *dysrationalia*. Stanovich defined dysrationalia as *the inability to think rationally despite adequate intelligence*. Although leaders in the field promptly dismissed the concept with amusement (Sternberg, 1993, 1994), Stanovich's notion of irrationality as a separate learning disability points out the extent to which poor reasoning skills characterize the thinking of some of our students with ELN.

Students who have different subcategories of learning disabilities differ in their ability to reason. Schiff, Bauminger, and Toledo (2009) found that students with nonverbal learning disabilities demonstrate significantly more difficulty with analogical reasoning than do their peers without ELN or their peers with verbal learning disabilities. Students with learning disabilities demonstrate less coordinated thought structures than do their nondisabled peers; in addition, they are less likely to employ second-order logical structures than are their peers. They also display operational logic structures significantly less often than do their peers on mathematics tasks.

The problems persist. College students with dyscalculia differ significantly from their nondisabled peers in reasoning ability (McGlaughlin, Knoop, & Holliday, 2005). In addition, college students diagnosed as having learning disabilities demonstrate difficulty in learning to use logic and require explicit instruction in thinking skills—instruction that they may not receive in college (Utzinger, 1982).

Memory Problems

Mnemonic problems are generally present in students with learning disabilities (McNamara, 1999), and they continue to be investigated. In fact, Boudah and Weiss (2002), writing in the ERIC Digest *Learning Disabilities Overview: Update 2002,* called memory problems one of five common problems of students with learning disabilities. Likewise, writing in the ERIC Digest *Nonverbal Learning Disability: How to Recognize It and Minimize Its Effects,* Foss (2001) listed memory problems as one of the four difficulties she identified.

D'Amico and Passolunghi (2009) conducted a two-year longitudinal study investigating how well students with learning disabilities in mathematics could retrieve both mathematical and nonmathematical information from long-term memory. The students with ELN and their matched controls differed markedly in the speed with which they could retrieve information from memory. This finding applied to both the numerical and nonnumerical information, even though the students were disabled only in mathematics.

Swanson, Xinhua, and Jerman (2009) compared short-term memory and long-term memory among students with a broad range of ages, reading abilities, and IQ scores. They found significant differences in both types of memory between those students who had reading disabilities and those students who did not. The differences persisted across age groups and IQ scores.

Mnemonic problems affect students' performance across the curriculum, not only in reading and mathematics. Teachers in the social studies and sciences have noted the need for memory strategies for students with disabilities in those areas, too (Steele, 2007; Ward-Lonergan, Liles, & Anderson, 1998). Keyword mnemonic strategies have been found to significantly increase the social studies achievement of secondary students who were English Language Learners in an inclusive secondary classroom in a racially diverse, large, urban high school (Fontana, Scruggs, & Mastropieri, 2007). The course of study involved nationalism, imperialism, World Wars I and II, and the period between the wars; the vocabulary included words such as *ecumenism, protectorate,* and *reparations.* Scruggs and Mastropieri (2007) reviewed a variety of approaches to teaching science to students with ELN and stated that mnemonics instruction is an extremely effective and robust feature of good instruction for such students when teaching content knowledge. The studies that they reviewed involved the use of mnemonics instruction in paleontology, geology, chemistry, and biology.

Memory is important in every area of life, not only in academics. McNamara (1999) argued that memory problems contribute to the social relationship problems of students with learning difficulties. Being unable to remember social conventions, particularly when required to think on their feet, creates relationship difficulties for students with ELN. Forgetting appointments, dates, and promises all cause social difficulties—sometimes rupturing relationships.

Like the other characteristics of students with learning problems, mnemonic difficulties do not end with graduation. Adults with learning disabilities continue to experience problems with mnemonic functions (Jordan, 2000). Like the memory problems of our students, those of adults can be devastating, especially when they involve employers' demands, policies, or expectations.

Metacognition Problems

Metacognition, as discussed by A. L. Brown (1975, 1978, 1979) and J. H. Flavell (1971, 1979, 1999) in their extensive work on the subject, particularly in the area of reading comprehension, refers to thinking about thinking and controlling thinking; metamemory (thinking about and controlling remembering), meta-attention (thinking about and controlling attention), and metacomprehension (thinking about and controlling comprehension) are closely related to metacognition.

Students with ELN tend to be passive learners who are unaware of their own learning processes (Wang, 1987); they fail to monitor their own learning. For example, Garcia and Fidalgo (2008) examined the metacognition of middle school students with and without learning disabilities who were engaged in the writing process. The students who had learning disabilities were far more passive in the writing process, demonstrating far less self-monitoring of their writing than did peers and spending less time on pre-writing activities, revision, and the editing of their work.

Poor metacognition results in mnemonic difficulties, transfer and generalization problems, reading comprehension problems, and a host of other difficulties (Brown & Palincsar, 1982; Wong, 1985). We have all had students say, "But I read the chapter!" when they performed poorly on examinations. True, they pronounced the words on the pages, but they did not monitor whether they understood the meanings embedded in the words they pronounced. Typical learners would have realized that they did not understand what they were reading, and they would have employed strategies to improve their comprehension.

In *Research on Interventions for Adolescents With Learning Disabilities: A Meta-Analysis of Outcomes Related to Higher-Order Processing*, Swanson (2001) noted that metacognitive instruction produced large positive benefits for learners. This supports the large-scale study of learning strategies that students use in science, mathematics, and reading that Chiu, Chow, and Mcbride-Chang (2007) conducted. In their investigation of metacognitive and other strategies employed by 158,848 students in 34 countries, the researchers found that those students who used metacognitive strategies when they studied mathematics or science outscored peers who used other learning strategies.

Metacognition is critical for academic success across the curriculum. Wang, Haertel, and Walberg (1993/1994) used a knowledge base of 11,000 statistical findings to identify the magnitude of 28 categories of influences on student learning. Only classroom management was more influential on student learning than was the teaching of metacognitive strategies.

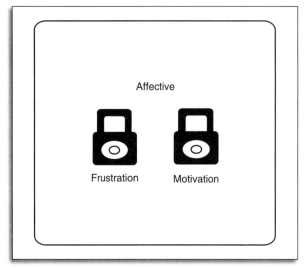

Metacognitive training extends beyond academics. For example, metacognitive training in social skills improves the social adjustment of incarcerated boys with learning problems and reduces the anger behavior and aggressive acts of elementary, middle school, and high school boys with anger management problems (Larson & Gerber, 1987; Smith, 1992).

In the context of our classrooms, we can use metacognitive strategies that will increase students' achievement in our discipline. That is good news. But the better news is that when we teach students to use metacognitive strategies, we may contribute to improving their lives both inside and outside of the classroom.

THE AFFECTIVE LOCKS

Frustration and Motivation Problems are the Affective Locks that bar our students' entry into the vault. Frustration and Motivation Problems are the direct result of Input and Information Processing/Retention Problems. Only by helping students unlock the previous locks can we help them unlock these barriers. But the phenomenon is cyclical in nature. Once we help them unlock these locks, our students will be better able to unlock the previous locks and, at the same time, the Persistence/Production Problems Lock.

Frustration

Writing in an ERIC Digest, Bergert (2000) noted that frustration is an early warning sign of learning disabilities; the frustration difficulties are evident in both academic and social arenas. As early as 1968, Beckman identified low frustration tolerance as a behavioral characteristic of children with learning disabilities. Toro, Weissberg, Guare, and Libenstein (1990) found that the poor social problem-solving skills of children with learning disabilities were complicated by their low frustration tolerance, and Murray and Whittenberger (1983) cautioned that frustration with learning problems contributed to the problems of many aggressive, severely behavior disordered children. In addition, Scime and Norvilitis (2006) found that students with Attention Deficit Hyperactivity Disorder not only became frustrated with difficult mathematics problems more easily than did their peers, but that they knew that they were more easily frustrated than nondisabled students were.

As early as 1978, Kronick noted that frustration characterizes the life experiences of adolescents with ELN both inside and outside of the classroom. But the problem of frustration does not end when high school does. Mays and Imel (1982), writing in an ERIC Fact Sheet, noted that low frustration tolerance is one of nine observable characteristics of adults with learning disabilities, and Lancaster, Mellard, and Hoffman (2001) reported that college students with learning disabilities reported frustration as one of their six major difficulties. (The other difficulties were concentration, distraction, test anxiety, remembering, and mathematics.) Even high ability students with learning disabilities who have earned college degrees have noted their frustration with certain academic areas.

Having learning problems frustrates our students who cope with them day in and day out, every day of their lives. Thank goodness we can help prevent much of their frustration when we use good inclusive practices.

Motivation Problems

The Input and Information Processing/ Retention locks prevent our students from being able to learn our disciplines, but they do teach them one thing: helplessness. In fact, the Motivation Problems Lock could easily be called the Learned Helplessness (Seligman, 1975) Lock because learned helplessness contributes to our students' low achievement motivation.

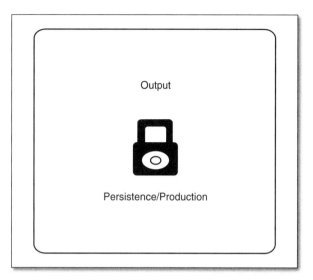

Low academic achievement motivation is a characteristic common to our students with ELN. In general, students with ELN tend to be extrinsically—rather than intrinsically—motivated to complete schoolwork, and of the various types of learning problems that students experience, our adolescents with learning disabilities demonstrate lower achievement motivation toward schoolwork than do their peers who have emotional disorders (Fulk, Brigham, & Lohman, 1998; Okolo & Bahr, 1995).

But some students with learning disabilities are highly academically motivated. Those students who are highly academically motivated are intrinsically, rather than extrinsically, motivated to excel in school (Dev, 1998). Also, many students who are not academically motivated are motivated in nonacademic areas. In areas in which they experience success, students with ELN are highly motivated (Adelman & Taylor, 1990). We have all known students who brag that they have worked for hours without food, rest, or sleep to master a complicated video game.

Learned helplessness appears to be at the root of low achievement motivation in students with disabilities (Valas, 2001). After repeated failures, students learn that they cannot succeed in school. This attribution becomes so deeply embedded that they may passively or actively refuse to try to achieve in schoolwork. A large-scale study in Sweden revealed that the more helpless a student feels, the more the student withdraws from engagement in school, the more depressive symptomatology the student exhibits, and the more the student engages in rule-breaking behavior (Määtt, Nurmi, & Stattin, 2007).

Once established, learned helplessness tends to persist, but fortunately, we can help combat learned helplessness by making assignments more approachable. Success breeds motivation.

THE OUTPUT LOCK

The Output Lock refers to Production Problems. However, we include the Persistence Lock with the Output Lock because combining them is intuitively appealing. Our students' problems with persistence are most observable when we have required them to produce some product.

Persistence/Production Problems

Persistence is a critical attribute for academic success. Somers, Owens, and Piliawsky (2008) investigated the predictors of academic success among 118 urban African American high school students. Personal persistence and educational intentions were the most powerful predictors of academic success of the multiple individual and social variables examined.

Our students with ELN often experience difficulty persisting in and completing classroom assignments and homework. Their teachers rate them as less persistent than nondisabled students and as deficient in quantity and quality of story production as compared to their nondisabled peers. In addition, while most students enjoy doing projects, students with ELN have difficulty completing them (Graves, Semmel, & Gerber, 1994; Salend & Gajria, 1995).

Adolescents and young adults with disabilities have difficulty completing their education; they comprise one of the three categories of students most likely to drop out of high school (the others being foreign-born students and those who were retained in one or more grades). Wave 2 of the National Longitudinal Transition Study published by the U.S. Department of Education in 2006 revealed that 28% of students with disabilities dropped out of high school; the group with the highest dropout rate was the students with emotional disabilities: 44% of the students in that group left school without graduating. College students with disabilities are less likely to have completed their degree in five years than are their peers without disabilities, and numerous studies have noted that adults and adolescents with mild intellectual disabilities have difficulty with work completion (Hurst & Smerdon, 2000a, 2000b; McMillen, Kaufman, & Klein, 1997).

From elementary school through adulthood, our students struggle with persisting in and completing what they need to do. While we cannot help in every arena, we can use supportive teaching strategies that will help students with ELN complete assignments in our classrooms.

THE SUM TOTAL OF THE LOCKS

Metaphorically, we do not think that multiple locks represent an additive relationship; we do not even think that the relationship is multiplicative. Instead, we think that the relationship of multiple locks on a student's learning is exponential. As with many other things, a synergy takes place among the locks, and the total damage that they do to our students is greater than the sum of their parts.

The news is serious: The learning problem locks make life and learning difficult for students with ELN. Reading about them could discourage us. But that is counterproductive. What we must do is learn how to use keys to help our students open the locks. Then we can invite them into the stronghold, and even into the vault, and offer them a handful of jewels.

5

How Teachers Teach

Good Practices for All

Toby J. Karten

Special education research, because of its complexity, may be the hardest of the hardest-to-do science. One feature of special education research that makes it more complex is the variability of the participants.

—Odom et al., 2005

When classified students are included in classrooms, both special education and general education teachers are indeed challenged to figure out ways that students with special needs can learn skills and strategies in a whole-class environment as opposed to a small-group setting. Some teachers are under so much pressure, trying to do it all, while a few do not even try to adjust their way of teaching to reach a variety of learners. However, with the right attitude and support, all students can learn and be successful.

First off, educators must buy in, and know that students do not know. Some educators feverishly try to teach every aspect of a concept without intermittently stopping the learning and assessing the knowledge. Students need to practice, apply, and test out the *new stuff.* Teachers, assuming that the students *know the lesson,* often allow misconceptions to escalate! It may sound ridiculous, but some teachers need to do less. When teachers observe and listen to the verbal and body language of their students, they are more attuned to their students' needs, even before formal assessments are given. Classified students in inclusive classrooms are often quite good at *feigning* their understanding with the correct body language, such as direct eye contact or even nodding their head, without actually *getting the concept.* Frequent observation and assessment of their knowledge, such as asking students to paraphrase their understandings with informal questions, is a valuable and revealing strategy. Sometimes, educators, paraeducators, and even parents want to help, but they instead enable students by doing more than the students do on their own. Good practices also include letting students realize their levels and mistakes, before the learning is corrected by an adult. This accurate self-reflection can then yield compensatory strategies for students to develop under teachers' and families' coordinated auspices.

Keeping this in mind, grade-level teachers sometimes get quite caught up in what can be dubbed as *speed teaching*. Here's an example: From Monday to Friday, we will learn all about igneous rocks. Next week's lesson will uncover sedimentary rocks, while the following week, we'll dig up facts about metamorphic rocks. After that, it's time to launch forward with astronomy. Okay, we all like to reach for the stars sometime in our lives, but where are the connections? By the time you deal with the next topic, most students have forgotten the prior learning, since they— forgive the pun—no longer have rocks in their head. Quite a classroom avalanche!

Next, here's a huge bonus of inclusion. Instead of singling out students within the room for specialized instruction, drill, redrill, or just about any needs governed by the *paper IEP* or the *commonsense IEP* (it's educationally prudent), why not teach the skill or strategy to the whole class? For example, my students, when formerly pulled out for instruction, recorded and graphed their test grades for all subjects during each marking period in a folder with their name on it, which was kept in a separate room. This metacognitive grading system helped them to stay on track and visually see which subjects and areas they needed to improve. I was then faced with a conundrum: How do I let them continue to record their grades when they are no longer pulled out, but, as their program currently states, included in the classroom full time, with two teachers supporting them? My answer was simple: Why not let entire classes record their grades too? Couldn't this metacognitive strategy benefit the general education students as well?

Another time, I was concerned with students completing long-range assignments on time. In this instance, I collaborated with my coteacher, and we decided that the entire class would be given monthly calendars to track upcoming school events, tests, assemblies, reports, and anything else. This general educator continues to use monthly calendars with all of his students, classified or not! The wonderful side effect of inclusion is that it benefits the "regular" kids too. Good practices are not exclusive to only those students with IEPs!

The appropriate delivery ensures the successful mastery of any set of teaching/ learning objectives. So what constitutes appropriate learning objectives? They need to be spiraling, vertically and horizontally aligned, student-based, interdisciplinary, standards-based, content-driven, and challenging, thereby allowing students of all levels to reap successes. Consequently, well-designed instruction allows students to generalize, apply, and connect learning principles to their lives. Teachers not only teach, but also have the instructional power to create lifelong learners, instilled with the joy of knowledge, or the *joie de learning.* Teachers who give step-by-step explanations avoid the rushed instructional pace that sometimes leads to nowhere quickly! Modeling examples and frequently checking baseline knowledge is crucial. All students benefit from creative teachers whose delivery and communication systems advocate and propagate the idea that learning is meaningful, *including inclusive classrooms!*

Most important is that the classroom is not a teacher-centered one, but rather one that fosters long-term student learning and achievements leading toward mastery of the general education curriculum. When it's student-centered, individual needs are addressed, aiding curriculum connections. Connecting to real-world issues through problem-based learning infuses the classroom with

Table 5.1   ICES: Inclusion Communication Exchange System

	Inclusion	*Communication*	*Exchange*	*System*
Nouns	involvement infusion interactions	consistency concepts collaboration	expertise emotions equity	supports students strengths
Verbs	involve interact improve	communicate collaborate coteach	evolve empower educate	support spiral structure
Adjectives	inclusionary interdisciplinary interactive	consistent critical conceptual	evolutionary effective emotive	supportive successful specialized
Adverbs	infectiously interactively intelligently	collaboratively cognitively conceptually	eventually emphatically effectively	supportively systematically skillfully

knowledge that goes way beyond the textbook facts and concepts. In addition, the availability of multimedia equipment awakens learners with instant information in an interactive way by having the students partner with available technology. Classroom communications are vital, as shown with this ICES chart.

MATCHING CONTENT TO DELIVERY

Just compare the next two items. One is a pictorial chart titled *Inclusion Strategies That Work!* The other one is a numbered list titled *Valuable and Applicable Things to Do in All Classrooms on a Daily Basis.* Notice that the basic content is the same, but the presentation differs. Which one would you prefer to use to best deliver the information? How does your brain process each of these two items? Now think about how you instruct your students. Can the same concept be delivered differently? Was the learning material in any way sacrificed by the accompaniment of the visuals? Picture your own handouts!

COLLABORATION, COTEACHING, AND PREPARATION

> *Clearly there are many paths. . . . It is only through the combined efforts of general and special educators in collaboration with parents that schools move toward inclusive practices and ultimately strengthen teaching and learning for all students.*
>
> —Burstein, Sears, Wilcoxen, Cabello, & Spagna, 2004

> *Due to greater numbers of students with disabilities receiving instruction in general education classrooms, the need has increased to provide training for general educators to meet the needs of a diverse range of students.*
>
> —Harriott, 2004

Figure 5.1   Inclusion Strategies That Work!

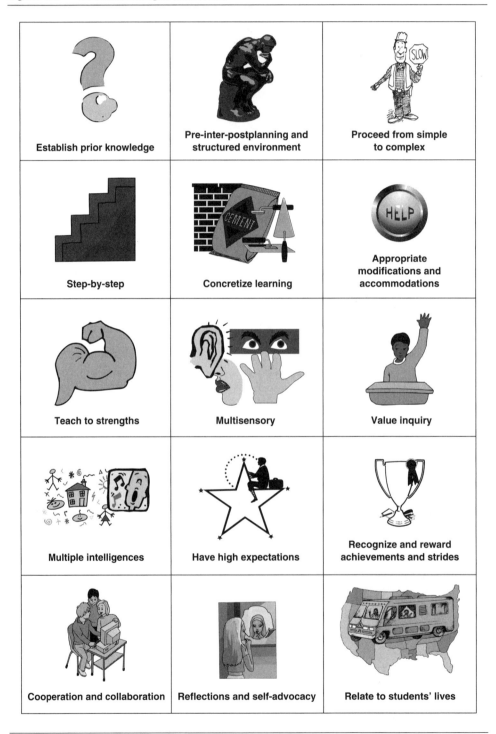

SOURCE: Adapted from Karten, T. (2005). *Inclusion strategies that work!* Thousand Oaks, CA: Corwin.

Figure 5.2   Valuable and Applicable Things to Do in All Classrooms on a Daily Basis

1. Establish prior knowledge.
2. Preplan lessons with structured objectives, allowing for inter-postplanning.
3. Proceed from the simple to the complex by using discrete task analysis, which breaks up the learning into its parts, yet still values the whole picture.
4. Use a step-by-step approach, teaching in small bites, with much practice and repetition for those who need it.
5. Reinforce abstract concepts with concrete examples, such as looking at a map while walking around a neighborhood or reading actual street signs.
6. Think about possible accommodations and modifications that might be needed, such as using a digital recorder for notes or reducing or enhancing an assignment.
7. Incorporate sensory elements: visual, auditory, and kinesthetic/tactile ones.
8. Teach to strengths to help students compensate for weaknesses, such as "hopping" to math facts, if a child loves to move about but hates numbers.
9. Concentrate on individual children, not syndromes, with a growth vs. deficit paradigm.
10. Provide opportunities for success to build self-esteem.
11. Give positives before negatives.
12. Use modeling with both teachers and peers.
13. Vary types of instruction and assessment, with multiple intelligences and cooperative learning.
14. Relate learning to children's lives using interest inventories.
15. Remember the basics such as teaching students proper hygiene, respecting others, effectively listening, or reading directions on a worksheet, in addition to the 3 R's: *Reading, 'Riting,* and *'Rithmetic.*
16. Establish a pleasant classroom environment that encourages students to ask questions and become actively involved in their learning.
17. Increase students' self-awareness of levels and progress.
18. Effectively communicate and collaborate with parents, students, and colleagues, while smiling—it's contagious!

SOURCE: Adapted from: Karten, T. (2005). *Inclusion strategies that work!* Thousand Oaks, CA: Corwin.

> *Special and general educators must work together to ensure that the highest possible number of students with exceptionalities successfully access the important concepts and skills in the general education curriculum.*
>
> —Kozleski, Mainzer, & Deshler, 2000

Some partnerships and corporations continue productively for years, while others dissolve as quickly as a rain puddle in the afternoon sun. The question here is, why? Compromises, ownership issues, effective division of work responsibilities, academic preparation, knowledge of appropriate instructional strategies, and degrees of flexibility influence collaborative relationships. Everyone needs to be involved in the planning, decisions, and training, including not only the teachers, but also administration; related staff such as educational assistants and speech pathologists; art, music, gym, and foreign language teachers; nurses, occupational therapists, mobility trainers, and physical therapists; and, of course, families and students too! Training needs to begin in preservice courses with proper instructional strategies and knowledge that is then applied in educational settings.

So, how can you describe the climate in a classroom that practices effective collaboration? That question is as easy to answer as comparing the climate of totally different countries, such as Vietnam, Switzerland, Tanzania, and Argentina. So many factors influence climate, such as topography, location in relation to the equator or poles, nearby bodies of water, and so on. Now, what influences classroom collaboration? Changing climates in school classrooms are influenced by some of these factors:

Teachers' preservice training: "I had no preparation for this in my Education 101 course" or "Oh, I remember learning about collaboration" or "I am proficient in this subject matter!"

Prior experiences in and out of education: "I firmly believe there's no *I* in the word *team*" or "I'd prefer to figure this out myself!"

Controlling vs. flexible (*Gumby-like*) personalities: "No need to be a Frank Sinatra here; we can do it *Our Way!*" or "It's my class, not yours!"

Self-confidence levels: "I'm a good teacher, and it's okay if someone else shares his or her knowledge with me so we can both learn from each other" or "Just who do they think they are, questioning what I do!"

Attitude toward students: "I know that they can succeed, if we . . ." or "This is just a waste of time. *Those kids* belong in a separate class, so I can really teach!"

Administrative support: "How can we plan together, if the only shared planning time we have are those casual, impromptu meetings in the restroom?"; "How do they expect us to teach when all they care about are standardized test grades?"; "What does it mean that we only have to provide an *appropriate* education vs. the best education?"; or "So much more is accomplished in an atmosphere of collegial respect when the central office and supervisors listen to, understand, respect, and support staff needs." "Let's listen to and respond to our teachers' everyday classroom concerns, aside from just evaluating their performances. We will provide ongoing training for all staff to help students with disabilities succeed in general education classrooms."

Defining roles: "Not sure what I should be doing here"; "How can that teacher treat me like his personal secretary? I can do more than make copies"; "There should be equality in the classroom, and that doesn't just go for students!"

Bridges can be built to do the following:

- Include children in general education classrooms, removing distinctions between general and special education students
- Collaborate between general and special education teachers and all staff to intermingle personalities and workloads
- Close the achievement gap and benefit all students
- Ensure that teachers are allotted time to conduct meetings to discuss past, present, and future lessons (including staff such as speech pathologists and occupational therapists)
- Connect the learning to the home environment, enlisting families and guardians as allies and partners in the education of their children

Today, special and general educators must collaborate to figure out ways that all students can and will be successful in school and in their futures by creating and instilling high expectations for all. Specific time needs to be spent on effective classroom designs, along with models of instruction that include collaboration and coteaching. Collaboration encompasses all school personnel, families as partners, and transitions between grades and schools.

The following highlights some coteaching issues that need to be addressed (to circumvent possible oil-and-water relationships between teachers):

Figure 5.3   Collaborative Survey to Promote Productive Relationships

Write some brief thoughts about ....

Classroom Modifications and Accommodations:

(Varying learning objectives, requirements, instructional materials):

Curriculum Concerns:

Teacher Knowledge of Subject Matter:

Instructional Style:

Methods of Testing/Grading:

Varying Classroom Rules/Organization Preferred:

SOURCE: Adapted from Karten, T. (2005). *Inclusion strategies that work!* Thousand Oaks, CA: Corwin.

Figure 5.4

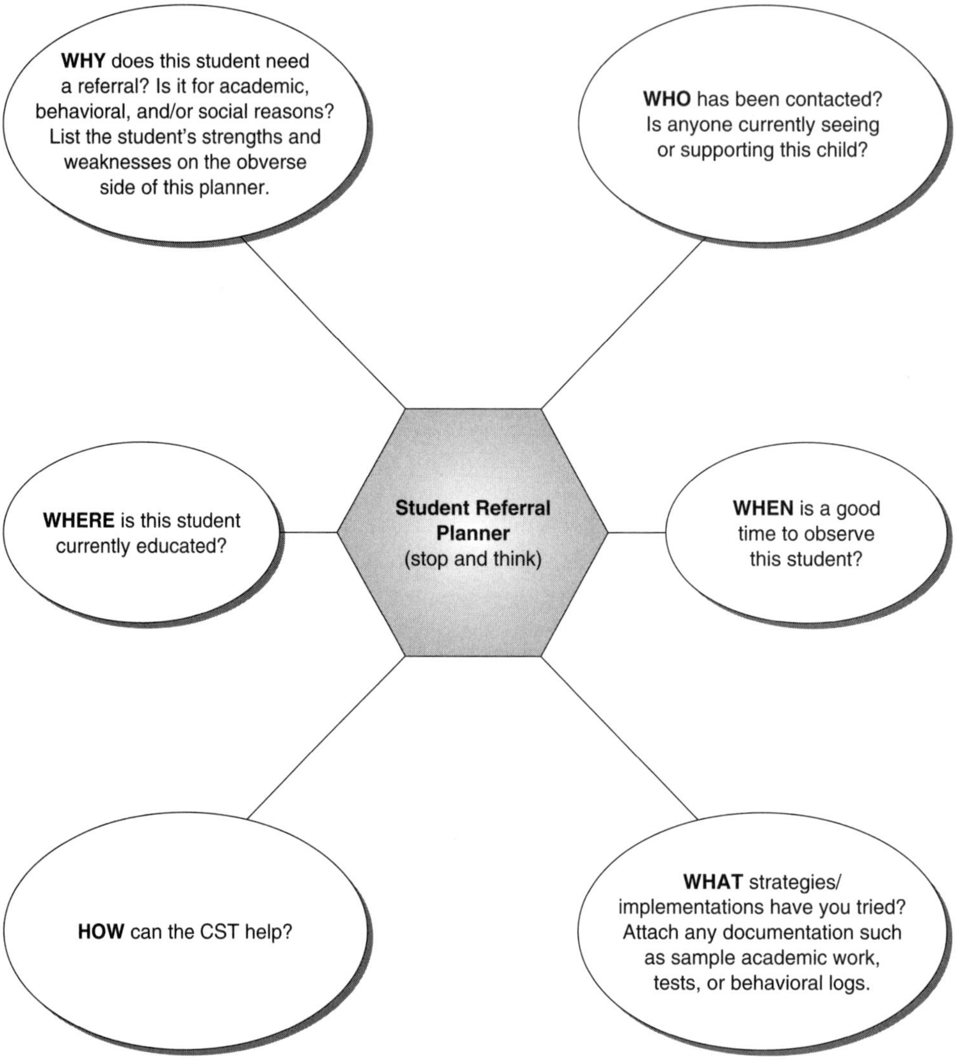

WHY does this student need a referral? Is it for academic, behavioral, and/or social reasons? List the student's strengths and weaknesses on the obverse side of this planner.

WHO has been contacted? Is anyone currently seeing or supporting this child?

WHERE is this student currently educated?

Student Referral Planner (stop and think)

WHEN is a good time to observe this student?

HOW can the CST help?

WHAT strategies/implementations have you tried? Attach any documentation such as sample academic work, tests, or behavioral logs.

Teacher: _____   School: _____

Student's Name: _____   Primary Language: _____

Teacher Contacts: E-Mail: _____   Phone: _____

Date: _____

Increasing Communications

Teamwork with instructional support teams (ISTs), student study teams (SSTs), child study teams (CSTs), and related services reduces miscommunication and includes all staff and teachers in the planning stages.

Joie de Learning

Structured lessons are necessary for students to understand the standards-based curriculum, since many learnings follow a sequence. Yet holding on to the teacher's manual as if it is the educational bible omits the spontaneity in the learning process. Just like rote memorization of facts negates application of learning and the generalization of concepts, *rote teaching* negates students' understandings and thwarts instructional passion. Doing the same lessons, year after year, is boring for the students if the teacher cannot exhibit enthusiasm about the subject matter as if it was his or her first time teaching it. When you walk into classrooms with excited learners, the following things happen:

The first question they ask as you hand out a paper is *not*

"Is this for homework?" but "Wow! What's this about?"

When you ask students to write, they *don't* say

"How long should it be?" but "Could I write more?"

When you assign only one novel chapter to read, the students voraciously forge ahead because they are enjoying the book.

Okay, maybe I am being overly melodramatic here, but the point is that many students do not care about the learning because they think it's just *stuff* they need to know for the test. To many students, school is not fun; it's a chore, and to some it's even a necessary evil that they are compelled to attend. Anticipation sets the classroom stage for a classroom audience that is ready and excited to learn. Teachers in some cases need to be educational performers, who can convince students that this *stuff* is not only worth knowing, but downright interesting!

$$\textbf{J}\text{oy}$$

$$\textbf{O}\text{f}$$

$$\textbf{I}\text{nvolvement in}$$

$$\textbf{E}\text{ducation}$$

$$\textbf{D}\text{oes}$$

$$\textbf{E}\text{qual}$$

$$\textbf{L}\textsc{earning}$$

Nothing Taken for Granted

Some teachers work in a linear manner: "After Math Lesson 1.3, we'll move ahead to 1.4, then 1.5, 1.6, 1.7, 1.8, 1.9, and then comes the Chapter Test." If the schedule is not followed, some teachers are fearful that the class will fall behind in their learning. There are valid arguments for such a regimented pace; however, this type of teacher is assuming that no regression or *learning amnesia* has occurred and that the whole class has the exact same prior knowledge on every given topic. Before moving on to the next lesson, taking a few minutes to review prior learning and allow for student connections is time well spent. Teachers teach, students listen; teachers teach, students forget; teachers test, students fail. Nothing can be taken for granted with today's classroom of diverse learners if a successful outcome is the ultimate goal!

Here are some examples of this *forgettable* scenario:

- Having students identify the location of continents on maps without determining if they know the difference between a continent and a country
- Adding, subtracting, multiplying, and dividing decimals without making the connection to how and when decimals appear in our daily lives
- Giving weekly spelling tests that do not define the words and failing to review them at a later date to maintain competencies
- Teaching about patterns without identifying patterns around us— e.g., nature, clothing, foods—or making real-life connections
- Giving instruction on the Linnean classification system, without teaching about how to classify common objects that surround us
- Teaching about the crisis in the Middle East without addressing past economic, political, and religious issues, or explaining the difference between these terms

These scenarios are given for teachers to realize that it is wise to

- Never assume students know the answers you think they should know
- Review prior learnings; it assists students in preparing for tests and high-stakes exams
- Ask varied questions and give frequent formal and informal evaluations to determine students' levels and to gauge pacing of your own lessons

Spiraling Objectives

So often, teachers are frustrated because it seems that some students with learning issues who are included in their classes are just not *getting it!* I use these words because I am actually paraphrasing the answer some students give when you ask if there are any questions: "I don't *get it.*" Well, what don't they get? If they cannot even define the *it,* then where do you proceed from there? Now, how do you as a teacher help them *get it?* And, if the curriculum spirals, won't these gaps hinder their future exposure to the same material? How will they *get it?*

Check yes or no to these *pedagocially ponderable* questions:

QUESTIONS	YES	NO
1. Was this student's prior knowledge increased?		
2. Even though this student did not receive a passing grade—e.g., 50% on an evaluation or test—did he or she master 50% of the material?		
3. Do you think this student will be more proficient when he or she learns about this topic, content area, or skill again?		
4. Is there a way to repeat this learning and somehow individualize instruction within the classroom—e.g., alternative assignment on the same topic—if appropriate support is given, such as a parent, peer coach, or paraeducator?		
5. Would assigning a peer coach be beneficial to both this child and his or her student mentor?		
6. Can the student chart his or her progress to take more ownership and responsibility for the learning?		
7. Is the student experiencing more accomplishments than frustrations with his or her inclusion experience in your class?		
8. Has physical inclusion allowed this child to develop a more positive self-image, which has translated to increased self-confidence and motivation?		
9. Are you experiencing personal or professional growth by having this child included in your class?		

The major point here is that inclusion has academic and social merits. The spiraling curriculum adds on to each student's differing prior knowledge, when they see the same topic with broadening concepts in future years. The curriculum exposure that they receive within the general education classroom, although not always geared to individual levels, allows for increased instruction on subject matter that in the past was very often deleted from specialized programs conducted in separate classrooms. Spiraling curriculums set the stage for spiraling brains that shelve or file the information or facts for a while. If the initial instruction included research-based strategies, such as kinesthetic learning with meaningful engagement, then *déjà learning* occurs. Now the prior learning is more apt to be retrieved from or added to the child's file of *stuff I heard before!* Equally important here are the social benefits of inclusion. Even though there are no standardized tests for social improvements, these gains are truly immeasurable. The spiraling curriculum also includes spiraling life skills that lead to independent living decisions, fostered by increased social interactions with peers. Students develop, observe, and model emotions. The *hidden curriculuum* develops character education with rewarding extrinsic and intrinsic behavioral choices! Social and academic growth are utterly compatible classroom objectives.

VERTICAL AND HORIZONTAL ALIGNMENTS

Picture an apartment building with an elevator or stairs. Well, that's comparable to the vertical alignment of objectives from one grade to the next. Now picture a house with a wraparound porch, and you have a scenario of horizontal alignment. Students, like apartment or home dwellers, are school residents who strive to master grade-level standards and objectives. Seeing what preceded or follows that grade in a fund of knowledge, or on the prior or next learning level, allows teachers to review facts and concepts if gaps are evident. Educators can now easily shift gears and accelerate to more challenging levels when different grade-level competencies are displayed. Elevators have a menu of floor choices!

Baseline, Advancing, and Challenging Assignments

Now think about a large apartment building with many families living together on different floors under the same roof. Well, today's classrooms are inhabited by *learning tenants* who are classmates instructed by the same teacher, but they too reside on different *learning floors.* Production of student clones who have identical knowledge negates the nature of what we know about learning. Teachers may have a baseline of knowledge that they want students to learn, but all students will not master these objectives at the same time, since they all did not begin on the same level, nor do they all achieve understandings at the same pace. Some students need more repetitive learnings, while others thrive when given challenging assignments. So, how does a teacher handle these differences in a classroom of diverse learners? Well, when I coteach in a math class, I deliberately introduce a difficult topic and expose even the lower learners to the more challenging assignments, not to frustrate them, but to include them in the learning. Surprisingly successful results often follow!

Never assume that a student with learning needs is not capable of achieving bigger strides on different topics. Each child displays varying achievements based on complexities of assignments, interest levels, instructional presentations, and sometimes just their moods, mind-sets, or even the weather on that particular day! How teachers teach is affected by the content, objectives, and skills they hope students will understand and gain, as well as their own proficiency with the content. In addition, who is in the class most definitely affects the pace, instructional delivery, classroom design, modifications, assessments, and varied activities required for the students to master that megalist of skills and objectives. Delivering this knowledge to students with different abilities becomes a rewarding experience when you as the teacher help those children increase their baseline knowledge and then move on to more advanced and challenging levels. It's quite a view from the school's penthouse!

The following chart, which is to be used as a planner, points out that teachers are not only instructing topics, but students as well. Fill in the skills and objectives as well as the students instructed, then look back at the accommodations chart in Chapter 1 and see which learning, behavioral/social/emotional, perceptual, and physical suggestions apply.

Grades	Skills and Objectives	Students with ...						
K–2								
3–5								
6–8								
9–12								

Skills and Objectives:

A. Word Decoding
B. Word Encoding
C. Reading Comprehension
D. Writing Skills
E. Literacy
F. Language Skills
G. Listening Comprehension
H. Math Computations
I. Problem Solving
J. Perceptual Activities
K. Everyday Math
L. Consumer Education
M. Measurement
N. Pattern-Based Thinking
O. Critical-Thinking Skills
P. Biology
Q. Chemistry
R. Physics
S. Earth Science

T. Map Skills
U. World Cultures
V. Ancient Civilizations
W. Citizenship
X. Environment and Society
Y. Geography
Z. Economic Literacy
AA. Understanding Government
BB. Cultural Awareness
CC. Media
DD. Music/Art Education
EE. Visual Information
FF. Physical Education
GG. Family Life
HH. Technology
II. Career Education
JJ. Self-Management
KK. Study Skills
LL. Other Skills/Topics

Delivered to students with

1. Above Average Skills
2. Asperger Disorder
3. Attention Deficit/Hyperactivity Disorder
4. Auditory Processing
5. Autism
6. Cerebral Palsy
7. Communication Disorder
8. Conduct Disorder
9. Deafness/Hearing Loss
10. Depression
11. Developmental Disorder
12. Dyscalculia

13. Dysgraphia
14. Dyslexia
15. Obsessive Compulsive Disorder
16. Oppositional Defiant Disorder
17. Physical Impairments
18. Specific Learning Disability
19. Tourette's Syndrome
20. Traumatic Brain injury
21. Twice-Exceptionality
22. Visual Impairment
23. Other Needs

These two lists must be collated for classroom learning achievements to occur. Teachers teach subjects, but the first consideration must be teaching the

Figure 5.5

FIRST:

WHOLE

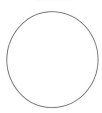

Everyone in the class could

- listen to the same speech, lecture, story, poem, or mathematical word problem
- look at the same picture prompt related to the content
- chorally read or write a story together on chart paper
- have a group discussion about . . .
- be introduced to science and social studies vocabulary or unfamiliar reading/language words or terms
- preview and discuss what skill(s) the lesson will focus on (e.g., scientific method, time lines, decimals, finding the main idea, how to improve writing by substituting words)
- be involved in a teacher demonstration or experiment, while handling concrete objects or appropriate lesson-related manipulatives

NEXT:

PART

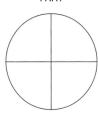

Students can work with smaller groups, partners, or individually,

- completing an assigned reading or writing task
- creating a product based upon what was learned (e.g., poem, story, short skit, illustrating captioned pictures, crossword puzzle, word search, solving given problems, reenacting an experiment, researching on the computer, reading and learning more about . . .)

Learning under teacher's auspices now exists for all students. During this time, the teacher walks around supervising or instructing smaller groups or individual students while recording observations and individual needs evidenced.

THEN:

WHOLE

again ☺

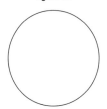

Together, the class becomes a whole unit again, while individual students, teachers, partners, and groups share

- what else they learned or discovered about the topic from a book, computer, other student, teacher, self
- a finished product created
- what they now know, giving specific details
- what they still wonder about
- questions about the material presented

It's basically a time for all learners to celebrate their discoveries and progress with each other, while validating and reflecting upon their own learning.

SOURCE: Karten, T. (2005). *Inclusion strategies that work!* Thousand Oaks, CA: Corwin.

students. Yes, there are curriculum mandates, but without individual student consideration, lessons become meaningless rather than beneficial academic experiences for both teachers and students of all levels. In inclusionary classrooms, this becomes a more challenging task, but a feasible one, when the learning needs of individual students are known and addressed before standards are applied.

Classroom Structure

So how can educators simultaneously address different objectives?

INTERDISCIPLINARY LESSONS

Learning must address students' interests, curriculum objectives, classroom structure, and the changing legislative dictates. Interdisciplinary lessons are certainly a way to meaningfully relate to different students' strengths, motivation, and the standards. Not every lesson needs to include every subject, but equally true is that every subject does not exist on its own. For example, if math is a student's least favorite subject, then this student might be turned off by anything that deals with numbers or problem solving. However, suppose this particular student loved to write short stories. Couldn't you somehow tap into this student's preferred intelligence, and couple the math instruction with writing strategies?

A growing body of research in the fields of mathematics education and literacy supports the inclusion of children's literature into the teaching and learning of mathematics.

—Ward, 2005

Words and images have the power to communicate analytical reasoning and insight and at the same time connect math to a world of things—nature, science, art, and stories—that matter to kids.

—Tang, 2003

	Writing/Art	*Reading*	*Science*	*Social Studies*
M A T H	Choose words from the glossary in the back of the math textbook to create a *math story* each month. For example, October's story could be about patterned pumpkins exponentially increasing. Then draw pictures that illustrate your math stories! In 3–5 sentences, explain the steps you used to solve the word problem. Can you draw a sequence of pictures that accompany each step? Exchange problems with a classmate and see if you could solve each other's problems.	Cut out or highlight mathematical words and pictures from articles and ads in magazines and newspapers. Design your own shopping coupons with words and pictures that offer consumer discounts. Create a bound classroom math collage or scrapbook with mathematical captions that refer to characters in recent stories read.	Find math in nature; e.g., symmetry, shapes, angles, trees, and other *environmental math.* Design an experiment that uses math; e.g., charts, graphs, probabilility, decimals, measurements. Be certain that the experiment includes the scientific process.	Investigate mathematical operations across cultures. Do they have different ways of adding, subtracting, dividing, or multiplying? What was math like in past civilizations across the world? Identify the currency, values, economy, and trade rules in different countries.

S C I E N C E	Reading/Writing	Technology	Math	Cultures
	After conducting research on your favorite scientific topic in biology, earth science, physics, or chemistry, write a play with this scientific theme. Write out the alphabet from A–Z in a column on lined paper and try to think of as many science words as possible that begin with each letter.	Create a Web search for your classmates on your favorite topic. First ask the teacher to approve your chosen sites, then gather information and compose 10 questions, which your peers will answer. View the site www.brainpop.com to see if there's a science-related movie about the concept you are now learning.	Choose some math formulas and plug them in to solve some everyday scientific situations. Think of how math and science go hand in hand in scientific experiments. Research how many mathematicians were also scientists.	How do some cultures view science vs. religions? Create a time line of different scientific discoveries and inventions. Then list the country in the world where the discovery or invention began. Explore how scientists from different cultures communicate and share ideas.

This chart offers some interdisciplinary connections with standards addressed, using math as an example. Remember, not every lesson needs to include every subject, but if the connections are feasible, then crossing over to another discipline does not dilute the present one. Interdisciplinary lessons strengthen concepts, beyond relying on the textbook as the only means of instruction. Here's an ongoing example with math. More interdisciplinary lesson ideas follow here and in a later chapter.

National standards addressed: *NCSS:* Understand global connections and interdependence, cultural diversity, and how human beings view themselves in and over time. *NCTE and IRA:* Adjust use of spoken, written, and visual language for communication while participating in literacy communities.

National standards addressed: *NRC:* Increase ability to conduct scientific inquiry and understandings of the environment. *NCTM:* Monitor and reflect upon problem solving, spatial relationships, connections, representation, and communication.

National standards addressed: *NCSS:* Understand individual identity and development along with interactions among groups and institutions. *NCTE and IRA:* Read, interpret, and comprehend a wide range of materials. Use techological resources. Employ sound-letter coresopondence and sentence structure. *NRC:* Understand relationships between science, technology, and society. *NCTM:* Connect mathematics to other contexts and understand the language of math.

National standards addressed: *NCSS:* Understand how human beings view themselves in and over time. *NCTE and IRA:* Accomplish a purpose with written language to exchange information. *NRC:* Increase ability to conduct scientific inquiry and understanding of science as a human endeavor. *NCTM:* Apply spatial reasoning and visualization.

	Science	Music	Physical Education	Art
R E A D I N G	Dissect the story you read, pretending one of the main characters is a scientist conducting an experiment. Cooperatively decide what experiment the character would conduct if he or she was a scientist. Plug in all of the details of the scientific method steps of your *fictional scientific character*. Identify the following: hypothesis materials procedure observation/results conclusion	Pretend that the book or story you just read is being made into a movie. You are in charge of deciding the musical score for the movie. Pick what songs or musical pieces will be the chosen. Decide when the pieces will be played. Be certain that the songs and music reflect the book's mood.	Create a dance or team game your book's characters could play. Decide the rules and steps for the dance or noncompetitive (fun) game.	Design a storyboard for the novel you have just read. You can use clip art or draw your own pictures. Other classmates can sequence your pictures or retell the story using your pictures as their prompts. If you prefer, you can sculpt your characters using clay or whatever other medium you desire.

Chapter Review Questions/Activities

1. What additional points would you add to the list of 18 Valuable and Applicable Things to Do in All Classrooms on a Daily Basis?

2. Cooperatively design an interdisciplinary lesson similar to the reading, science, and math ones modeled in this chapter. Vertically place your main topic or concept in the first column, and then list the headings of subjects you'd like to include and touch upon in the following four. Then make the connective multisubject lesson happen!

3. Use these words in an *educationally instructive* paragraph:
   a. baseline knowledge
   b. advancing knowledge
   c. challenging assignment
   d. vertical alignment
   e. horizontal alignment

6

What Is Co-Teaching?

Richard A. Villa, Jacqueline S. Thousand,
and Ann I. Nevin

Susan Cushman

Topics Included in This Chapter:

- What co-teaching is not
- What is co-teaching?
- The elements of co-teaching
- Importance of systemic supports

We just found out that we are expected to co-teach. What is co-teaching? What is it not? What elements or variables need to be in place so that we know we are really co-teaching? Is there a process that will help us successfully co-teach? The answers to these questions are discussed in this chapter.

■ WHAT CO-TEACHING IS NOT

Although the concept of co-teaching is not new in education, there are many teaching arrangements that have been promoted in the history of American education that may look like co-teaching. If you are a person who learns from nonexemplars, then the following discussion may be helpful.

Using your own experience as a guide, can you think of nonexemplars for what co-teaching is not? We can think of several from our experience.

Co-teaching is not one person teaching one subject followed by another who teaches a different subject. Many teachers are familiar with this structure if their students travel in groups within a departmentalized administrative framework. In this case, however, the teachers often do not have time to plan or evaluate instruction. Instead, they are responsible for covering the subject matter individually within their curriculum areas (e.g., science), and then the math teachers who are then replaced by the language arts teachers and so on.

Co-teaching is not one person teaching one subject while another person prepares instructional materials at the photocopier in the teachers' workroom or corrects papers in the teachers' lounge. This is a familiar arrangement for those teachers who have the luxury of working with a paraprofessional, a parent, or a community volunteer in the classroom.

Co-teaching is also not occurring when one teacher conducts a lesson and others stand or sit by and watch. This often happens when there are observers or volunteers who come into the classroom with no specific function or assignment.

Co-teaching is not happening when the ideas of one person prevail for what is to be taught or how it will be taught. This type of structure often occurs when a group of would-be co-teachers defer to the eldest, to the person with the most presumed authority, or to the person with the most convincing voice.

Finally, co-teaching is not simply the assignment of someone to act as a tutor. For example, the early schoolmistresses and schoolmasters in one-room schoolhouses were known to use older students to help teach younger students. It is not known to what extent the older student had input in the selection of the lesson, design, and delivery of the lesson, and so on. Many of those student helpers went on to normal schools to become teachers themselves. In this case, the student was an assistant teacher often assigned to teach individuals or groups of pupils while the schoolmistress taught another individual or group.

Instead, the twenty-first-century notion of co-teaching places it within the context of some of the most innovative practices in education. The reassignment of existing personnel to co-teaching teams results in a knowledge and skill exchange among team members and higher teacher-to-student ratios, outcomes that benefit more students than the individual student in need of intensive instructional support. Skrtic (1991) considers this a dynamic structure in which complex work is more likely to be accomplished and novel instruction is are more likely to be crafted to meet individual student needs.

WHAT IS CO-TEACHING? ■

Co-teaching is two or more people sharing responsibility for teaching some or all of the students assigned to a classroom. It involves the distribution of responsibility among people for planning, instruction, and evaluation for a classroom of students. Another way of saying this is that co-teaching is a fun way for students to learn from two or more people who may have different ways of thinking or teaching. Some people say that co-teaching is a creative way to connect with and support others to help all children learn. Others say that co-teaching is a way to make schools more effective. Co-teaching can be likened to a marriage. Partners must establish trust, develop and work on communication, share the chores, celebrate, work together creatively to overcome the inevitable challenges and problems, and anticipate conflict and handle it in a constructive way.

THE ELEMENTS OF CO-TEACHING ■

Our definition represents an integration of our firsthand experiences with other school-based teams that actively support students in heterogeneous learning environments (Villa and Thousand 2004) and our reading of the literature on cooperative group learning (Johnson and Johnson 1999), collaboration and consultation (Fishbaugh 1997; Friend and Cook 2002; Hourcade and Bauwens 2002; Idol, Nevin, and Paolucci-Whitcomb 1999), and cooperation (Brandt 1987). Enhancing the initial definition presented in the previous paragraph, a co-teaching team may be defined as two or more people who agree to do the following:

1. Coordinate their work to achieve at least one *common, publicly agreed-on goal*

2. Share a *belief system* that supports the idea that each of the co-teaching team members has unique and needed expertise

3. Demonstrate *parity* by alternatively engaging in the dual roles of teacher and learner, expert and novice, giver and recipient of knowledge or skills

4. Use a *distributed functions theory of leadership* in which the task and relationship functions of the traditional lone teacher are distributed among all co-teaching team members

5. Use a *cooperative process* that includes face-to-face interaction, positive interdependence, interpersonal skills, monitoring co-teacher progress, and individual accountability

Each of these factors is explained in more detail in the following sections.

Common, Publicly Agreed-On Goal

Many co-teachers begin with an agreement to achieve one instructional event, such as a school play, as a team. Their successes then lead them to agree to co-teach instructional thematic units for a six-week period of time, perhaps culminating in a schoolwide celebration. Over time, they see that their unique expertise, skills, and resources are needed for more extensive periods of time, thus leading to more formal co-teaching assignments.

Shared Belief System

Co-teachers agree that not only do they teach more effectively, but their students also learn more effectively. The presence of two or more people with different knowledge, skills, and resources allows the co-teachers to learn from each other. Often individuals decide to become co-teachers as a result of taking inservice courses in specific instructional methods such as cooperative group learning or differentiated instruction. Having a shared language to discuss teaching and learning is both an outcome and a necessary component of co-teaching.

Parity

Parity occurs when co-teachers perceive that their unique contributions and their presence on the team are valued. Treating each member of the co-teaching team with respect is a key to achieving parity. Co-teaching members develop the ability to exchange their ideas and concerns freely, regardless of differences in knowledge, skills, attitudes, or position. Soliciting opinions and being sensitive to the suggestions offered by each co-teacher is especially important when there is a perception of unequal status because of position, training, or experience. Parity between a teacher and a paraprofessional, for example, could be demonstrated when the paraprofessional uses his or her unique knowledge to enhance a lesson developed with the teacher. Reciprocally, the teacher is in an expert role when the paraprofessional imitates a teaching-learning procedure that the teacher has demonstrated. The outcome is that each member of the co-teaching team gives and takes direction for the co-teaching lesson so that the students can achieve the desired benefits.

Distributed Functions Theory of Leadership

Nancy Keller, an experienced co-teacher from Winooski, Vermont, states that as a member of a co-teaching team, "I do everything a normal teacher would do except that now there are two or more people doing it" (personal communication). What is important about this statement is the implicit recognition that co-teachers must agree to redistribute their classroom leadership and decision-making responsibilities among themselves. This phenomenon of role redistribution in which the functions of the traditional lone leader or lone teacher are divided among members of a team is known as the *distributed functions theory of leadership* (Johnson and Johnson 1999). There are functions or jobs that occur before, during, and after each lesson; co-teachers must decide how they will distribute these jobs from one lesson to the next. Some responsibilities must occur daily, others weekly or periodically, and still others once or twice a year. Teachers decide how the content will be presented—for example, one person may teach while the other(s) facilitates follow-up activities, or all members may share in the teaching of the lesson, with clear directions for when and how the teaching will occur. Another decision involves identifying the teacher who communicates with parents and administrators. Some co-teachers decide that co-teaching team members will rotate that responsibility. Still another decision involves describing how co-teaching team members will arrange to share their expertise; some decide to observe one another and practice peer coaching. Remember, when co-teachers make these decisions, they will experience more success if they use the cooperative process described in the next section.

Cooperative Process

There are five elements that facilitate cooperative processes: face-to-face interactions, positive interdependence, interpersonal skills, monitoring co-teacher progress, and individual accountability. Each of the five elements is now defined in more detail.

Face-to-Face Interactions

Face-to-face interaction is an important element for co-teachers as they make several important decisions. Co-teachers need to decide when and how often they will meet as well as how much time meetings will take during school hours. They need to decide when others (e.g., parents, specialists, paraprofessionals, psychologists) should be involved. They also need to develop a system for communicating information when formal meetings are not scheduled (e.g., a communication log book at the teachers' desk, Post-it notes on the bulletin board of the classroom). Face-to-face interactions are necessary for co-teachers to make these and other critical decisions.

Positive Interdependence

Positive interdependence is the heart of co-teaching. It involves the recognition that no one person can effectively respond to the diverse psychological and educational needs of the heterogeneous groups of students found in typical twenty-first-century classrooms. Co-teachers create the feeling that they are equally responsible for the learning of all students to whom they are now assigned and that they can best carry out their responsibilities by pooling their diverse knowledge, skills, and material resources. To establish positive interdependence, co-teachers can establish a common goal, create rewards for their success, and divide the labor of the delivery of instruction.

Interpersonal Skills

Interpersonal skills include the verbal and nonverbal components of trust, trust building, conflict management, and creative problem solving. Such social interaction skills are needed for achieving the distribution of leadership functions and for ensuring that no child is ignored. Individual co-teachers will find that they are functioning at different interpersonal skill levels, depending on their previous training, personality styles, and communication preferences. Effective co-teacher partnerships encourage each member to improve his or her social skills by giving feedback and encouragement to each other.

Monitoring Co-Teacher Progress

Monitoring refers to the process of frequently debriefing about the successes and challenges of co-teaching lessons. Co-teachers check in with each other to determine whether (1) the students are achieving the lesson's learning goals, (2) the co-teachers are using good communication skills with each other, and (3) the learning activities need to be adjusted. Methods of monitoring can range from very simple to more complex. For example, some co-teachers use a checklist on which they each literally check off their agreed-on responsibilities. Some co-teachers set up a brief, 15-minute meeting each day while their students are at recess to discuss the three aspects of monitoring (goals, communication skills, adjusting the activities). Co-teaching team members also can take turns sharing accomplishments, reporting on what each one contributed to the success of the lesson, and making suggestions about what might need to be changed to improve the lesson.

Individual Accountability

Individual accountability is the engine of co-teaching. It is clear that co-teaching is effective based on the actual delivery of skills and knowledge by each co-teacher. Individual accountability is a form of acknowledging the importance of the actions from each co-teacher. Individual accountability in co-teaching involves taking time to assess the individual performance of each partner for one or more of four purposes. One purpose is to increase partners' perceptions of their contributions to the co-teaching endeavor. A second purpose is to provide partners with recognition for their contributions. Yet another is to determine whether any adjustments need to be made in any of the partners' co-teaching roles and actions. A final purpose is to identify when one or more of the partners may need assistance (e.g., some modeling or coaching, access to additional resources or supports) to increase effectiveness in the performance of assigned roles and responsibilities.

You will see how the five elements of the cooperative process operate in varying degrees for each of four approaches to co-teaching—supportive, parallel, complementary, team teaching—that are defined in Chapter 3 and illustrated in Chapters 4 through 7.

■ IMPORTANCE OF SYSTEMIC SUPPORTS

Administrative support is another reason for the successful and beneficial outcomes of co-teaching. Beneficial outcomes increase when the school principal or assistant principal works with the faculty to provide systematic professional development, establish coaching and mentoring opportunities for learning new ways of working together, and arrange master schedules so that co-teachers can teach and plan together. An important aspect of administrative support is realizing that new roles and responsibilities emerge as a result of changing the way that teachers, paraprofessionals, related services personnel, and students work together. Parts II and III of this book illustrate the new roles and relationships that co-teaching affords adults and students. In Part IV, you learn about professional development and logistical and administrative supports that promote systematic development of co-teaching (Chapter 10). Chapters 11 and 12 of Part IV offer guidelines for meshing planning with co-teaching activities and tips for communicating and managing conflict so that you thrive rather than merely survive with your co-teachers. In the Epilogue, you meet two middle level teachers who show how they developed a shared voice through their individual and shared professional development activities. We hope you can agree that, although systemic support is important and valued, your individual action is even more important—you know that you can take action even in the absence of systemic supports. We are always inspired by Margaret Mead (an American anthropologist) who writes, "Never doubt that a small group of thoughtful, committed people can change the world; indeed it's the only thing that ever has." We hope you count yourself as one of those people.

7

Teaching Core Curriculum to Students With Moderate to Severe Intellectual Disabilities

June E. Downing

KEY CONCEPTS

- Response to Intervention (RTI) may require more extensive adaptations and accommodations for students with severe disabilities.

- Individualized adaptations are typically needed to make the core curriculum meaningful and accessible.

- Teachers must identify the Big Ideas in each lesson to determine what to teach students with severe intellectual disabilities.

- Individualized needs can be blended into general education lessons.

- Students with moderate to severe disabilities can and should be actively involved in the group lesson.

- Systematic instruction of individualized skills will be needed and can occur in a variety of teaching arrangements.

In this chapter, several examples will be given that demonstrate what is important to teach different-aged students and how to do that in general education classrooms. This chapter will use the information presented in previous chapters and demonstrate its applicability to the general education classroom under different teaching arrangements. First, the concept of a student's response to intervention will be described with application to students with moderate to severe intellectual disabilities. This discussion will lead naturally

---

into the importance of meaningfully adapting core curriculum at different grade levels. Numerous suggestions for appropriate accommodations for different students will be given. Then, the focus will turn to the specific skills that the student is to learn and how those are linked to and embedded in the broader curriculum. Finally, systematic instruction procedures will be highlighted for teaching the student the targeted skills during general classroom instruction. The chapter will conclude with the importance of teaching students to generalize the skills they have learned.

■ RESPONSE TO INTERVENTION

Response to Intervention (RTI) is a process of determining how well students are responding to the instructional environment and instructional strategies used in the general education classroom (Gresham et al., 2005). Strategies are perceived along a continuum from universal measures to increasingly more intensive and extensive based on the needs of the student. Typically associated with students having learning disabilities, the RTI process involves careful observation of students receiving evidence-based practices to determine if they are performing significantly below same-age peers. More intensive intervention is applied with ongoing monitoring to determine if students who do not respond as intended should be evaluated for special education services (Fuchs, Mock, Morgan, & Young, 2003). RTI keeps the focus on the quality of instruction provided to all students and its effectiveness for individual students rather than on deficits inherent in a student. When RTI is implemented effectively, it should result in a more coordinated service delivery and improved learning for all students (Cummings, Atkins, Allison, & Cole, 2008).

Although much less researched and utilized, RTI applies to students with moderate to severe disabilities. Instead of looking at disability labels and automatically assuming instruction must occur in a specialized environment, the process of RTI looks at how the student responds to increasingly more intense instruction within the general education classroom. For some aspects of any lesson, the student with moderate or severe disabilities may respond quite appropriately to the general instruction used with the entire class (e.g., the animated reading of an interesting story with pictures shown to all students). Other aspects of the lesson may involve information that the student cannot respond to given a typical or universal approach (e.g., directions to write a brief essay on a social studies topic). When this occurs, more intensive instructional approaches will be needed to ensure adequate responding from the student. The student does not have to be removed to a specialized setting but will need a more individualized approach to be successful.

■ THE CRITICAL NEED TO ADAPT CURRICULUM TO MAKE IT MEANINGFUL

Core curriculum becomes increasingly abstract in nature, relying on considerable verbal abilities and preceding basic skills, especially as the student enters secondary education. Students with moderate to severe intellectual disabilities should not be excluded from abstract curriculum, but will need for it to be adapted to be accessible. Considerable literature exists on adapting core curriculum for students with severe disabilities (Clayton, Burdge, Denham, Kleinert, & Kearns, 2006; Downing, 2008; Janney & Snell, 2004; Ryndak & Ward, 2003). At times this can be a very simple adaptation, such as learning to recognize pictured vocabulary words in a high school Spanish class while the rest of the class works on Spanish composition using the same vocabulary. At other times it can be more challenging, such as learning class rules while the rest of the government high school class learns about legislation. Careful thought and planning are needed to ensure that the adapted lesson clearly reflects what the class in general is learning and the link to the required standards for that class and grade level is strong. Furthermore, the curriculum must be made meaningful to the student with moderate to severe intellectual disabilities, so that the student can understand the relevance to his or her life. Adapting the curriculum, therefore, is not something that can be done haphazardly, but must have some forethought and conceptual planning. All members of the team can assist in this effort, although the primary individuals responsible for such planning are the general and special educators. Family members and paraprofessionals also can be very helpful in providing suggestions as well as material adaptations.

IDENTIFYING THE *BIG* IDEAS ■
FROM CORE CURRICULUM

Core curriculum is clearly defined by each school, school district, or state and closely follows national guidelines tied to standard forms of assessment. Schools and/or school districts use approved texts for language arts, math, science, and social studies that cover the respective curriculum and provide ideas and guidelines for teachers when presenting the material to their students. All students should have access to the material, although some will need additional interpretation of the information to make it meaningful.

Interpreting the curriculum for students with moderate or severe disabilities and identifying the big ideas for learning requires the attention of teachers prior to instruction. Knowing what to address for each student with moderate or severe disabilities requires knowledge of the student, the content, and performance standards expected of same-age students. Whatever the subject, it is important to reduce the complexity of detail and determine what main idea or ideas will be taught to a given student (Parrish & Stodden, 2009). The student will have access to all the information taught, but specific and direct instruction will focus on the big ideas identified for that student. Vocabulary related to and explaining these ideas may need to be greatly simplified and reduced in quantity as well. The goal for the student will be to master these big ideas and related vocabulary and not the breadth and depth of content expected of students without severe disabilities. Federal guidelines for students taking alternate assessments allows for a reduction in breadth and depth of the content targeted for assessment (U.S. Department of Education, 2005).

The following examples of different subject matter as well as different grade levels will be used to highlight the process used to identify the big ideas from core content. Information presented at grade level will be stated followed by the interpretation of that information for a particular student. The interpretation and resulting information to teach will vary per student. Instead of becoming bogged down in each detail provided, the intent is to paint a big picture of important general knowledge that will improve the student's ability to better understand the world and communicate that understanding to others. Doyle and Giangreco (2009) stress the importance of being actively involved in the general education classroom and learning the relevant vocabulary to improve interaction skills.

Example 1. Lesson Topic: Prohibition

Class: 11th-Grade American History

Students read a text with the following information in it:

Promoting Moral Improvement

Other reformers felt that morality, not the workplace, held the key to improving the lives of poor people. These reformers wanted immigrants and poor city dwellers to uplift themselves by improving their personal behavior. Prohibition, the banning of alcoholic beverages, was one such program.

Prohibitionist groups feared that alcohol was undermining American morals. Founded in Cleveland in 1874, the Woman's Christian Temperance Union (WCTU) spearheaded the crusade for prohibition. Members advanced this cause by entering saloons, singing, praying, and urging saloonkeepers to stop selling alcohol. As momentum grew, the union was transformed by Frances Willard from a small Midwestern religious group in 1879 to a national organization. Boasting 245,000 members by 1911, the WCTU became the largest women's group in the nation's history. (Danzer, de Alva, Krieger, Wilson, & Woloch, 2007, p. 513)

Interpretation: A long time ago, people thought it was bad to drink alcohol. Bad things happened when people drank a lot. So, a large group of women got together and tried to get people to stop drinking alcohol. Finally, it became a rule that no one could drink alcohol.

Vocabulary words to be taught: people, women, bad, a lot, work, hurt, drink, large. Pictures and actions would be used to help identify words such as *people, women, alcohol, drink, hurt, police.*

Example 2. Finding Unknown Values

Class: 10th-Grade Algebra

Students might read word problems related to determining unknown values such as determining how much more room a student will have in his bedroom if his parents are planning to increase the length of the room by four feet and the width of the room by three feet. They will need to develop the polynomial expression that will represent the area of the new bedroom: $(x + 4)(x + 3)$ to $(x^2 + 7x + 12)$.

Vocabulary words to be taught: bedroom, wall, floor, bed, pictures, CD player, chair, clothes, big or bigger, more, and the numbers 3, 4, 7, 12.

Pictures would be used to show the smaller room and the bigger room and the items that are typically found in a bedroom.

Example 3. Lesson Topic: Acids and bases

Class: Eighth-Grade Science

Students in this class read the following section of their text.

> Carbonate ions contain carbon and oxygen atoms bonded together. They carry an overall negative charge (CO_3^{2-}). One product of an acidic reaction with carbonates is the gas carbon dioxide.
>
> Geologists, scientists who study Earth, use this property of acids to identify rocks containing certain types of limestone. Limestone is a compound that contains the carbonate ion. If a geologist pours dilute hydrochloric acid on a limestone rock, bubbles of carbon dioxide appear on the rock's surface. (Frank, Little, & Miller, 2009, p. 100)

Interpretation: Things that are alive are made up of very, very small things called atoms. Like a magnet, some of these very small things are negative (–), and some are positive (+), and they can push away or pull together.

Some men and women, called scientists, study rocks. They can pour an acid, which is something you can't drink, onto a certain rock, called limestone. If bubbles appear on the rock or limestone, they know that there are small atoms called carbonate ions in it.

Vocabulary words to be taught: rock or stone, pour, small, big, drink, bubbles, men and women, push and pull (– and +). Pictures and real rocks with something to produce bubbles, as well as magnets and magnetic items, would all be used to explain the big ideas.

Example 4. Lesson: The Boston Tea Party

Class: Fourth-Grade Social Studies

In their social studies text, students read the following passage with a picture or two.

> Many people think Samuel Adams planned what happened next. On the night of December 16, 1773, about 150 members of the Sons of Liberty dressed as members of the Mohawk tribe and marched down to Boston Harbor.
>
> At the harbor, hundreds of people were gathered on the docks to watch. When members of the Sons of Liberty arrived, they boarded the ships, broke open more than 300 chests of tea, and threw it all overboard. Their angry protest became known as the Boston Tea Party. (Harcourt, 2007, p. 311)

Interpretation: A long time ago, some men didn't like what was happening to them, and they got angry. They dressed up like Indians with paint on their faces and feathers in their hair and got on some ships that didn't belong to them. The ships belonged to the British, the people wearing red, who made them angry. They opened up a lot of boxes that had tea in them, and they threw the tea into the ocean. This happened in a city called Boston, and it was called the Boston Tea Party. It really wasn't a party, but a lot of people were there.

Vocabulary words to be taught: red, tea, boxes, ship and/or boat, men, Indians, paint, feathers, watch, throw, ocean, party, angry, people. Pictures and real objects such as tea bags and feathers will be used to teach the main concepts. These concepts will also be acted out to promote greater understanding.

Those responsible for identifying big ideas from grade-level content must receive some training to be effective (Spooner, Baker, Harris, Ahlgrim-Delzell, & Browder, 2007). Practice performing such interpretation should help to ease the initial challenge experienced. Once curriculum has been adapted, it can be saved, stored on disks, shared with other teachers in the district, and used for future students. For example, Figure 7.1 shows an adapted lesson on animal adaptations for a fourth grader who does not read in a conventional manner and needs easier concepts highlighted with pictorial support. Knowing in advance what curriculum will be taught at a given age may make it possible for teachers to seek the support of other team members to assume some responsibility for adapting parts of the curriculum. These can be saved, modified, and reused over the years for any student needing such adaptations.

■ AVOIDING ISOLATION IN GENERAL EDUCATION CLASSROOMS

Although outcomes of learning may be different, instruction should not remove the student from class activities. Wehmeyer, Lattin, Lapp-Rincker, and Agran (2003) found that even when middle school students with cognitive disabilities were learning in the same classroom as peers, they often would be working with a paraprofessional on separate work. When accommodations in both instruction and instructional materials are quite extensive due to complex cognitive, sensory, physical, and behavioral challenges, a tendency may exist to separate the student from students without disabilities even though students are all in the same classroom. If the student has an adult providing individualized and systematic instruction, such separation can easily occur. For example, a general educator may be leading the class in a large group discussion, and a paraprofessional may be working with a student with severe and multiple disabilities near the back of the classroom on unrelated IEP objectives. In this case, the student may need to block out the verbal instruction from the classroom teacher as well as questions and responses from his classmates, while also attending to the visual and auditory instruction on unrelated or vaguely related work. To avoid this type of instruction from occurring (or from occurring with any regularity), the educational team must be sure that planning for lessons includes all students in the class activities and reflects Universal Design for Learning (UDL).

Figure 7.1	Adaptation for a Fourth-Grade Lesson on Animals

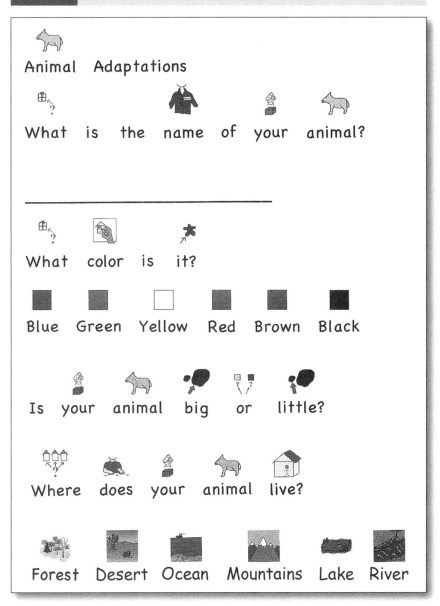

Made with PixWriter from Slater Software, Inc. Adaptation by Susie Speelman.

UDL is a process of creating learning activities and environments that are accessible to all students. General and special education teachers plan lessons from the onset (not as an afterthought) so that students of different abilities can be actively involved in the lessons (Rose & Meyer, 2002, 2006). Teachers plan to present information in different modalities (e.g., demonstration, acting out, pictorial information), plan for students to access more information through different means (e.g., reading, listening, experimenting), and plan for students to demonstrate what they have learned in different ways (e.g., writing, oral presentations, PowerPoint presentations, skits). Although universal design for learning considers all students' needs, those students with more complex disabilities will likely need additional accommodations (Dymond et al., 2006). These students are at greater risk for being isolated within general education classrooms unless more intensive support is available. For example, in a high school English literature class, students are studying the poems of T. S. Eliot. Students with learning disabilities, behavioral challenges, and mild intellectual disabilities may need a graphic organizer to help remember and better understand the use of tone, vocabulary, and analogies. They may also need prewritten notes with occasional blanks for them to fill in missing key words as the teacher discusses the material. Students with more severe intellectual (as well as other concomitant) disabilities will need pictorial material to identify what the poem is about and what it relates to as well as pictorial information of facial expressions to demonstrate understanding of the tone of a poem. As Shumaker et al. (2009) state, students may need more direct support, but they can still learn in general education classrooms given the necessary support strategies.

Ohtake (2003) presented an argument that greater class membership could be attained for the student with severe disabilities through increasing levels of class participation. She proposed four levels of contribution to the class' functioning that might help to describe a classroom and the degree to which a student with severe disabilities is an actively learning member and recognized as such by fellow classmates. These four types of contributions include *thematic,* where a student is working on related material but is not actively contributing to the lesson of the class; *social,* where a student is able to share related information to the class; *contributing,* where a student is giving direct feedback or information to assist the class in learning; and *distinctive,* where the student is adding unique and important information to the lesson of the class. Ohtake urged that classroom lessons be changed to allow for greater participation on the part of the student in the class activity to assuage the isolation that can occur even when students are physically a part of the class.

Isolation is most likely to occur when large group instruction is the teaching arrangement and the student has limited communication skills to participate. As described in Chapter 2, including the student by starting different parts of the discussion with simple questions asked of the student that lead to more abstract and in-depth questions for the rest of the class is one way of avoiding the isolation of the student with severe disabilities. The student is periodically called on to offer information to the class discussion that is used to broaden the topic and provide more comprehensive information from others in the class. For example, a biology teacher might call on a student to respond to the question of what plants need to grow. The student has three items presented in front of him (an eraser, dry erase board, water can). When the student picks up the water can, the teacher thanks him, "Yes, that's correct A. J., water," and then asks the rest of the class to explain how water impacts the plant and what happens if there is insufficient water to the plant.

This contribution from the student furthers the discussion and challenges all of the students to learn important information.

Another option for enhancing the contribution of the student to the entire class is to call on the student to assist in demonstrations or to carry a sample of the lesson to each student in the class for a closer look. Such a contribution may be particularly helpful for the student who needs to get up from the seat and move on a regular basis and for the student who is working on using a wheelchair or walker effectively or who needs to stand and weight bear and practice walking. Such participation by the student also supports efforts to teach following directions and appropriate social behavior. The teacher may also call on the student to help pass out papers, collect homework, or replace books on shelves. All such activities assist the teacher and class functioning and allow the student the opportunity to move meaningfully around the room.

Individual Student Considerations

Unique characteristics of every student need to be considered when adapting curriculum and determining the best way to help that student learn. Students come to school with different life experiences, different familial supports, different languages, cultural experiences, needs, and strengths. No one curriculum will address every student's needs and each one will require adaptations and accommodations to learn as effectively and efficiently as possible. Working with the student and the family of the student to determine the best ways of making the curriculum meaningful and relevant is essential.

Physical Considerations

Students come to school with vastly different means of using their bodies to move, manipulate items, and sit or stand. Some students may need to concentrate on using their bodies, which takes time and effort away from doing schoolwork. Typically, more time must be allotted the student who has physical limitations and needs to plan movements to carry out tasks. Efforts should be made to avoid requiring substantial physical concentration while simultaneously teaching cognitive tasks (e.g., expecting the student to maintain a sitting balance while also answering comprehension questions about a story). The balance required in independent sitting can be worked on while the student is expected to do less (e.g., listen to a story, watch a play, or cheer for a team during PE).

Students may need physical support to control their movements to respond as expected. Physical and occupational therapists on the team can provide valuable input regarding most effective positions and positioning equipment for the student, as well as which movements are most reliable and under the control of the student (Szczepanski, 2004). Movements over which the student has greatest control should be used to indicate responses. A student may use an elbow, thumb, head turn, eye gaze, knee or foot motion, or any body part to respond to a question. Teachers need to present information in such a way that students have easy access to it and can act upon it as efficiently as possible. If movements by the student require excessive effort, it may impact the willingness of the student to actively participate in lessons. Therefore, the amount of concentration and effort required of the student to perform physical skills should always be considered when planning the student's active participation in class.

Students with physical disabilities will need their prescribed positioning and other adaptive equipment in general education classrooms where they are learning. They should not need to go to a special room in order to access such essential equipment. Students may need standers for vertical positioning and weight bearing, computers with adaptive keyboards, and specialized software. Assistive technology can be very supportive of the learning of many students with a variety of disabilities, not just physical. For example, Figure 7.2 shows a fourth grader using his augmentative communication device that is interfaced with a computer to help him complete his modified work. The amount and type of assistive technology and all adaptations and accommodations are determined individually for each student as part of the IEP.

Visual Considerations

Students may have varying amounts of functional vision or no vision remaining that can compound difficulties in learning. A visual impairment may make it difficult to see things clearly at a distance (myopia) or make it difficult to see things up close (hyperopia). Some students have lost some or most of their visual field,

| **Figure 7.2** | A fourth grader using his augmentative communication device to write on the computer |

Photographer: Kristina Zeider

making it difficult to detect the presence of certain information. A few students may learn better through their sense of touch and other remaining sensory input. Whenever a student has a significant visual impairment, adaptations must be made that will ensure access to the material (Downing, 2003). For some students, enlarging material will prove helpful, as well as adding color and presenting in a specific visual field. Figure 7.3 shows large alphabet stamps for writing that can be helpful for students with a visual impairment or for students who just need materials enlarged and less complex. Other students may need the information decreased in size so that they can see the entirety. Simplifying the background and highlighting the relevant information often helps students who have difficulty differentiating the foreground from background stimuli. For those students unable to presently make use of visual information tactilely relevant items that represent concepts will need to be used.

Figure 7.3 Alphabet stamps as an adaptation for writing

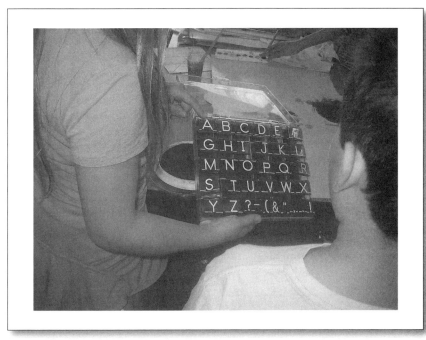

The vision teacher who is on the educational team for this student should be able to read visual reports and make recommendations for material accommodations, seating preferences, most appropriate lighting, and important ways to make use of other sensory input when teaching. Accommodations will need to take into account the visual impairment as well as the cognitive and physical disability, if any. The ability to make use of visual information can vary throughout the day for a student due to fatigue, medication levels, or unknown reasons, and therefore, such information is important for the teaching staff to know. How information is presented to the student will depend on a number of variables, including a student's visual skills and ability.

■ DETERMINING PROMPTS TO USE
FOR A PARTICULAR STUDENT AND LESSON

Each student is unique as is each teaching situation and each skill to be learned by that student. Therefore, determining prompts to use must be planned as a team for each different skill and teaching situation. The team will need to consider what prompts work best for the student and under what conditions. Prompts that provide the most information to the student (taking into account cognitive and sensory disabilities) should be used, especially when teaching new skills. What's informative for one student (e.g., a visual cue) may not provide any information to another student (a student who does not make use of vision).

Prompts should also be selected based on their tolerance by the student and their lack of intrusiveness as the goal is to support students to learn, not to force them through activities. Physically manipulating the student to perform tasks does not necessarily relate to the student's understanding of the task or the need to do it independently (Riley, 1995). Likewise, prompts that draw undue negative attention to the student and stigmatize that student should not be used. Modeling appropriate interactions with students is critical for facilitating positive peer interactions (Carter, Cushing, & Kennedy, 2009). For example, the use of juvenile versus more adult pictures to teach basic skills would not be appropriate in a middle school or high school class (e.g., using pictures of little children and toys versus pictures of young adults or teens and cars, cell phones, etc. when discussing consumerism). The goal is to help students demonstrate their competency as much as possible. The use of juvenile material undermines such a goal.

Finally, prompts used with the student must not distract the teacher or other students or disrupt the learning process in any way. Using loud vocal prompts with a student during a teacher's lecture to the class would not be appropriate. Planning with the general educator clarifies when certain prompts can be used and when other prompts would be more appropriate. Table 7.1 lists questions to consider regarding different prompts to use with students. Table 7.2 provides an example of how specific prompts as part of a simultaneous prompting strategy are employed during large group instruction in a tenth-grade English class.

Table 7.1	Determining the Types of Prompts to Use in General Education Classrooms

What prompts work best for the student?
Which prompts provide the most information?
Are any prompts intrusive and/or disliked by the student?
Will any prompt stigmatize or draw negative attention to the student?
Will any prompt disrupt the class or distract the teacher?
Do all those supporting the student know how to provide the prompts and when?

Table 7.2	Teaching Plan for a 10th Grader on Finding the Author's Voice Using Simultaneous Prompting

Indiana 10th-Grade Reading Standard: Comprehension and Analysis of Literary Text
Performance Objective: Explain how voice, persona, and the choice of narrator affect the mood, tone, and meaning of text.
When Ms. Kleinert is lecturing about author voice and reading different pieces of literature, use the pictorial emotions to show Jadin the following:

1.	When students are doing their research on author voice, put the three emotion cards in front of him and tell him what each one is (use your own tone of voice and facial expressions to make it clear).
2.	Read a short poem or short section of a story stressing the tone of the words with inflection, facial expressions, and emphasize certain words (sorrowful, delighted).
3.	Tell the student what the tone is and touch that facial expression. (Repeat this three times with different tones, using all three emotions—happy, sad, angry.)
4.	Read one of the previously read sections or poems again and ask Jadin if it's one of the three emotions, holding them up for him as you label them.
5.	With no pause, guide his hand toward the correct answer using your hand under his forearm and tell him what the answer is.
6.	Follow this same procedure for the other two poems or sections that have different emotions of the author.
7.	Then, rearrange the three emotion cards so that they are in different places and read three different poems or sections (depending on time). Use the same prompt as described.

*Collect data on Jadin's performance before instruction—that is, read a poem or section and ask him to tell you if it's happy, sad, or angry. Do not prompt.

A Tale of Two Students

Two very different students will be used to explain more clearly how student characteristics impact teaching strategies. Kim is a fourth grader who loves books, appliances, puzzles, and silhouettes. He is nonverbal, moves very quickly, has a short attention span—especially for things he doesn't find interesting—and is labeled with severe autism and intellectual disabilities. Another fourth grader, Jeremiah, has quite different characteristics. He loves interactions with his peers, is a country music fan, and loves *Indiana Jones* movies. He has limited movement of his body and a severe visual impairment. He uses objects and some pictures to communicate and has a difficult time retaining new information. He uses a wheelchair, a stander, and adaptive seating.

Given their different strengths, interests, and needs, these two students learn somewhat differently and require different teaching strategies and supports. In general, Kim does better with limited and short verbal cues, paired with pictorial information, modeling, and visual gestures. He does not need a long wait time to respond, and in fact, can lose track of expectations if a wait time is more than about three seconds. He performs better with quick models from the teacher and clear, direct instructions. He dislikes being touched or manipulated in any way.

Jeremiah, due to his limited movement, slow processing, and severe visual loss, needs time to understand expectations, visually examine materials, make mental connections, and then act on them. A teacher working with Jeremiah needs to wait at least 10 seconds before providing more information (other prompts). Jeremiah appreciates verbal information about what he is examining as long as it is not too extensive or abstract. He often requires physical support under his forearms and elbows to stabilize the movement and allow him more accurate and controlled movement of his hands. He needs enlarged pictorial and written material with limited detail and a simple (dull) and contrasting background.

Since Kim likes to grab materials and throw them, it is better to block incorrect responses (e.g., cover the wrong options), redirect to the correct option, and quickly move on. Belaboring a particular response is not what Kim responds to. He does better using lots of different materials that address the same concept. He needs multiple opportunities to master a skill, but he likes to move through trials quickly with the focus on the materials and limited verbalizations.

The pace for Jeremiah, on the other hand, is considerably slower. Since he only sees a very small amount of information at one time, he needs time to carefully piece it together. Furthermore, once he's determined a correct answer, it takes him time to plan how to move his body to make his decision clear to others (e.g., typically by placing his whole hand on the answer). Due to these somewhat extreme differences in student learning style, teachers must be able to adapt readily and adjust their teaching strategies accordingly to be most effective.

■ EXAMPLES OF STUDENTS RECEIVING DIRECT INSTRUCTION ACROSS GRADES AND INSTRUCTIONAL ARRANGEMENTS

In general, teaching in any environment, but certainly in general education classrooms, requires certain preplanning. Teachers will need to determine how to (1) teach the target skills (share the information with the student), (2) check for acquisition (comprehension), (3) maintain acquired skills (review), and (4) generalize skills learned to other environments. The following detailed examples address the first two requirements and describe how a class and particular subject are being taught. A student with a moderate to severe intellectual disability is an active member of each class. What this student is learning as well as how the information is being taught during the whole class activity also is described. The intent of these several examples across subject matter, grade level, and teaching arrangements is to provide suggestions for addressing the needs of other students with similar disabilities in general education classrooms.

Once skills have been taught, a periodic review of the material to check for maintenance of skills also is needed. Brief reviews can occur at the start of class lessons and during lectures. Reviewing learned skills is critical to maintain a strong base from which to develop more skills. At the end of this chapter, the additional need to teach students to generalize what has been learned in one environment to other environments and situations will be discussed. For each of the lessons described, the team has considered the related content standards, the related skills that the student is to learn, adapted materials and prompts that will be needed to support student learning, and how progress will be measured. A list of questions that educational teams may wish to consider to support learning in general education classrooms can be found in Table 7.3.

Table 7.3 Steps to Consider When Teaching in General Education Classrooms

1.	What is the class learning and what standard(s) does it relate to?
2.	What skill(s) is the student to learn and how does it relate to age-level standards?
3.	What materials will be needed to highlight the critical information/skill to be learned? • Will the adapted materials be cognitively and physically accessible? • Will the adapted materials be culturally sensitive? • Will the adapted materials resemble materials/subject matter used by others in the class? • Will distracters be used (information that doesn't go with the subject)?
4.	How will the adapted materials be presented to the student? How will you get the student's attention? How will the adapted materials be used?
5.	What prompts will be used to teach the target skill(s) and in what order?
6.	How will the student's behavior be reinforced?
7.	How will mistakes be corrected?
8.	How will the student be taught during different instructional arrangements in the room (e.g., large group, small group, pairs, independent work)?
9.	What other ways will the student interact with the class that may be unrelated to the targeted skill?
10.	How will data be collected on acquisition of the targeted skill(s)?
11.	How will skills be maintained and generalized to other environments and situations?

■ SMALL GROUP INSTRUCTION

The use of small groups to teach students allows the teacher to become more acquainted with the skill level of a smaller number of students, who can serve as role models and support one another. Small group instruction also builds cooperative working relations, as students must share ideas, make decisions as a group, work toward a common goal, and compromise. Soukup, Wehmeyer, Bashinski, and Bovaird (2007) identified the small group teaching arrangement as one variable that was supportive of a student's access to the core curriculum. Researchers have identified numerous benefits (i.e., higher achievement and greater productivity, valuing of diversity, improved social skills, higher self-esteem, and greater ability to cope with adversity) as a result of small group instruction that is cooperative in nature (Salisbury, Palombaro, & Hollowood, 1993). In addition, learning vicariously, by watching other students in the group, has been documented for students with severe disabilities, making this instructional arrangement potentially more efficient than one-to-one instruction (Colozzi, Ward, & Crotty, 2008; Falkenstine, Collins, Schuster, & Kleinert, 2009). The following examples of small group instruction are provided to demonstrate how students with moderate or severe intellectual disabilities can be successfully educated using this teaching arrangement.

Small Group Instruction—Middle School

In Mr. Edwin's sixth-grade math class, students are learning simple algebraic equations to find unknown quantities. Mr. Edwin typically presents a story problem related to something of high interest to the class (e.g., movie plots) and represents some part of it as an algebraic equation. This is done as a whole group lesson and addresses the national standard of using mathematical models to represent and understand quantitative relationships. He presents three to four different examples and then divides the class up into pairs and gives the class a page of problems to work on.

Derrick, a student in this class, is learning to recognize which of two numbers is larger (this relates to the math standard stated above). During the large group lesson, he is asked by the teacher to select a problem for the class. He does this with the use of a magnetic wand that he moves over three to four problems written on different pieces of paper with a paper clip on each one (magnetic). As the problem is being discussed, the two numbers in the problem are used to help Derrick determine which is larger. For example, in one problem Mr. Edwin writes $5x + 3x = $ ____. The numbers 5 and 3 are then used with Derrick to determine which is larger. If two-digit numbers are used, then the first digit is used to teach Derrick. Derrick sits at a table with five other students at the front of the room and in easy reach of the teacher.

The occupational therapist (OT) working with Derrick writes the two numbers on two separate cards and asks him to first point to each number as she says them. This is just to check to ensure that he still remembers the numbers and to make him feel successful. Then she asks which of the two numbers is larger. After a five-second wait to give him a chance to respond, she counts out five pictures of items related to the problem Mr. Edwin is teaching and places them over the number 5. She then counts out three pictures of items and puts them over the number 3. Then she asks Derrick again which is larger. If he points to the 5, she praises him and then listens to what problem the classroom teacher is on and does another problem with Derrick in the same way but with different pictured items (e.g., starships from the movie *Star Wars*).

If he doesn't respond after five seconds or responds incorrectly, the OT tells Derrick that he was wrong and highlights (spreads out) the five pictured items and moves the three pictured items closer together, repeats the number of each, while pointing to it. Then, she asks which number is more—which has more items. He is praised if he chooses the correct answer, and the picture items are lined up next to each other to give feedback and help him clearly see it. If after five seconds he does not choose or makes an error, he is given corrective feedback (e.g., "No, that's the three. Five is the larger number."). The OT will model and verbally explain the correct response twice (changing the location of the two numbers). Then she will change the position of the numbers and items and ask once more (waiting five seconds). If correct, he will be praised and shown why he is right. If not he will be told the correct answer and asked to find the 5.

The instruction by the OT is done quietly while Mr. Edwin is demonstrating to the class the solution of the algebraic equations. Sometimes the OT can offer several opportunities to select the larger of two numbers, using Mr. Edwin's examples and sometimes only one or two. If Derrick picks the correct number following the first request to do so, he receives credit for recognizing the larger number. The data sheet shows the two numbers being compared and the number that Derrick chose after the first question is circled (not after all of the prompts). This data is used to determine his progress toward meeting his IEP goal.

When Mr. Edwin divides the class into pairs, Derrick joins one pair of students and with the OT's support (and when she leaves, Mr. Edwin supports) continues to work on this skill using numbers in his group's assignment. He has pictured items (each on a separate small card) that go with the story problems, and his peers present different ones (three at a time) and ask him to decide which one they'll do first. Derrick enjoys this interaction, which typically results in some teasing about his choice. It also provides a brief break from the math work, which seems to help him. The procedure described above of least-to-most prompts with constant time delay is used to teach Derrick because this is not a new task for him and he is beginning to identify the correct number without several additional prompts.

Small Group Instruction—Elementary School

In a first-grade classroom, students are assigned to groups during language arts to work on different skills. One group of five is reading a story with the classroom teacher, one group of five is working with the special educator on decoding skills related to words in the story, another group is working with a parent volunteer on creating different endings to the story, and the rest of the class is working independently on reading or unfinished work. All groups are composed of students with diverse skills and ability.

In the group facilitated by the special educator, one of the five students is a curious young boy who loves pictures, especially of dinosaurs, and enjoys imitating his peers. He is nonverbal, has Down syndrome, and has a mild to moderate hearing impairment. The group is working on identifying initial, medial, and final blended sounds in words. For example, the special educator will ask the group to tell her where the *ch* sound is in words such as *witch, chicken,* and *kitchen.* In this group, Daniel is shown three pictures and is asked to listen to the teacher and then find the picture of the word that she has said. Once he has done this, the teacher uses the correct picture to ask the others in the group where the sound being targeted occurs. For example, Daniel is presented with pictures of a potato, a sandwich, and apple. He is asked to find the sandwich, and when he does, the rest of the group is to state that the *ch* sound occurs at the end of the word. Then they make sure everyone can spell the word correctly. Since Daniel also is working on recognizing initial letters, he is shown the three words that go with the pictures and asked to find the *s* for sandwich.

The special educator is responsible for the learning of all students in this group and must make sure that the pace of the lesson is appropriate for covering the necessary material. After showing Daniel the three pictures and naming them while pointing to each one, she waits three seconds for a response. If no response or an incorrect one, she'll quickly remove one picture and ask again while tapping each picture and stating its name. If no response in three seconds (or an incorrect one), she'll describe what each is and then asks him again. If correct, she'll praise him and go on with the rest of the group. If incorrect, she'll ask a peer to correct him and let him know which is the correct answer. She uses a least-to-most prompting strategy in this manner since Daniel recognizes the task and is beginning to become more accurate connecting the spoken word with its pictorial referent. He does not need a long wait time and typically responds immediately if he knows the answer. This procedure goes quite quickly and does not slow the group excessively. At times, the teacher will ask a classmate to describe the pictured items to Daniel to offer some practice in this skill.

Learning to recognize pictures and their meanings helps Daniel in his communication goals. Pictured items are used (either as the correct answer or distracters) that Daniel can make use of in communicating with others throughout his day at school and at home. His hearing loss interferes with his ability to clearly understand others in his environment, and so this lesson teaches him to listen and to associate what he hears with the pictured referent. Identifying letters and letter-sound associations are basic phonetic skills to aid him in creating his own messages.

Small Group Instruction—Middle School

In Mr. Benton's seventh-grade social studies class, students are learning about the Constitution and in particular, the Preamble to the Constitution. They are studying the introductory phrase of "we the people," learning what it means and comparing to other countries as well. They are also learning that federal laws supersede the power of individual states. In general, Mr. Benton uses small group instruction to explore issues in his class. After a brief introduction to the topic, he divides the class into small groups of five students and asks them to respond to questions he has selected.

Small group instruction works well for Jordan who has a harder time attending in a large group. Jordan has a very curious nature and is highly mobile. He loves to move quickly from one activity to the next. He is nonverbal and has difficulty interacting with his peers, although he often remains close to two of the boys in his group. Jordan uses picture and word symbols to communicate as well as vocalizations, a loud "no," a few gestures, and body movements (e.g., reaching, shoving, running off, kicking, and pinching). He writes by sequencing pictorial information, and he is learning to choose from different sticky labels to sign his name.

While the group explores policies in other countries, comparing and contrasting democratic societies to dictatorships, for example, a special educator provides some guidance and also provides additional support to Jordan. Pictured information is downloaded and printed from the Internet by the group and used by Jordan to identify a single leader (one man) as opposed to a large group of people. He is also learning about voting (by marking a ballot or raising one's hand) and that the greatest number of votes determines the outcome. Since Jordan often wants to ignore the group's wishes and do what he wants, this is an important lesson for him. Vocabulary words he will learn include *people, leader, vote, majority* or *most, America,* and his state, *Wisconsin.* The lesson for Jordan will involve social studies, math, reading, and writing. It relates to Wisconsin's standard in Political Science and Citizenship—specifically to identify and explain democracy's basic principles, including individual rights, responsibility for the common good, equal opportunity, equal protection of the laws, freedom of speech, justice, and majority rule with protection for minority rights.

Different members of Jordan's group assume the role of recorder, facilitator, and timer. The group decides what will be written in response to Mr. Benton's questions and decides on how many and what countries to explore and compare. All students vote, and the special educator asks the students if that is democratic or not and what would be another way to decide. When hands are in the air, Jordan is asked to count them and is given two very different numbers to identify the correct count. A peer tells him that they are voting, and he is shown a picture of people with their hands raised. The number of votes is placed on the country, and Jordan is helped to place them on a number line by matching numbers to determine which country received the majority (or most) of the votes. This occurs several times so that Jordan gets to practice the concepts of voting and determining the majority vote.

Since Jordan moves at a fairly quick pace and is easily distracted, the special educator (and anyone providing direct instruction) must keep the instruction moving with few if any delays. To ensure that Jordan is successful and does not get confused or just randomly selects any option provided to him, a simultaneous prompting procedure is used. The special educator gives Jordan four or five pictured vocabulary cards at a time and verbally labels them as Jordan looks at each one. She will repeat them for the several minutes that Jordan shows interest in manipulating the pictures. As the group formulates ideas and records them, simple sentences are written for Jordan to reflect these ideas (e.g., "A dictator is one *person* who rules."). The vocabulary word for Jordan is left blank, and Jordan is asked to find the word that completes the sentence. He is given two options placed in front of him, the sentence is read by a peer, and the special educator taps the correct vocabulary word picture as it is said. Jordan picks up the correct card (which was tapped) and is shown where it goes in the sentence. He is praised for completing the sentence. The same vocabulary and concepts are used in different ways as the lesson progresses during the week. However, before instruction begins, a quick probe is done to see if Jordan can identify any of the vocabulary words.

Small Group Instruction—10th-Grade Biology Class

Mr. Drapper's biology class has been studying DNA, the scientists who discovered DNA, and the impact on diversity. This work relates to a life science standard on the theory of biological evolution, and students must understand why genetic variation within a population is essential for evolution. The subject of study is a weeklong unit, and the class has been divided into small groups to study for the upcoming test. Mr. Drapper moves around to the different groups, checking on their progress and responding to questions.

Brad is a 10th grader in this class with severe intellectual disabilities who has a few words but typically uses alternative and augmentative forms of communication (e.g., gestures, body movement, facial expressions, and pictorial and written symbols). Brad has physical delays, which slow his movements and make his speech hard to understand. Brad is well liked by his classmates who provide a fair amount of natural support. Brad works with three of his classmates and the additional support of a peer tutor.

As Brad's group discusses the scientists responsible for the discovery of DNA and the process they undertook and ask questions of each other, Brad also works on his IEP objective of recognizing the big ideas of topics. Brad is asked to draw a number from a pile of number cards and give it to a peer of his choice in his small group. The number on the card relates to a prewritten question that the peer tutor has. The peer tutor reads the question, and the peer that Brad handed the number to must provide an answer. The peer tutor asks the others in the group if they all agree with the response or not and can refer to the answer that he has. At the same time, Brad is asked to find (from three pictorial/ written options) which one is a scientist or which one is a man who is trying to find answers. The pictures are very different from one another to simplify the task.

A progressive time delay procedure is being used with Brad so that when initially asked to find the man or scientist, there is no wait provided and he is told which one is the correct picture. A zero wait of this nature is provided for the first four trials during one class, and then the wait is increased to two seconds following the direction to find the man. The three pictorial options are scrambled after every trial so that the correct response will be in a different location and Brad must carefully view each option before responding. If Brad responds within the two-second time delay by looking in the direction of the correct picture card and beginning to move his hand toward this card, then the wait time is increased to four seconds. If correct, Brad is praised and his response is reaffirmed. If incorrect, he is told what to look for in the correct response, and one of the options is removed to make the decision easier. The peer tutor assumes responsibility for ensuring the wait time increases as Brad seems to better understand the task, although the peers in his group are encouraged to give him feedback following the trials.

LARGE GROUP INSTRUCTION ■

Teachers may wish to present information to all students at once and to discuss the subject matter as a large group. Large group instruction can occur at any grade level, although it may be more prevalent and last longer in duration in secondary schools where students typically have longer attention spans. In a study observing 19 elementary students, Soukup et al. (2007) investigated ecological variables contributing to students with disabilities accessing the core curriculum. They found that students with intellectual and developmental disabilities had greater access to the core curriculum when in general education classrooms and large group instruction than when in specialized settings. The following are examples of large group instruction for different classrooms and subjects, with specific attention provided for ways to teach a student with moderate to severe intellectual disabilities during such a teaching arrangement.

Large Group Instruction—Ninth Grade

Mr. Keith's and Mr. Tybok's ninth-grade economics course is undertaking a unit on budgeting. This cotaught class by Mr. Keith (general educator) and Mr. Tybok (special educator) is very popular with a number of students. In a large group, the two teachers present different information on income, debits, and how to set up a personal budget. Mr. Keith and Mr. Tybok use lots of humor in their lectures, playing off one another, and also encouraging active student participation by having students come to the front of the room and "role play" a certain amount of income from a job and necessary as well as frivolous expensive items. The entire class can then visualize the necessity of earning enough money to obtain desired goods. Following the whole group lesson, the teachers break the students into groups of two or three students and have them work on a computer game on balancing a budget. Both teachers move around the room responding to various students' needs for assistance.

Mohammed really enjoys Mr. Keith's booming voice and his teasing nature. He also loves the attention of Mr. Tybok but doesn't care for the subject matter. His parents want him to learn some basic money concepts, and so this class offers that opportunity. Mohammed has a moderate to severe bilateral hearing impairment with a severe intellectual disability. He is nonverbal but uses his facial expressions, body language, vocalizations, objects, pictures, and a few signs to communicate. Mohammed tends to get frustrated when he isn't sure what is expected and pulls away from people and throws items when this happens. Mohammed sits at the front of the room, near the middle so he can see his teachers and they have easy access to him.

Mr. Keith always calls on Mohammed to help demonstrate concepts in the class. Mohammed will be shown pictures of certain jobs with dollar amounts attached (credit or income) or various items with price tags (debits), and he will choose which one he wants to portray. He holds the sign while standing in front of the class. The manual sign for his choice will be modeled for him several times by Mr. Tybok, the paraprofessional, or speech and language pathologist (whoever is supporting this class), and the entire class will use it along with other signs they've learned (e.g., MONEY, 1, 10, 100, 1000, FOOD, CDs, CAR).

During parts of the whole-group instruction when both teachers are teaching various aspects of budgeting, Mohammed works on sorting pictures of necessities (housing, clothing, food, transportation), jobs (with income amount attached), and desired items (computer games, CDs, TVs, movie tickets). He sits close to a classmate who is really interested in learning sign and enjoys interacting with Mohammed. On the back of each pictured item or job is a picture of the manual sign. Mohammed's classmate looks at the sign and then produces it for Mohammed and asks him which pile to put it in. This peer also uses the pictured cards to respond to teacher questions regarding income and expenses. The peer prompts Mohammed to continue working by moving a pictured item toward his hand and gesturing toward all three piles signing *WHERE? WORK, WANT, NEED?* Since this peer is also taking notes, one of the two teachers will check on Mohammed's performance, correct mistakes, and offer praise. If he has made a mistake, the correct response will be modeled, followed by a similar item that he is to sort.

Large Group Instruction—High School

In Ms. Juarez' 11th-grade Spanish class, students are expected to take notes and orally participate in the group's lesson (vocabulary, grammar, sentence structure, idioms). Typically, Ms. Juarez begins her class with a short review from the previous class, asking different students to respond to her questions. Then she'll spend some time introducing the new subject matter and will demonstrate, write on the dry erase board or Smart Board, and show pictures pertaining to new vocabulary or phrases, having the class repeat after her. She infuses a great deal of humor into her lessons, and students appear to enjoy her class. Ms. Juarez will often divide the class into pairs to work on their pronunciation, use of vocabulary, and syntax. At this time, she will either work individually with students on certain skills, or she will move around the room, helping pairs of students.

Estrella is a student in this class who comes from a Spanish-speaking family and loves hearing Spanish. She also loves the humor in the class and the interactive nature. Although Estrella does not use speech, she does have vision and enough mobility to use her fist to indicate messages through large pictorial/written cards. Her goals for this class include vocabulary development, spontaneous communication, appropriate interactions with peers, and emergent literacy skills. Estrella uses pictured/labeled cards in English to respond to questions, and her peers must provide the Spanish oral interpretation.

In this class, Estrella works with either the special educator, a paraprofessional, a high school peer tutor, or at times the classroom teacher, Ms. Juarez. Her support person depends on the schedule for that day or week. For the purpose of this example, she is working with a peer tutor. The peer tutor does not get credit for the Spanish class but does earn high school credit for serving as a student assistant to the class. This student has been trained by the general and special educators to demonstrate specific prompts that are the most effective for Estrella without over-supporting her. This student also is responsible for gathering data on Estrella's specific goals and reporting back to both teachers.

During the large group review, Estrella sits next to a student who is a high achiever and benefits from the support from this student. When the teacher asks a review question, the student will raise her hand if she knows the answer and also whispers to Estrella to identify a certain word or phrase in English. Estrella is to look at her three picture/word cards and move her hand to the correct one. When Estrella has made her choice (e.g., by putting her fist on one picture/word card), the peer tutor will gesture to the teacher who may or may not decide to call on her. If she is called on, the student next to her will state in English which one she chose and then will be expected to also respond in Spanish. If incorrect in her selection, the teacher will give her feedback and ask for another student to respond. Many students make mistakes and receive similar feedback, so Estrella is not singled out as the only one not knowing the answer.

The peer tutor and others who work directly with Estrella have learned a systematic prompting strategy of most-to-least prompts to teach her new vocabulary words when others are also learning new content. During this part of the large group instruction when the teacher is presenting new information, two quite different pictured representations are placed in front of Estrella, and the correct option is tapped and labeled or described as Estrella's arms is guided toward this option with a prompt to her elbow. When vocabulary words are reviewed at the beginning of each lesson, the support person will present two pictorial options and wait for a few seconds to see if Estrella starts to identify the correct word. If not, then those words will be used in further instruction.

During those times of the class when students are working individually or in pairs to practice their skills, much more attention and time is paid to helping Estrella understand the vocabulary and how to use it. Each new picture/word card is shown to her, and its label in English is given as well as what the word means and how it is used. Examples related to Estrella's life are provided. For example, if the word is *house* (*casa* in Spanish), then the picture is shown to her, pointing out features of a house, that it is where people live (sleep, eat, play), and that she lives in a house as well. To check for comprehension, the peer tutor will read simple sentences, omitting the last word so that Estrella has the opportunity to choose the correct vocabulary word (e.g., Estrella lives in a nice pink _____). The vocabulary Estrella is learning is used on her communication displays and in other class subjects.

Large Group Instruction—Elementary School

The first graders in Ms. Pierce's class are studying different authors and their writing styles. One author being studied is Laura Joffe Numeroff, who wrote a series of books based on amusing contingencies such as *If You Give a Mouse a Cookie, If You Give a Pig a Pancake,* and *If You Give a Moose a Muffin.* These popular books for young readers can be used to help children predict outcomes as well as learn a specific writing style by a given author. Ms. Pierce uses a Big Book to read to the entire class as a group, with the students sitting on a rug around her. She asks students to identify where they would find the author of the story, the illustrator, and what these terms mean. As she reads the story, she stops frequently to ask the group questions about what they are hearing, make predictions using pictorial cues, and learn new vocabulary. Standards being addressed include but are not limited to the following: identify the author and illustrator and the roles of each; identify the main idea of a story; make predictions based on evidence; and with assistance, make inferences and draw conclusions about setting and plot based on evidence. Students must be quiet and pay attention, raising their hands to ask questions or respond to questions from the teacher. Following the large group reading of the story, Ms. Pierce has the students create their own stories based on this writing style.

Bashir, a first grader in this class, enjoys stories but due to his blindness, misses out on the colorful illustrations. Although Bashir has a lot to say, he is nonverbal and uses objects and parts of objects as well as facial expressions and vocalizations to send his messages. Bashir is positioned on the floor very close to the teacher so that she can touch him at times to maintain his attention. Family members and other members of the team have gathered various objects that relate to the story as well as those that do not relate (distracters). A peer in his class has a pet mouse and that has been brought to the class for Bashir to understand what a mouse is—its size, how it feels, moves, smells, and sounds it makes. He has been told that the mouse in the story is not real and that mice really don't speak. As the story progresses, Bashir is shown various objects that go with the mouse's requests. Many of these are common objects that Bashir has encountered before. Objects are held on a simple tray in front of Bashir who feels these objects and responds to teacher questions by touching or grasping one of the options. A parent volunteer sits close to Bashir, but to the side, so that she doesn't obscure their visual access to the Big Book. This parent will repeat the question asked by the teacher to Bashir and guide his hands with a finger under his right wrist to each object while labeling them. Then she'll return his arm to midline, remind him of the question, and ask him to touch the object that is his choice. What he chooses can respond to the teacher's question regarding what is a certain vocabulary word or what the students predict will happen in the story. When a question is asked that has a correct response, the number of items placed before Bashir are reduced in number to two or three so he has less to remember and a better chance of choosing the correct item. When it is time to write their own stories, Bashir is given a prewritten form with fill in the blank options. The parent volunteer reads the story to him and offers him various object choices to make his selection. She provides the same physical cue on his wrist as previously stated. She writes in his choices as he selects them and then reads the entire story to him when they are finished. As Bashir becomes accustomed to this type of prompting, the person supporting him will repeat the teacher's question but fade the wrist prompt to his forearm and then to a nudge of his elbow. The goal is for Bashir to hear the teacher's questions and touch the correct answer without physical prompts.

Large Group Instruction—12th-Grade English Literature

In Ms. Jacobs' 12th-grade English literature class, students are studying the plays of William Shakespeare. Ms. Jacobs typically offers some preview information to the whole class, discusses Elizabethan style of English, and asks the class to compare different scenes to their current experiences. Then students get into groups of five to work on various scenes that they will enact for the class.

During the large group instruction and reading of *Romeo and Juliet*, Cody receives support from a peer tutor. (A special educator and speech-language pathologist also support on other days of the week.) As the play is discussed, the peer tutor interprets the story for Cody using small paper figures of key characters and focuses on relevant vocabulary such as *boy, girl, love, mother, father, friends, party, dance,* and so on. The peer tutor uses the paper figures to act out the action and writes out related simple sentences. The tutor also encourages Cody to use the figures of key characters to act out a scene with him since he particularly likes to manipulate items while he is learning. Cody has some letter recognition and knows some letter and sound associations, so he is asked by the peer tutor to identify some of the words in sentences he's written. At times, the teacher will direct simple questions to Cody, such as "How did one of the men get badly hurt?" and Cody will respond by acting out the swordplay. He also raises the paper figures to respond to questions related to specific characters.

When students break into groups to work on their various scenes, Cody is given an active role that involves a few lines that he says using a small voice output device. Cody's own speech is very difficult to understand, so the voice output device is used to more clearly support his efforts. Cody particularly enjoys using props (such as fake swords, masks) to engage him more in the activity.

When Cody is working on recognizing the vocabulary words that relate to the play during large group instruction, the person providing support asks him to identify a specific word (e.g., dance) from four options. He is given three seconds to find the word and then is shown the correct word (if he didn't identify it correctly). The letters in the word are pointed to as they are pronounced to help him decode the word. An effort is made to ask him to identify the same word at least three times per class as it naturally emerges during the discussion of the play (not three times in a row). Constant time delay of this nature has been effectively used with Cody in other lessons and seems to be effective during this large group lesson as well.

■ PAIRED INSTRUCTION

Considerable research has investigated the effect of students working in pairs to enhance both students' learning (see Carter et al., 2009). In this arrangement students are paired with another student as determined by the teacher to learn new skills, review skills, work cooperatively to complete projects, and study for exams. Classwide Peer Tutoring (Greenwood, Arreaga-Mayer, Utley, Gavin, & Terry, 2001) represents one type of peer buddy learning where all students in a class are engaged in a cooperative learning arrangement with another student. The teacher can decide how long specific students will be paired together during the academic year and will change the pairings based on various factors. The following serve as examples of paired instruction.

Paired Instruction—Second Grade

Mrs. Henney's second-grade class is studying plants and plant life in science. The text has many colorful pictures, which help a number of students in the class, especially those who are English language learners. Mrs. Henney makes frequent use of buddy learning—pairing students to work together—and the class has shown steady progress. Students get materials from a side table and then get with their partner to follow the directions and prepare their seeds in dirt, water, write their names on tape and add to the cup, and find a location on the windowsill for their plant. Then they complete a worksheet, which requires students to read and fill in missing words in the two paragraphs on plants.

Rika, a student with severe intellectual and physical disabilities, works with her partner, Shana, to complete the activity. Shana holds up the pictorial and written directions for Rika to see while the teacher goes over the activity with the class. Then she asks Rika if she wants her to push her wheelchair to get the materials, and Rika smiles or slightly nods her head to say yes. A list of materials with accompanying pictures is used to help Rika identify what will be needed. As the two girls collect their materials and put them on Rika's wheelchair tray, the general educator shows Rika two items and asks her which one is needed (one is offered as a distracter). Rika is to look at the item on the list of materials (e.g., dirt and not an eraser). Mrs. Henney models the first two options for Shana, who then asks Rika the same question for the last two items. If Rika looks at the irrelevant item, Shana will tell her that it's not correct and shows her the list of needed items. Mrs. Henney will point to the picture or word of the item that she needs, and Shana will repeat the question, holding up the two items. After four seconds of no response, or if Rika looks at the incorrect item, Shana will put the correct item in front of her and tell her what it is and that it is what they need. Mrs. Henney will hold up the list and point out the similarity between the picture and the item to help Rika make this association.

When the two girls follow the written and pictorial directions to plant their seeds, Shana performs the physical steps (since Rika does not possess the physical ability to assist), while Rika is asked which step to perform. She does this by looking at the appropriate item. For instance, if the step involves filling a paper cup with dirt, Shana holds up the dirt and a marker or some other distracter and asks Rika which one goes in the cup. With the pictorial directions supported vertically near Rika, she is to check the directions and then look at the correct item. If she looks at the incorrect item, Shana will wave the correct item in front of her, correct her verbally, and then perform the step. Mrs. Henney checks on all groups of students, and when she gets to Rika and Shana, she makes sure Rika is being asked each step. She'll also point out the similarity between picture and object as well as the label under the picture to draw her attention.

The same procedure is used when the girls need to complete the worksheet on the science activity. Shana will do the actual writing for both girls, but Rika will be asked questions during this aspect of the task so that her opinion is included. For instance, when the worksheet calls for the rationale for putting the plant in a certain spot in the room, Shana will show Rika a picture of a window with bright sunlight coming through and a picture of a box and ask her where they put their plant. If Rika looks at the picture of the window, Shana confirms her decision and adds that plants need light, not dark places. If Rika makes a mistake, Shana will tell her why it's wrong and show her the correct answer.

Paired Instruction—11th-Grade English Literature

This English literature class is studying poetry and the conventions used by various authors to create a very personalized tone for their poems. The class is also exploring the use of more sophisticated vocabulary words to more precisely convey mood and tone. In particular, the standard being addressed for this lesson targets the elements of literature and requires students to identify, analyze, and apply knowledge of the structures and elements of literature. Students are to demonstrate the ability to evaluate the authors' use of literary elements, such as theme (moral, lesson, view, or comment on life). Mrs. Holbrook is the English literature teacher and makes use of buddy learning or paired instruction in her class to assist students in their productivity and learn about giving peer feedback. She typically pairs students for nine to ten weeks, depending on the activities to be completed and how well students work together. For this lesson, student pairs have selected different poets to study and present their findings on their author's use of language to the class.

One eleventh grader in this class, Beth, is learning to read text at approximately a second-grade level and to express herself more effectively. She has a moderate level of intellectual impairment and is fairly shy with others. Working with one peer is much easier for her than working in a larger group given her shyness and tendency to withdraw from group involvement.

Beth is working with Janet, a classmate who does not have special needs but often struggles with her own academic achievement. The special educator, Ms. Brodsky, provides support to this pair of students, as well as other pairs.

Janet and Beth are researching Walt Whitman and how he conveyed his point of view in his poems. Ms. Brodsky helps both students interpret the poems, asking them what they think certain vocabulary means. Janet will read a poem and then ask Beth what emotion he's trying to express. Beth will express her opinion, saying that he's sad, happy, hopeful, angry, or being silly. If no response after a three-second pause, Ms. Brodsky will show her these emotion words written on cards and ask her to select the best one for the poem. Janet must decide if she agrees with Beth or not and then tell her why and make note of representative phrases that support their decisions. She explains what these phrases mean to Beth. Ms. Brodsky will write these explanations out for Beth using words at her reading level while Janet makes notes for the presentation using the poet's actual words. If Ms. Brodsky is helping other students, Janet writes the phrases for Beth to read. For example, in the poem, "O Captain! My Captain!" the line "The port is near, the bells I hear, the people all exulting" might be explained to Beth as "The boat is coming back home and everyone is happy." Rephrasing different lines and defining certain words seems to help Janet's understanding of Whitman's use of language as well.

Beth is to read the short phrase. If she doesn't read the words, Ms. Brodsky or Janet points to the first letter and ask her to think of the sound it makes. If this doesn't help her to identify the word, she is given the first sound(s). If this prompt doesn't help her, then the word is read to her. Once she has finished the phrase, she is asked to repeat it more quickly for fluency and enhanced comprehension. When her partner has written several points to make regarding the poet and his use of language, using actual phrases, she asks Beth if she agrees or wants to make changes or additions. Janet may read other poems and ask Beth if they should be added to their presentation.

When they practice their presentation, Beth will read the title with support from Janet and will state a certain tone or viewpoint held by the poet. Beth reads this information with Janet or Ms. Brodsky using least-to-most prompts as described earlier, and Janet will add to each introduction by Beth with examples from Whitman's poems. In this manner, Beth works on her verbal expressions, vocabulary development, and reading skills, while meeting class expectations.

Paired Instruction—Third Grade

Toni's third-grade class is studying Mexico for their social studies unit. They have been reading about Mexico in their textbook, and class time essentially involves working with a partner to investigate various aspects of the country. Mr. Felix, the third-grade teacher, has shared some information on geography, size, culture, language, customs, food, and music and has let various pairs of students further investigate a topic using books, travel pamphlets, and the Internet. Mr. Felix offers individual attention to the paired students to guide their learning. A culminating activity will be for all students to make short presentations to the class on their chosen topic.

Toni is working with a favorite classmate, Chloe. Toni loves bright colors and is learning to identify pictures that are enlarged to account for her visual impairment. She is very expressive and usually has a big smile that draws others to her. Toni uses a wheelchair and is learning to use an adapted keyboard to access the computer.

Since Toni loves music and often attends for longer periods of time if she can listen to music during a lesson, Toni and Chloe opted to investigate the music of Mexico. A parent of a classmate who used to live in Mexico has offered to help the girls. This mother brings in some CDs of Mexican singing artists as well as some Mexican rhythm instruments. Having the actual tactile items to relate to pictorial information helps Toni to understand what is being conveyed.

Toni's objectives for this lesson are to differentiate Mexican style of music from other forms, identify Mexican rhythm instruments from other kinds of instruments by the sound they make, recognize what instrument produces what sound, and which adjective best describes the music (e.g., happy, fast, slow, sad). Her partner's objectives involve investigative research, use of different media, comparing and contrasting Mexican music with other types of music, especially Mariachi music, and writing and oral skills involved in the final presentation.

Various sounds from CDs and instruments, the actual items, as well as verbal and physical prompts will be used to help Toni reach her objectives. The person supporting Toni will also guide Chloe in her research and will encourage interactions between the two girls as needed. Chloe has learned to seek Toni's input on a regular basis, so little external prompting is typically needed. When Chloe finds and plays Mexican music on the Internet, she tells Toni to listen and will ask her if she likes it or not. Toni will typically respond with a facial expression. Chloe will show Toni maracas and xylophone, both of which she plays and labels. She'll tell Toni that the maracas are typically what she will hear in Mexican music.

While Chloe works on the computer searching for information, the vision teacher teaches Toni the information she needs to learn. She plays a CD or shakes the rhythm instruments and tells Toni what she is doing. She describes the music (fast, upbeat, slow, etc.). She repeats this several times, asking Toni to use the instruments or use her switch to turn on the CD player. She will also ask Toni to play the rhythm instruments fast and then slow. She guides Toni's hand under the wrist while saying fast or slow. When Chloe plays some music and asks her if it's fast or slow, the vision teacher will give Toni an instrument and ask her to show Chloe if it's *fast* or *slow*. She waits five seconds, then only using her thumb and forefinger, she moves Toni's hand with the instrument either fast or slow depending on the music and states what it is. She also does this if Toni shook the instrument, but the beat was incorrect. She intersperses this instruction with instruction on whether music is Mexican or of another country and what sounds belong to what instruments. She tells Toni the correct information and then models the correct response making the selection using the actual items (CDs or instruments). For example, she plays a CD of guitar music and presents Toni with a guitar and a small drum. She asks Toni to listen and then to touch the instrument making the music. She waits five seconds for a response and then tells her that it's the guitar and points to it. She encourages Toni to strum the guitar before moving on to another question. She will use a fading procedure of first slightly moving the correct item closer to her and then waiting for five seconds before telling her. When Toni is successful at this level of prompting, the teacher will fade to asking her about a characteristic of the correct answer (e.g., which one has strings) and then wait five seconds before telling her the answer. They then practice with different types of music and instruments. A small picture of the Mexican flag is placed on the Mexican CD, and she is learning to recognize that flag as Mexican versus another country's flag. The vocabulary she is learning (e.g., flag, fast, slow, loud, soft, music, happy) are words that she will also encounter in other subjects/activities (e.g., Pledge of Allegiance, PE, music) and that she will need to use on her augmentative communication device when interacting with others.

■ GENERALIZATION OF SKILLS TAUGHT

The situations described earlier for different students, grade levels, subject matter, and teaching arrangement are specific to the lesson being taught. However, the skills learned should be applicable (or somewhat applicable) to many different lessons. The concepts, vocabulary, reading and math skills, and so on taught in one class or subject should not be restricted to this one learning environment. Skills learned in one class must also be taught across different people, different situations, and different environments. If skills identified are important to teach the student in one class, they should also be important in other classrooms or environments (e.g., lunchroom, playground, library). Identifying the big ideas or major concepts of a lesson should have broader application than the one lesson or unit currently being taught.

The transfer of knowledge and skills to different environments cannot be left to chance for students with moderate to severe intellectual disabilities but must be explicitly taught (Albin & Horner, 1988; Westling & Fox, 2009). The student needs to be taught how, when, and where the knowledge can be applied. For example, when learning about astronomy in science class, a student also needs to be taught to go outside at night (not during the day) to look for stars. A TV science program on astronomy also can support the transfer of knowledge from school to home. Such information can be incorporated into conversation books about students' interests.

Vocabulary words learned during a language arts class may be the same words studied for spelling and may be very important words to identify on an augmentative communication device. The words *boys* and *girls*, for example, may appear in a story being read in class, appear on the restroom doors, can occur in math as part of story problems, and can emerge during a social studies unit. The same can be said for the recognition or sequencing of numbers. They may be targeted in a math class but can certainly be an important aspect of stories being read in language arts, appear on doors of the school, appear on clocks, and appear in science and social studies depending on the topic. By highlighting similar information across classrooms and subjects, the student has more opportunities to practice these skills and more opportunities to respond to similar stimuli but in different environments and activities.

SUMMARY ■

Specific and systematic instruction is quite possible to provide within general education classrooms and is a necessary component of successful inclusion. Students with moderate and severe disabilities do not leave behind their unique needs when entering a typical classroom. They still need supports to learn. Carefully identifying important skills to teach a given student within core content for all students is the first step. Then systematically providing prompts, feedback, and a fading strategy to help the student master identified skills needs to occur.

Different students require different prompting strategies depending on physical, sensory, and cognitive strengths as well as the demands of the task. In addition, the teaching style and arrangements used during a given lesson have an impact on prompting strategies to use. The different scenarios described in this chapter covered a wide age range, ability level, and subject matter to show systematic instruction in general education classrooms. To ensure that the skills learned in these classrooms remain in the student's repertoire and are generalized to different environments where needed requires further instruction as well as opportunities for practice.

Learning from different instructors also is important in the education of students with moderate or severe disabilities. Students may have several different team members who will share responsibility for their learning. Therefore, Chapter 5 will discuss the potential members of the team who may be providing systematic instruction in different activities and lessons. When many different individuals are involved in instruction, collaboration and cooperation are important considerations. Teaming of this nature and the need for training will also be discussed.

8

Determining and Implementing Valid and Appropriate Testing Accommodations

Spencer J. Salend

I know I need testing accommodations to pass and graduate. I think they help me show others what I have learned. But some of them are unnecessary and embarrassing. Sometimes the person giving me the test gives me hints I don't need. I hate it when they make me leave the classroom to take a test. It makes me feel different, and the other kids always ask me why I have to leave.

—A student with a disability

Although I understand the need for some testing accommodations, some of them are inappropriate and unfair. They change the nature of my tests and give students with disabilities an advantage over other students. I wish they would consult me and consider the other students when making decisions about testing accommodations.

—A general education teacher

I was very disappointed, confused, and angry. I worked with the IEP team to identify the testing accommodations my son should receive. We listed them in the IEP and I assumed he would receive them, especially for the state tests. Then they told me the state says he can use only state-approved testing accommodations when taking the state tests. What about the other testing accommodations he's supposed to receive? He uses them to take his teachers' tests. Why can't he use them for the state tests?

—A parent of a student with a disability

Some of our students' families are very savvy. They are used to getting what they want, and many of them want their children to have the advantage of having testing accommodations when they take tests to improve their chances of getting into college.

—A special education teacher

(Continued)

(Continued)

Although it has caused us to focus more on students with diverse and special needs, NCLB places an overreliance on standardized testing and forces schools to adopt a one-size-fits-all approach. The judging of a school's success at making adequate yearly progress based on the results of standardized tests for different groups of students with special needs can make these students scapegoats, particularly students with disabilities. Testing accommodations related to IDEIA help us level the playing field for some of our students with special needs, and many of them are testing quite well. Unfortunately, many are falling farther behind.

—A school administrator

- What concerns do these individuals have about testing accommodations?
- What have been your experiences with testing accommodations?
- How would you and your school address these concerns?

As these comments indicate, there are many issues in determining and implementing appropriate testing accommodations (see Figure 8.1). Often these issues are interconnected and present challenges when deciding which of your students should receive testing accommodations, and in selecting and implementing valid testing accommodations for the different types of tests your students take (Ketterlin-Geller, Alonzo et al., 2007). This chapter helps you overcome these challenges by offering a variety of best practices you and your colleagues can use to determine and implement valid and appropriate testing accommodations for your students. Specifically, this chapter addresses the following questions:

- What are the elements of valid testing accommodations?
- What are the different types of testing accommodations?
- Who is eligible to receive testing accommodations?
- How are valid and appropriate testing accommodations for students determined?
- How can the implementation of testing accommodations be fostered?

Figure 8.1   Issues Related to Testing Accommodations

- Complying with NCLB and IDEIA
- Understanding what makes up valid testing accommodations
- Distinguishing between high-stakes and teacher-made testing
- Deciding who receives which testing accommodations
- Having a process for making decisions regarding testing accommodations
- Ensuring the implementation of identified testing accommodations
- Dealing with issues of fairness, appropriateness, and effectiveness
- Considering the acceptability (stigma) of testing accommodations

Source: From "Determining Appropriate Testing Accommodations: Complying With NCLB and IDEA," by S. J. Salend, *Teaching Exceptional Children, 40*(4), 2008, p. 15. Copyright © 2008 by the Council for Exceptional Children. Reprinted with permission.

Keys to Best Practice: Understand that valid testing accommodations should provide your students with access to tests without altering the content, constructs, or results of your tests or giving students an advantage over their classmates (Byrnes, 2008; Cox, Herner, Demczyk, & Nieberding, 2006; Edgemon, Jablonski, & Lloyd, 2006).

WHAT ARE THE ELEMENTS OF VALID TESTING ACCOMMODATIONS?

As some of the comments at the beginning of this chapter suggest, what makes a valid testing accommodation is often misunderstood. Valid testing accommodations are changes in the testing administration, environment, equipment, technology, and procedures that allow students to participate in testing programs and do not change the nature of the test (Byrnes, 2008; Cox et al., 2006; Edgemon et al., 2006). Valid testing accommodations are designed to provide students with access to tests without altering the tests or giving students an advantage over others. For example, having a proctor read test items would not be a valid testing accommodation on a reading test as it changes the nature of the test from reading to listening comprehension. However, it might be an appropriate testing accommodation for use on a mathematics test that is not designed to assess reading. Therefore, whether your students are taking state, districtwide, or teacher-made tests, an essential element defining a valid testing accommodation is that it must not change the test's content, constructs, and results.

WHAT ARE THE DIFFERENT TYPES OF TESTING ACCOMMODATIONS?

Because of the varied purposes of testing and the unique qualities of your students, it is important for you to be aware of a range of possible testing accommodations. Testing accommodations are usually categorized as relating to presentation and response mode formats; to timing, scheduling, and setting alternatives and to linguistically based factors (Salend, 2008). A range of possible testing accommodations is presented in Figure 8.2.

Many educators also consider grading alternatives and instruction to improve students' study skills as well as their test-taking strategies to be types of testing accommodation (we will discuss ways in which you can teach your students how to study and take tests in Chapter 4).

Recent advances in technology-based testing are offering new ways to design and implement all types of testing accommodations (Ketterlin-Geller, Yovanoff, & Tindal, 2007). Thus, technology provides alternatives to traditional testing formats and allows for the implementation of customized testing accommodations for individual students (we will discuss technology-based testing in Chapter 3).

Keys to Best Practice: Be aware of a range of presentation mode testing accommodations (Clapper, Morse, Thurlow, & Thompson, 2006; Edgemon et al., 2006; Elbaum, 2007).

Figure 8.2   Possible Testing Accommodations

(a) PRESENTATION MODE ACCOMMODATIONS

- Reading directions and items aloud
- Clarifying or simplifying language
- Repeating directions as necessary
- Listing directions in sequential order
- Increasing the spacing between items
- Highlighting changes in the directions
- Presenting only one sentence per line
- Using markers or masks to maintain place
- Using reminders

- Highlighting *key* words or phrases
- Organizing or sequencing items appropriately and logically
- Providing a sample of each item type
- Placing fewer items on a page
- Providing a proctor
- Offering aid in turning pages and maintaining place
- Presenting tests via signing or Braille

(b) RESPONSE MODE ACCOMMODATIONS

- Responding via native language or preferred mode of communication
- Providing extra space
- Using lined or grid paper
- Using enlarged answer bubbles or blocks
- Providing check sheets, graphic organizers, and outlines
- Providing a proctor to monitor place and the recording of answers

- Answering on the test
- Allowing students to dictate answers
- Fewer items per page
- Using multiple-choice items
- Giving oral exams, open-book tests, and take home tests
- Providing a scribe

(c) TIMING AND SCHEDULING ACCOMMODATIONS

- Giving more time or untimed tests
- Providing shorter versions of tests
- Allowing breaks as needed
- Adjusting the testing order

- Eliminating items or sections
- Varying the times of the testing sessions
- Scheduling shorter testing sessions
- Administering tests over several days

(d) TIMING, SCHEDULING, AND SETTING ACCOMMODATIONS

- Taking tests in small groups or individually in separate locations
- Allowing movement and background sounds
- Providing preferential seating arrangements (carrels)
- Providing adaptive furniture or equipment

- Eliminating visual and auditory distractions
- Delivering reinforcement
- Providing specific environmental arrangements (lighting, acoustics, sound amplification)

(e) LINGUISTICALLY BASED ACCOMMODATIONS

- Using understandable and familiar language
- Repeating orally based directions or items
- Teaching the language of academic testing
- Pairing items or directions with graphics or pictures
- Translating tests
- Allowing responses in native languages or dialects

- Offering review sheets and lists of important vocabulary
- Allowing use of bilingual materials (bilingual glossaries or dictionaries)
- Providing context clues
- Providing alternate ways to demonstrate mastery of test material
- Providing translators to administer tests

Source: From "Determining Appropriate Testing Accommodations: Complying With NCLB and IDEA," by S. J. Salend, *Teaching Exceptional Children, 40*(4), 2008, p. 17. Copyright © 2008 by the Council for Exceptional Children. Reprinted with permission.

Presentation Mode Testing Accommodations

Presentation mode testing accommodations involve changes in the ways test questions and directions are presented to your students. Possible presentation mode testing accommodations are presented in Figure 8.2(a).

One very popular presentation mode accommodation is having an educator read aloud the test's directions and items to students who experience difficulty reading text (Elbaum, 2007). Readers can improve their effectiveness and ensure the integrity of the test by following the guidelines presented in Figure 8.3 (many of these guidelines also are appropriate for scribes, proctors, translators, and interpreters).

Figure 8.3 Guidelines for Reading Tests to Students

Prior to the Test Administration

- Read and review the test and learn the definitions and pronunciations of unfamiliar terms and mathematical and scientific expressions and formulas
- Eliminate generic directions if they are not appropriate for the testing situation
- Make sure that testing materials are organized and presented in a way that makes it easy for you to access and follow
- Review testing materials to understand all of the administration conditions associated with the test (i.e., allowable and prohibited test administration actions)
- Distribute testing materials to students in accordance with the test's directions

During the Test Administration

- Refrain from alerting students to their errors and confirming correct responses
- Avoid providing assistance, cueing, and engaging in actions that impact the student's answers such as

  o Reminding, prompting, coaching, and teaching students
  o Unnecessarily highlighting or paraphrasing important information
  o Changing your voice
  o Explaining vocabulary, concepts, and visuals
  o Clarifying and elaborating on parts of the test

- Read only approved parts of the test (e.g., reading passages and questions assessing reading comprehension can impact the validity of those items by making them into measures of listening comprehension)
- Read all of the text on the test including directions, examples, and items
- Establish an appropriate pace that includes reading all parts of the question before soliciting and acknowledging the student's answer(s)
- Reread the entire question when asked to repeat a question to make sure that critical parts of questions are not inadvertently highlighted
- Consider facilitating the validity of the test administration and the rereading process by making a digital recording of the test administration (e.g., replaying questions that have been asked to be repeated)
- Use your voice to highlight key parts of questions that are printed in boldface, italics, or capitals
- Spell synonyms and other words requested by the student (if permissible)
- Redirect off-task comments from the student
- Observe students for signs of fatigue as reading tests tends to make the testing experience longer and more tiring

---

Source: Adapted from Clapper, Morse, Thurlow, & Thompson (2006).

Test Proctors

Some students will require the assistance of a proctor (Cox et al., 2006). In the case of deaf or hard-of-hearing students, the proctor should be a professional who can sign and interpret oral directions and translate their answers (Clapper et al., 2006). Proctors can help students take tests by

- reading, repeating, or simplifying the test directions and items;
- adjusting the pace at which the test is administered;
- noticing when students tire and modifying the testing schedule and administration accordingly;
- responding to student questions about the test;
- turning pages for students who have motor difficulties;
- assisting students in maintaining their place; and
- prompting students to pay attention and sustain their effort.

Like readers, scribes, interpreters, and translators, proctors should be careful not to give students cues, hints, and additional information that may affect their answers.

Keys to Best Practice: Be aware of a range of response mode testing accommodations (Byrnes, 2008; Clapper et al., 2006; Cox et al., 2006; Edgemon et al., 2006).

Response Mode Testing Accommodations

Response mode testing accommodations refer to changes in the way students are asked to respond to test items or determine their answers. Possible response mode testing accommodations are presented in Figure 8.2(b).

Accommodations for Students With Writing and Speaking Difficulties

Since most tests require written or oral responses, your students with writing and speaking difficulties may particularly benefit from adjustments in the ways that they can respond to test items. To minimize difficulty in transferring responses to separate answer sheets, you can have students

- mark their responses on the test protocol,
- use enlarged answer bubbles, or
- fold test pages and position the answer sheet so that only one page appears at a time.

In addition to giving oral answers in lieu of written responses, your students with writing difficulties can be given tests that are formatted to

- contain fewer items per page,
- provide extra space between items,
- present items on lined or grid paper,
- have a larger space in which to write test answers, and
- use multiple-choice questions rather than essay items.

Your students with verbal difficulties can write or indicate their responses in alternative ways. For example, deaf and hard-of-hearing students can respond via sign language, and students with physical disabilities can respond through use of eye movements (Clapper et al., 2006).

Responding to Essay Questions

You can take several actions to try to make sure that writing difficulties do not severely impact your students' ability to demonstrate their mastery of the content being assessed on essay questions. You can provide these students with check sheets, graphic organizers, or outlines listing the components that can guide them in organizing their essays and make sure they have sufficient time to draft and write their answers. On essay questions where the focus is on content, students can be provided with graphics and resources that allow them to take notes and prepare responses to essay questions (Chapter 3 provides a range of technology students can use to answer essay questions). For example, when students are asked to compare concepts, you can provide them with an outline of a compare-and-contrast chart, and when students need to discuss the relationships between concepts, you can provide them with an outline of a semantic web.

When grammar, spelling, and punctuation are not important components in grading, students can dictate their responses into a digital audio recorder or take an oral exam. However, keep in mind that oral exams can be intimidating. To minimize anxiety, you can give students opportunities to practice responding orally and allow them to use visual aids and manipulatives to supplement their answers.

You can structure your administration of essay items by using alternate forms of essays such as open-book tests and take-home tests. During open-book tests, students are permitted to use their books and notes to answer essay questions. Take-home tests, which allow students to use a range of resources to complete essay questions, are good ways to motivate students to apply the important concepts and topics to problem-based essay questions. However, when using take-home tests, you need to establish rules and procedures that ensure that your students do not write excessively long responses and that they do not receive assistance from others.

Scribes

When appropriate, students can be asked to dictate their responses to a trained scribe. During testing, a trained scribe should

- establish that students, not scribes, are responsible for reading all parts of the question to themselves;
- make a verbatim record of students' dictated responses, beginning each sentence with a capital and ending each sentence with a period;
- keep their copy of the response hidden until students indicate that they are finished dictating their response;
- refrain from editing students' responses and questioning, correcting, and coaching students; and
- use index cards marked with letters or numbers to allow students to indicate their choices on objective tests such as multiple-choice and true-false questions (Clapper et al., 2006).

Scribes may want to make a digital recording of the session to ensure that student responses were written as dictated and that no assistance or prompting was provided to students.

When your students use a scribe, it is important for them to understand that they are responsible for reviewing their dictated verbatim responses in terms of formatting, grammar, punctuation, word choices, capitalization, and spelling of words than contain more than two letters, and to make or direct the scribe to make changes. Therefore, your students who use scribes should practice how to use the services of a scribe before taking tests. If the students' final responses are difficult to read or a response must be recorded in a test booklet, scribes may record the responses in the desired format.

Keys to Best Practice: Be aware of a range of timing, scheduling, and setting testing accommodations (Byrnes, 2008; Cohen, Gregg, & Deng, 2005; Elliott & Marquart, 2004).

Timing, Scheduling, and Setting Testing Accommodations

Some of your students may need timing, scheduling, and setting accommodations. These accommodations are particularly helpful when your students

- have problems with processing information and being on-task or motivated;
- require additional time to use specialized testing techniques (such as dictating answers or reading test items aloud);
- need specialized testing conditions (such as special lighting, acoustics, or equipment or furniture);
- have physical conditions that cause them to tire easily;
- experience test anxiety; and
- take medications that are effective only for a limited amount of time or have side effects that affect performance.

A range of possible timing and scheduling alternatives are available for your students who need them (see Figure 8.2[c]). Students can be given additional time or shorter versions of tests. The scheduling of tests also can be adjusted for your students by

- allowing them to take breaks more frequently,
- modifying the order in which specific parts of test(s) are administered,
- breaking the testing session into several shorter periods, and
- administering tests over several days or at times students are most likely to be productive.

A variety of setting alternatives also are available for your students. While some students may perform better when they take tests in a small group or individually in a quiet location free of distractions, other students may need to have preferential seating arrangements, to move around, or to have some type of background sounds. Your students with physical disabilities may require adaptive furniture or devices, and your students with sensory impairments and attention difficulties may need specific environmental arrangements, specialized lighting, acoustics, or sound-field amplification systems. Some students may need preferential seating so that they are near you, another adult, or a positive role model and in a nondistracting classroom location. Your students who need assistance in maintaining their motivation may benefit from a separate testing location that provides them with verbal praise or tangible and activity reinforcers and allows you or others to monitor their behavior and performance.

Keys to Best Practice: Be aware of a range of linguistically based testing accommodations (Albus, Thurlow, Liu, & Bielinski, 2005; Herrera, Murry, & Cabral, 2007).

Linguistically Based Testing Accommodations

In addition to the previously mentioned testing accommodations, several specialized linguistically based accommodations can be used when testing your students who are English language learners (see Figure 8.2[d]). Since language proficiency can affect students' test performance, you can foster comprehension of test items and directions by

- using familiar and easy-to-understand language,
- reading and repeating directions and items, and
- pairing items and directions with culturally appropriate pictures and graphics (Herrera et al., 2007).

You can allow your students who are English language learners to use individually designed simplified bilingual dictionaries, glossaries, and word lists. When using these types of materials, it is important for you to make sure that they provide only direct translations of words and do not offer definitions or explanations of key terms and concepts. You can allow these students to show mastery of test content in other ways, such as with projects completed by cooperative learning groups or via the use of drawings, charts, manipulatives, demonstrations, or drama (Albus et al., 2005).

Translation

When appropriate, your students who are English language learners can take translated and alternate language versions of tests, be provided with translators to administer tests, and be permitted to respond in their native language or dialect. However, it is important for you and your colleagues to realize that translation does not remove the bias that may exist in tests. Thus, if you give translated test items that include questions that do not relate to your students' learning and cultural experiences and developmental and language levels, they will still struggle to answer them correctly, whether they are answering in English or their native language.

Keys to Best Practice: Be aware of grading alternatives and use them cautiously and occasionally to motivate your students and reinforce their efforts to succeed on tests (Brookhart & Nitko, 2008; Salend & Garrick Duhaney, 2002; Stern & Avigliano, 2008).

Grading Alternatives

In addition to the accommodations during testing we just discussed, you can consider whether to use a variety of grading alternatives when scoring students' tests. These alternatives, which should be used cautiously and only occasionally to motivate all of your students and to reinforce their efforts to succeed on your tests, include the following:

- Eliminate certain items, especially those items that you and your students find confusing, tricky, or unnecessarily difficult.
- Award partial credit for aspects of answers that are correct and for showing correct work.
- Offer extra-credit opportunities. It is best to make extra credit an integral part of the test rather than making it an option after the test has been administered, because extra credit should not be used to help students compensate for poor test performance that is due to their lack of effort.
- Give bonus points for specific questions. Informing students that there are secret bonus point questions on tests can motivate students to give detailed and complete answers to all test questions.
- Allow students to earn back points by correcting incorrect answers using their notes and textbooks, or retaking test questions that they answered incorrectly.
- Deduct points for incorrect answers. Some teachers do this to discourage students from guessing and to prepare them for high-stakes tests that use similar scoring procedures.
- Adjust how you grade essay responses. When the mechanics of the written response are not the elements being tested, you can give students some credit for an outline, web, diagram, or chart in lieu of writing a lengthy response. You also can modify your penalties for writing errors or assign your students separate grades for content and mechanics. For example, if an essay response on a social studies or science test is correct in terms of the content but contains numerous misspelled words, you can give your student separate grades for content and spelling (Brookhart & Nitko, 2008; Salend & Garrick Duhaney, 2002; Stern & Avigliano, 2008).

These options can be used judiciously to motivate students periodically to expand their learning and demonstrate their mastery of concepts. When considering these options, be careful that you do not inadvertently excuse students from studying and preparing for tests. Some teachers set rules relating to the number of times students can use these options, the maximum grade a student can receive for a test that was originally below a certain level (e.g., grades on retakes cannot exceed 80%), and the types of items that cannot be retaken (e.g., extra-credit items cannot be retaken).

Giving Students Choices

Some teachers try to make their grading fairer by giving students choices (Salend, 2008). When using objective test items, consider giving students the option of writing a justification of their response to items for which they are unsure of the answer. You can then use their justification to award partial credit to students whose justifications make sense or to eliminate confusing test items.

You also can give students the opportunity to select the type of test they take. For example, you can organize your tests so they offer students choices in responding to items. Thus, a test can consist of 25 items with varying formats, and students can be directed to respond to any 15 of them in whatever format they choose. Those students who are proficient at multiple-choice items but who have difficulty with essay questions can select more of the former and fewer of the latter. Similarly, you can create several equivalent versions of a test such as a multiple-choice test, an essay test, an oral test, and a test containing a variety of items. Your students can then select the test version that best fits their strengths and challenges.

Cooperative Group Testing

Another alternative way to grade your tests is through *cooperative group testing* (Pomplun, 1996; Salend, 2008). Cooperative group testing involves having your students work collaboratively on open-ended problem-solving activities that typically have a variety of solutions. Each group of students creates one product, which reflects the contributions of all group members. You then grade this product, with each student in the group receiving the group grade. For example, to test students' mastery of material related to amphibians, students can work in groups to complete an open-ended test or an activity related to different amphibians.

When using cooperative group testing, concerns about the equitable contributions of each member of the group can be addressed in a variety of ways. You can have each group keep a log that lists the group's activities, including a summary of each group member's contribution and effort. As part of their grade, students can be randomly asked to respond individually to questions about their group's test.

You can employ a *two-tiered testing system* (Gajria, Giek, Hemrick, & Salend, 1992; Salend, 2008). This method involves students completing a test in collaborative groups, with each student receiving the group grade. Following the group test, students individually complete a second test that covers similar content. You can reverse the order of the tests and have students initially complete the test individually and then in a collaborative group with their classmates (Michaelson & Sweet, 2008). You can then choose to grade students by giving them a separate group and individual testing grade, averaging or weighting their group and individual grade together into one grade, or giving them the option of selecting their higher grade.

WHO IS ELIGIBLE TO RECEIVE TESTING ACCOMMODATIONS?

Keys to Best Practice: Work with the multidisciplinary team to determine if your students are eligible to receive testing accommodations under IDEIA or Section 504 and whether students should take general grade level assessments or alternate assessments (Byrnes, 2008; Edgemon et al., 2006; Ketterlin-Geller, Alonzo, et al., 2007; Towles-Reeves, Kleinert, & Muhomba, 2009).

Not all students are eligible to receive testing accommodations. Typically, your students who have been identified by a multidisciplinary team as having a disability under IDEIA or Section 504 are eligible to receive testing accommodations. There are four levels for assessing your students with disabilities under NCLB and IDEIA with the vast majority of them being tested at Levels 1 and 2 (see Figure 8.4).

Figure 8.4   Levels for Assessing Students With Disabilities Under NCLB and IDEIA

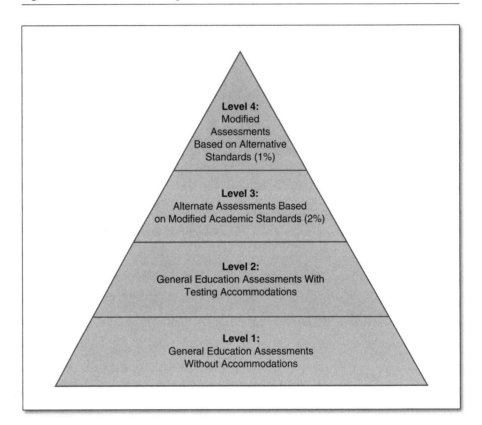

Level 1: General Education Assessments Without Testing Accommodations: At this level, your students with disabilities participate in high-stakes testing programs aligned with statewide learning standards by taking the same general grade-level assessments and teacher-made tests as their classmates without disabilities. Level 1 students typically

- require relatively few instructional accommodations to access the general education curriculum and
- are likely to achieve grade-level proficiency in the same time frame as their classmates without disabilities.

Level 2: General Education Assessments With Testing Accommodations: At this level, your students with disabilities take the same general grade-level assessments and teacher-made tests as their classmates without disabilities but with testing accommodations. Level 2 students have many of the same characteristics as Level 1 students. However, they typically require you and their other teachers to implement more instructional accommodations to help them access and master the general education curriculum in a time frame that closely resembles their peers.

Level 3: Alternate Assessments Based on Modified Academic Standards: Rather than taking the general education assessments and teacher-made tests that their classmates take, Level 3 students take alternate assessments based on *modified academic achievement standards.* These modified academic achievement standards address challenging but less difficult grade-level content from the general education curriculum. For example, Level 3 students might take less rigorous grade-level content tests that have multiple-choice items with fewer choices or reading tests that ask them to read fewer passages. These modified standards and alternate assessments are designed for use with your students with disabilities who

- do not have a significant cognitive disability,
- have access to grade-level content instruction,
- have IEPs that include goals addressing grade-level content standards, and
- are not likely to reach grade-level proficiency in the same time frame as their classmates without disabilities.

Level 4: Modified Assessments Based on Alternate Achievement Standards: Level 4 students take modified assessments that relate to *alternate achievement standards* that are not as complex as the state's grade level achievement standards or your teacher-made tests. The modified assessments include work samples and the collection and documentation of products of student learning via teacher observation. They may take the form of audio and video digital recordings of students performing various activities related to alternate achievement standards. In most states, these collections of student work are linked to statewide standards and evaluated via performance assessment, portfolios, or through use of a checklist or an instructional rubric (we will learn more about these types of assessments in Chapter 5). These modified assessments are designed for your students with significant cognitive disabilities who

- take a class for reasons other than mastery of the general education curriculum,
- require extensive instructional modifications, and
- are not able to participate in high-stakes testing even with testing accommodations.

Once your individual students are identified as eligible for testing accommodations, you and your colleagues can use the following guidelines to determine which testing accommodations are valid and appropriate for them.

HOW ARE VALID AND APPROPRIATE TESTING ACCOMMODATIONS FOR STUDENTS DETERMINED?

Keys to Best Practice: Decisions regarding the use of specific testing accommodations should be determined individually for your students based on their unique characteristics and learning strengths and challenges (Byrnes, 2008; Brinckerhoff & Banerjee, 2007; Edgemon et al., 2006).

Rather than being disability based, decisions regarding the use of specific testing accommodations should be determined individually for your students and related to information about their unique characteristics and learning strengths

Figure 8.5 Resources for Selecting and Implementing Testing Accommodations

1. National Center on Educational Outcomes Special Topic Area: Accommodations for Students with Disabilities (www.cehd.umn.edu/nceo/TopicAreas/Accommodations/StatesAccomm.htm)
2. *How to develop state guidelines for access assistants: Scribes, readers, and sign language interpreters* (Clapper et al., 2006).
3. *Survey of teacher recommendations for accommodation* (Ketterlin-Geller, Alonzo et al., 2007).
4. *The assessment accommodation checklist* (Elliott, Kratochwill, & Schulte, 1998).
5. *Dynamic assessment of test accommodations* (Fuchs & Fuchs, 2001).

and challenges (Brinckerhoff & Banerjee, 2007; Byrnes, 2008). This means that testing accommodations for your students with disabilities should be based on each student's characteristics so that the testing accommodations

- match the instructional accommodations that support student learning,
- comply with state and districtwide policies, and
- are responsive to the perspectives of students and teachers.

It is important to be aware that your students may benefit from more than one testing accommodation and may therefore need packages of different types of testing accommodations (Edgemon et al., 2006). Resources to assist you and your colleagues in selecting testing accommodations for students with a wide range of disabilities are presented in Figure 8.5.

Keys to Best Practice: Testing accommodations should match the effective instructional accommodations regularly used by students in their daily classroom instruction (Cox et al., 2006; Ketterlin-Geller, Alonzo, et al., 2007).

Matching Testing Accommodations to Effective Teaching Accommodations

Your students' testing accommodations should match the effective teaching accommodations you use within your daily classroom instruction to support student learning. For instance, the instructional accommodation you use to help a student understand classroom directions also should be used to help the student understand test directions and items. You can use the following questions to gather information about your students and the teaching accommodations that support their learning:

- Does the student have sensory, medical, physical, or attention conditions that affect classroom performance? If so, what are these conditions and what strategies and resources are used to address them?
- Does the student exhibit academic and social behaviors that interfere with learning or the learning of others? If so, what are these behaviors and what strategies, classroom arrangements, resources, and technologies are used to address them?

- What instructional methods, approaches, strategies, specialized equipment, technology, materials, or classroom designs have been successful in supporting the student's learning?
- What instructional strategies, resources, and technologies are used to help the student understand directions and respond to classroom activities?
- What are the student's learning and testing style preferences?
- What instructional strategies, resources, and technologies are used to help students complete assignments?
- Does the student need additional time or motivation to complete assignments?

Keys to Best Practice: Comply with statewide and districtwide policies regarding testing accommodations (Byrnes, 2008; Cox et al., 2006; Elliott & Thurlow, 2006; Ketterlin-Geller, Alonzo, et al., 2007).

Keys to Best Practice: Differentiate between testing accommodations that are appropriate for high-stakes assessments and teacher-made tests and make these distinctions explicit via your students' IEPs and 504 accommodation plans (Byrnes, 2008; Salend, 2008).

Complying With Statewide and Districtwide Policies and Differentiating Between High-Stakes Assessments and Teacher-Made Tests

The types of testing accommodations used by your students will depend on your state's and district's policies and the types of tests they will be taking. This means that the testing accommodations available for use by your students will be guided by whether they are taking high-stakes assessments or teacher-made tests.

Testing Accommodations and High-Stakes Testing

In the case of students who need testing accommodations to participate in high-stakes assessment, it is essential to comply with state and districtwide policies regarding approved accommodations. In making these determinations, states consider whether the accommodation is appropriate and valid and would provide access by eliminating or lessening difficulties related to disability or second language acquisition without altering the test or providing an advantage over other test takers. Therefore, testing accommodations selected for use on high-stakes tests must be consistent with state and districtwide policies and must be provided under certain testing situations (Elliott & Thurlow, 2006). For instance, some states mandate that a testing accommodation be employed for a specific period of time in classroom instruction before it can be used during high-stakes testing. Some states also have provisions whereby multidisciplinary teams can seek permission from their state's department of education to allow individual students to use accommodations that are not listed as approved. Since accommodations allowed in one state may not be allowed in other states and policies vary from state to state, you and your colleagues should obtain information about your state's testing accommodations policies by contacting your state education department or visiting its Web site.

Testing Accommodations and Districtwide and Teacher-Made Testing

Although testing accommodations on statewide tests are determined by individual states, selections regarding appropriate testing accommodations for your classroom tests are made by you and your colleagues on multidisciplinary teams. Therefore, there is typically more flexibility when selecting testing accommodations for use by your students when they take districtwide and teacher-made tests. For example, while use of a thesaurus for a high-stakes statewide writing test may not be approved, you and your colleagues on the multidisciplinary team may determine that it is an appropriate testing accommodation for teacher-made tests in a range of content area classes. However, even when students are taking teacher-made and districtwide tests, testing accommodations should provide access without altering the test or giving students an advantage on the test. Keep in mind that there also may be districtwide testing policies that must be followed. To avoid the confusion, disappointment, and anger experienced by the parent at the beginning of this chapter, it is important to differentiate among testing accommodations that are used during the administration of state, districtwide, and teacher-made tests. It is essential to make these distinctions very clear to everyone, especially students and their families, by listing them on students' IEPs or 504 accommodation plans.

Keys to Best Practice: Make efforts to match testing accommodations used by students for teacher-made tests with those allowed for high-stakes tests so that students can become more familiar with the conditions they will encounter when taking high-stakes tests (Salend, 2008).

For most students, it is beneficial for the testing accommodations used for teacher-made tests and high-stakes tests to match each other. That way, students can become more familiar with the conditions they will encounter when taking high-stakes tests, and you can assess student performance with respect to how students are tested on high-stakes assessments.

Keys to Best Practice: Consider the perspectives of your students when selecting testing accommodations for them, including whether testing accommodations are fair, age appropriate, and do not adversely affect students or their classmates (Edgemon et al., 2006; Elliott & Marquart, 2004; Salend, 2008).

Considering the Perspectives of Students

Another important factor to consider when selecting testing accommodations is how specific accommodations are viewed by students. In terms of your students, it is important to make sure that testing accommodations are fair and do not adversely affect your students who receive them or their classmates. For example, many students might feel similar to the student quoted at the beginning of this chapter who felt that taking tests in separate locations was embarrassing, isolating, and stigmatizing. Additionally, it is essential that the testing accommodations you use with your students with disabilities are age appropriate.

Keys to Best Practice: Testing accommodations selected for students with disabilities should boost their performance and have a limited impact on the performance of their classmates (Bouck & Bouck, 2008; Fuchs & Fuchs, 2001).

It is important that testing accommodations selected for your students with disabilities give them a *differential boost* (Fuchs & Fuchs, 2001). In other words, the testing accommodations selected for your students with disabilities should boost their performance and, if used by their classmates, should have little positive effect on their classmates' test performance (Bouck & Bouck, 2008). For example, while having items read aloud can help students with reading difficulties, other students may find that it makes some test items more difficult and causes the testing session to be longer. If a testing accommodation benefits both your students with and without disabilities, you need to be careful to make sure it is not changing the nature of your test.

Keys to Best Practice: Consider the perspectives of teachers when selecting testing accommodations, including whether testing accommodations are valid, effective, easy to use, appropriate for the setting and student, and reasonable and whether they impact the integrity of tests (Cox et al., 2006; Edgemon et al., 2006; Elliott & Marquart, 2004).

Considering the Perspectives of Teachers

You and your colleagues' perspectives need to be considered when selecting testing accommodations. Therefore, when selecting possible testing accommodations for use with your students, you and your colleagues need to reflect on whether they are valid, effective, and appropriate by assessing whether and how specific accommodations affect the integrity of the tests and their administration. In addition, viewpoints about ease of implementation and reasonableness of specific testing accommodations should be examined by considering the extent to which you and your colleagues have the materials, time, resources, education, technology, and equipment needed to implement the testing accommodations.

HOW CAN THE IMPLEMENTATION OF TESTING ACCOMMODATIONS BE FOSTERED?

Keys to Best Practice: Foster implementation of the testing accommodations via students' IEPs and 504 accommodations plans including listing whether testing accommodations are appropriate for state, districtwide, and classroom testing, and the individuals, roles, resources, and preparation needed for implementation (Byrnes, 2008; Cox et al., 2006; MacArthur & Cavalier, 2004; Salend, 2008).

As we saw in several of the comments at the beginning of this chapter, there are times when testing accommodations are implemented inappropriately or unnecessarily. Therefore, you and your colleagues should consider the factors that foster implementation of testing accommodations by listing on IEPs and 504 accommodation plans

- which testing accommodations are appropriate for state, districtwide, and classroom testing;
- how these testing accommodations will be implemented;
- which individuals will be responsible for implementing the testing accommodations;
- what resources (materials, technology, locations, and equipment) will be needed to implement the testing accommodations; and

- what preparation will students and educators need to implement the testing accommodations (Byrnes, 2008; Cox et al., 2006; MacArthur & Cavalier, 2004; Salend, 2008).

For instance, while using a scribe can be an effective testing accommodation, many students may need instruction to teach them how to dictate to a scribe effectively. Similarly, educators who will serve as scribes, readers, proctors, and translators should be taught how to perform their roles effectively and appropriately (see Figure 8.3) and how to avoid giving students cues and additional information that may affect answers.

Keys to Best Practice: Evaluate your students' testing accommodations, and use this information to determine whether testing accommodations should be continued, revised, discontinued, or gradually faded out (Cox et al., 2006; Edgemon et al., 2006; Ketterlin-Geller, Alonzo, et al., 2007).

You can ensure the successful implementation of testing accommodations by using the guidelines presented in the introduction for continually evaluating them in terms of their validity, effectiveness, efficiency, fairness, and impact on you and your students. Effective testing accommodations can be continued if necessary, or gradually faded out so that your students with special needs take tests in the same ways as their classmates if possible. Similarly, efforts should be made to make sure that effective testing accommodations used for teacher-made tests match those allowed for high-stakes tests so that students can become more familiar with the conditions they will encounter when taking high-stakes tests. Testing accommodations that are not achieving their intended outcomes should be revised to make them more effective or discontinued.

SUMMARY

This chapter provided best practices for determining and implementing valid and appropriate testing accommodations for your students. These best practices allow you to respond to the many challenges you, your colleagues, your students, and their families face in responding to the testing mandates of NCLB and IDEIA. You can use the reflectlist (see Figure 8.6) to review the main points presented in this chapter and to examine the extent to which you and your colleagues are applying best practices to determine and implement valid and appropriate testing accommodations for your students.

COMING ATTRACTIONS

In addition to creating and grading valid and accessible teacher-made tests (see Chapter 1) and using the best practices presented in this chapter, you can enhance the effectiveness and inclusiveness of your teaching, testing, and assessment practices by

- using technology-based testing with your students (see Chapter 3),
- teaching effective study and test-taking skills and strategies to your students (see Chapter 4), and
- using classroom assessment to supplement your testing (see Chapter 5).

Figure 8.6   Reflectlist for Determining and Implementing Valid and Appropriate Testing Accommodations for Students

Reflect on your ability to determine and implement valid and appropriate testing accommodations for your students by rating the extent to which you are applying the following keys to best practices.

Keys to Best Practice	Often	Sometimes	Rarely	Never
I work with the multidisciplinary team to determine if my students are eligible to receive testing accommodations under IDEIA or Section 504.	☐	☐	☐	☐
I work with the multidisciplinary team to determine whether my students should take general grade level assessments or alternate assessments.	☐	☐	☐	☐
Testing accommodations for my students provide them with access to tests without altering the content, constructs, or results of my tests or giving them an advantage over their classmates.	☐	☐	☐	☐
I consider providing my students with a range of presentation mode testing accommodations.	☐	☐	☐	☐
I consider providing my students with a range of response mode testing accommodations.	☐	☐	☐	☐
I consider providing my students with a range of timing, scheduling, and setting testing accommodations.	☐	☐	☐	☐
I consider providing my students with a range of linguistically based testing accommodations.	☐	☐	☐	☐
I consider using a range of grading alternatives cautiously and occasionally to motivate my students and reinforce their efforts to succeed on tests.	☐	☐	☐	☐
Decisions regarding the use of specific testing accommodations for my students are individually determined based on their unique characteristics and learning strengths and challenges.	☐	☐	☐	☐

(Continued)

Figure 8.6 (Continued)

Keys to Best Practice	Often	Sometimes	Rarely	Never
Testing accommodations for my students match the effective teaching accommodations they regularly use in daily classroom instruction.	☐	☐	☐	☐
Decisions regarding testing accommodations for my students comply with statewide and districtwide policies.	☐	☐	☐	☐
Testing accommodations for my students during high-stakes and districtwide assessments and teacher-made tests are differentiated, and these distinctions are made explicit via their IEPs and 504 accommodation plans.	☐	☐	☐	☐
Efforts are made to match my students' testing accommodations for teacher-made tests with those allowed for high-stakes tests.	☐	☐	☐	☐
The perspectives of my students are considered in determining their testing accommodations.	☐	☐	☐	☐
Testing accommodations selected for my students with disabilities boost their performance and have a limited impact on the performance of their classmates.	☐	☐	☐	☐
The perspectives of teachers are considered in determining testing accommodations for my students.	☐	☐	☐	☐
The implementation of my students' testing accommodations is fostered via their IEPs and 504 accommodation plans.	☐	☐	☐	☐
Evaluation data are collected on my students' use of testing accommodations.	☐	☐	☐	☐
Evaluation data are used to determine whether my students' testing accommodations should be continued, revised, discontinued, or gradually faded out.	☐	☐	☐	☐

- How would you rate your ability to determine and implement valid and appropriate testing accommodations for your students?
- What aspects are your strengths?
- In what areas do you need to improve?
- What steps can you take to improve your ability to determine and implement valid and appropriate testing accommodations for your students?

9

Effective Home-School Partnerships

Bob Algozzine, Ann P. Daunic, and Stephen W. Smith

In this chapter, we

- review why home-school partnerships are important,
- describe characteristics of home-school partnerships,
- identify and describe effective home-school partnership programs and practices,
- describe critical features that support the implementation and effective use of home-school partnership programs, and
- review evidence of effectiveness of home-school partnership programs.

Parent involvement has been a core value in special education since the passage of the Education for All Handicapped Children Act of 1975. The law required schools to include parents of children with disabilities in educational program planning, decision making, and evaluation. Since this initial mandate, the role of families has changed significantly with each reauthorization of the law. The parents of children with disabilities are involved with their child's education on multiple levels. Part C of the Individuals with Disabilities Education Act of 1997 (IDEA) calls for family-centered services that address the need of the whole family of infants and toddlers with disabilities. Early interventions design and implement programs that use family strengths to facilitate the child's development and learning, while assisting the family in finding resources for meeting their needs. Such family-centered approaches are the recommended practices: they tend to encourage a sense of self-efficacy and greater parent satisfaction with services (Trivette, Dunst, Boyd, & Hamby, 1995).

Moreover, for children with disabilities ages 3 to 21 years, the law requires that parents are to be included in decisions regarding assessment, placement in special education, educational program planning, and confidential treatment of records, as well as whether to participate in mediation to solve disputes or not to participate at all. These are considered basic rights concerning the family's participation, but educators are encouraged to go beyond the minimum legal requirements to develop truly collaborative home-school partnerships (Smith, Gartin, Murdick, & Hilton, 2006), including offering meaningful opportunities to participate in their child's education at school and at home.

In addition to IDEA, the passage of the No Child Left Behind Act of 2001 (NCLB) expanded parental involvement and parents options with regard to their children's education. NCLB requires local school districts, working in collaboration with parents, to develop written polices for parent involvement. In addition, school districts are to strengthen teachers' and staff members capacity to work effectively with families, provide parents with material and training that will help them improve student achievement, and design and conduct parent involvement activities that help guide their children's learning. The goal of parental involvement as specified by by both laws is to maximize the learning potential of children.

The provisions in these laws and the research on the effects of parental involvement on school achievement clearly indicate the importance of schools and families working together, suggesting that the relationship is mutually supportive; that is, the relationship between families and schools is one in which both contribute and benefit. The current focus is on forming partnerships. Ideally, a home-school partnership is a collaborative relationship in which all partners are valued for their knowledge, judgment, and experiences to improve outcomes for students (Turnbull, Turnbull, Erwin, & Sodak, 2006).

THE IMPORTANCE OF HOME-SCHOOL PARTNERSHIPS

Epstein (2001) described three overlapping spheres of influence that are the major contexts for children's development and learning: the family, the school, and the community. Time, experiences in families, and experiences in schools control the degree of overlap among the three. Students engage in activities that influence their school success in all three areas and are influenced by their peers, teachers, and families. Ultimately, the theory hypothesizes that students will learn more when home, school, and community work together.

Research conducted over the last three decades provides a persuasive argument for the critical role that families play in facilitating their children's educational success. Several comprehensive reviews of the research on parent involvement (Fan & Chen, 2001; Henderson & Berla, 1994; Henderson & Mapp, 2002; Jeynes as cited in Jeynes, 2005) document the benefits to students in schools, including improved motivation, homework completion, and academic performance; fewer absences; increased self confidence; and higher graduation rates and rates of postsecondary education.

The benefits to schools have also been documented. One benefit is that schools with strong home-school connections are likely to exhibit higher levels of trust than those without, resulting in better student morale and a more positive climate (Hoy, 2002), better teacher morale, and higher ratings of teachers by parents (Decker & Decker, 2003). Building trusting relationships within schools makes them more inviting places for parents. Parents who feel that they can trust the professionals who work with their child are more inclined to participate in their child's education. When they feel welcomed in their child's classroom and school, parents participate in more informal and open communication with professionals (Soodak & Erwin, 2000).

Families and professionals can benefit significantly from each other. Hallahan, Kauffman, and Pullen (2008) posited that parents and teachers have a "symbiotic relationship" in which both groups can benefit from each other. As we know, parents have a wealth of information about their child in terms of background information and medical history that may help understand child learning and behavior. Working together, parents and teachers can determine child interests, strengths, and needs that are helpful to planning and implementing effective academic and social instruction. Parents can follow up on teacher instruction by helping at home with assigned tasks and behavior plans. Teachers, on the other hand, can enable parents to become more actively involved in their child's education by providing information on school progress, including them in the teaching and reinforcing of social skills, and helping them to stay abreast of opportunities for their children.

A belief in sharing the responsibility for educating children is a characteristic of home-school partnerships, which emphasize collaborative problem solving and shared decision-making strategies to provide students with consistent, congruent messages about learning and behavior. Building relationships and finding ways to work together to promote the educational experiences and school successes of all students is essential. In home-school partnerships, both parents and teachers are valued for their contributions to child growth and development.

PRINCIPLES AND KEY FEATURES OF HOME-SCHOOL PARTNERSHIPS

Because families, schools, and communities are so different, no single model for establishing home-school partnerships exists. In fact, if anything is true, it is that one size does not fit all when it comes to planning and implementing home-school connections. Partnerships are more effective if they are site-specific in development (Kagan, 1984). That is, school personnel, in collaboration with family members, determine the elements of their home-school program. Smith and colleagues (2006) offered the following set of interrelated principles to guide educators work with families of children with disabilities to develop partnerships:

- *Develop a sense of community.* When families and professionals feel they are a part of a community, they are more committed to its success. A school that promotes community building is dedicated to an open, welcoming, and accepting environment.
- *Promote equality between family members and professionals.* Considering the wealth of information parents have about their child, they must be recognized for their important role in their child's education. To establish equality, it is important to recognize parents as knowledgeable resources and value them as key to their child's success.
- *Share responsibility and decision making.* Shared decision making assumes that academic and social outcomes result from the interaction of qualities that the child brings from home with the qualities of the school. As such, family members should participate in decision making with regard to all aspects of schooling (i.e., they are recruited to be members of school advisory groups and school governance, as well as to plan for their own child's education). The notion of shared responsibility for educational outcomes is at the heart of home-school partnerships.
- *Consider family culture.* It is critical to recognize, value, and affirm the strengths of families, especially when families are from culturally diverse backgrounds. Boethel (2003), in reviewing the literature on diversity and school-family connections,

found that regardless of ethnicity, culture, or income, most families have high expectations for their children, and many are involved in their child's school programs. However, the form of that involvement on the part of families of lower socioeconomic status and/or of ethnic minorities generally differs from that of white, middle-class families. In addition, economic stressors will impact the extent and type of involvement among low-income families.

- *Focus on collaboration.* Collaboration is fostered when each partner shares a common goal of student success. Epstein's (2001) perspective of overlapping spheres of influences showed that families, schools, and communities have a common mission around children's learning. This common mission compels them to work together to produce the best outcomes for children.

- *Protect the integrity of the family.* The family is seen as a whole unit that collectively demonstrates strength and cohesion at multiple levels. Recognition of the family as a unit is crucial. Note that each family differs, and the primary caregiver for each child may not be a parent.

- *Improve family members advocacy skills.* Involving parents as partners recognizes that they are advocates of education and key resources to improve their child's growth and development. Families empowered as advocates for quality education, for their child and for all children, can also be supportive of needed systems change in today's schools (Shaheen & Spencer, 2001).

Christenson (2002) suggested that there are four important features of home-school collaboration:

1. Recognize that both home and school are microsystems that are used to operating autonomously. Collaborating with schools or families will require a change of beliefs about responsibility for teaching and learning, as well as growth and development.

2. Home-school collaboration is not restricted to a specific area. It may concern a child-centered issue (e.g., behavior, academic learning) or systems-level issue (e.g., school policy).

3. Home-school collaboration is a preventive rather than a remedial activity. The purpose of home-school collaboration is to improve student success and prevent conflict and alienation.

4. While parent-teacher relationships are crucial to student successful outcomes, home-school collaboration is a broader concept. It includes the primary home contact person, who may be a parent, grandparent, or even a neighbor. Likewise, school partners may be teachers, administrators, or other support personnel that contribute to the student's success.

In their analysis of 80 studies of parental involvement, Henderson and Mapp (2002) found that many forms of family involvement positively affect outcomes both socially and academically for children. They concluded that four aspects of home-school partnerships were evident across all studies:

Programs that successfully connect with families and community invite involvement, are welcoming, and address specific parental and community needs.

Parent involvement programs that are effective in engaging diverse families recognize cultural and class differences, address needs, and build on strengths.

Effective connections embrace a philosophy of partnership where power is shared—the responsibility for children's educational development is a collaborative enterprise among parents, school staff, and community members.

Organized initiatives to build parent and community leadership aimed at improving low-performing schools are growing and leading to promising results in low-income urban areas and the rural South. (p. 1)

CHARACTERISTICS OF EFFECTIVE HOME-SCHOOL PARTNERSHIPS

Research on effective home-school partnerships suggests that they have six central characteristics: communication, commitment, equity, respect, trust, and competency (Blue-Banning, Summers, Frankland, Nelson, & Beegle, 2004; Smith et al., 2006; Turnbull et al., 2010). Each will be discussed.

Communication

Communication is the foundation for successful home-school partnerships. The methods of communication that teachers, administrators, and family members use take many forms. The most important aspect of communication to keep in mind is that it is a two-way process. Families and school professionals have the opportunity to give input and be heard on all matters related to child outcomes and school policy. Communication between home and school should be positive, understandable, and respectful. Effective methods for communication take into consideration the cultural and linguistic backgrounds, lifestyles, and work schedules of families and school staff. Communication content to and from families can include information about the child, information on resources available to support the child in school and home, as well as school and family events. Effective communication style includes speaking positively and listening to one's partner.

While communication between home and school can take many forms, parent-teacher conferences are a regular occurrence in most schools and can be an extremely effective way to share information. These conferences are most successful if they are well planned and positive. Even if the conference focus is on poor achievement or behavior, teachers who are diplomatic and include positive information about the child will find parents are more willing to work together to solve the problem. If teachers present the attitude that they want each child to succeed, parents will respond positively and actively participate in a plan to help the child improve.

Scheduling conferences is crucial to success. Making times available that meet the lifestyles and schedules of families will increase attendance. Offering to come to their homes may be the only way to ensure meetings with some families will take place because of limited resources and transportation. It is important that the family is open to a home visit; they should know you are coming, and you should be cautious to avoid making them feel uncomfortable. When allowed, home visits can be very helpful in building the relationship, including mutual trust and reciprocity, because families see that teachers are willing to be flexible and supportive (Allen, 2008).

There are a number of other methods of communication between home and school. Home-note programs have been utilized to communicate with parents as part of a behavior management system when help is needed to reinforce certain behaviors. These are most successful if parents and teachers have agreed philosophically about the behavior management approach (Hallahan et al., 2008). Journals that go back and forth between school and home can help keep families and teachers apprised of important events. They are particularly useful with children with severe disabilities when they are well organized and jargon-free and include appropriate space for commenting. Also, procedures for their use should be agreed upon by teachers, therapists, and parents (Hall, Wolfe, & Bollig, 2003). E-mail is yet another form of written communication between home and school. Homework hotlines and homework Web sites are also becoming available in many schools. Although computer technology offers new streams of communication, schools will need to determine the appropriateness of their use based on their availability to the families in the school area. Communication methods are limited only by the imagination. Each school and classroom should investigate and use the methods that are most useful to the partners.

Commitment

Commitment refers to all members of the partnership sharing a sense of confidence in their mutual loyalty to the child and the family and a belief in the importance of the goals set for the child's success. This commitment goes beyond the point of service compelled by law. In their research, Blue-Banning and colleagues (2004) found that family members looked for an attitude of commitment from professionals that indicated their work was more than "just a paycheck." Other terms used to describe professionals who are committed are *flexible*, *available*, and *accessible*. For example, school professionals may arrange their own schedules so that families are able to get in touch with them or arrange times other than the workday to hold conferences. When professionals are willing to look beyond themselves, family members will see them as committed and are more likely to work with them to improve their child's educational outcomes.

Equity, Respect, and Trust

These three concepts are closely related. The concept of equality in home-school partnerships assumes that all partners have the same capacity to influence decisions made with regard to the child. When equity is apparent in the partnership, then family members, as well as professionals, are recognized for their knowledge, skills, and expertise. In promoting equality in the relationship, teachers work to understand the knowledge that family members have of their children, particularly experiences and cultural influences that may account for children's development, learning, and behavior, while providing opportunities for sharing this information.

When respectful partnerships are in place, each partner judges all others to be valuable members. In communicating with one another, respect is demonstrated when teachers, family members, and students treat each other with dignity (Turnbull, Turnbull, & Wehmeyer, 2009). Families suggest that respectful teachers are courteous to them (Blue-Banning et al., 2004). The simple gesture of calling parents by their last names or asking permission to use their first names is an example many parents appreciate. Other ways to be respectful of family members are being on time for meetings, acknowledging the time parents are taking to attend a meeting, and recognizing the contributions family members make to the discussion as important.

Respectful partnerships also honor cultural diversity. A number of barriers may limit home-school partnerships with families from culturally and linguistically diverse backgrounds. These include language differences, a lack of understanding of the American public school system, miscommunications, and past negative experiences with schools. Two possible solutions for these issues are interpreters and liaisons (Parette & Petch-Hogan, 2000). Liaisons with the community can help to inform family members, as well as build trust between school personnel and families. The liaison should be someone respected and trusted by the community. Interpreters can facilitate communication between home and school. It is essential that interpreters be adequately trained to ensure that information is exchanged accurately, and ideally they should have knowledge of the local community.

Honoring cultural diversity also includes developing a deeper understanding of and sensitivity to family priorities, needs, and resources (Parette & Petch-Hogan, 2000). To do this, school professionals need to understand cultural norms related to social behavior, family values, and communication styles (Harry, 2008) yet to do so without overgeneralizing specific characteristics to all families with whom they work. Allen (2008) described several school settings in which teachers worked with family members to address cultural differences. Activities included reading and discussing published cultural memoirs (i.e., autobiographies or short stories) and gathering photographs and other cultural artifacts to share.

As mentioned previously, a trustful environment is a necessity if home-school partnerships are to be successful. When parents feel they are welcomed to the table in a respectful manner and that their input is valued, their participation will be strengthened. Family members identify trust with regards to schools in three ways: reliability, safety, and discretion (Blue-Banning et al., 2004). Reliability refers to knowing that you can depend on someone (i.e., they will do what they say they will). For example, school professionals are reliable if they are careful not to make promises they can't keep. All parents need to know that their children are safe at school, and parents want their children to be nurtured and cared for both physically and emotionally (Baker, 1997/2001; Blue-Banning et al.). Finally, discretion refers to parents being certain that school professionals can be trusted with confidential information. We have discussed the value of information that parents and other family members share about their child that can benefit plans for the child's learning and behavior. As we encourage families to share this information, we must assure them that it will be treated with discretion.

The families that Soodak and Erwin (2000) spoke with stressed the importance of building trusting relationships between school professionals and families. To these parents, trusting relationships resulted from interactions that were open and mutually respectful. Parents felt welcomed to the school through a variety of formal opportunities to participate and through informal interactions with school personnel. Continued efforts to build respectful and trusting relationships sustain connections that support student learning (Allen, 2008).

Competency

Competency refers to being highly qualified for one's professional role (Turnbull et al., 2009). Several researchers have found that family members are very aware of the skill level of their child's teacher and other school professionals (Baker, 1997/2001; Blue-Banning et al., 2004). They want school professionals to demonstrate knowledge of "best practices," to be able to individualize instruction, and to differentiate instruction. Both NCLB and IDEA state that teachers should have high expectations for all students and that outcomes are driven by high educational standards. Parents have this expectation as well. Competent teachers are also lifelong learners who strive to improve their skills and are always open to new knowledge and experience.

While school professionals maybe extremely competent in their roles as teachers, related service providers, and school administrators, they may not have adequate skill in collaboration and team building to develop effective partnerships with families. Investigations of teacher preparation programs indicate that education on collaboration is limited (Broussard, 2000; Hoover-Dempsey, Walker, Jones, & Reed, 2002). Therefore, it may be necessary to provide this training as part of the design and development of a home-school partnership. Training provided to both teachers and other school personnel together may foster effective collaboration (Whitbread, Bruder, Fleming, & Park, 2007).

The principles for and characteristics of effective home-school partnerships indicate the complex nature of what may seem to be a simple endeavor. For schools to establish and maintain effective home-school partnerships, they must be willing to invest the necessary time and energy. Remembering that there is no "one-size-fits-all" approach to partnerships, schools will identify what teachers, administrators, staff, and family members determine to be the strengths, interests, and needs of their community and design appropriate strategies to respond. Once the partnership is established, members must regularly assess its effects based on the desired outcomes. While this approach may not be easily accomplished, the evidence clearly indicates the results for students (i.e., improved academic and social outcomes) are worth it.

HOME-SCHOOL PARTNERSHIPS AND CHALLENGING BEHAVIOR

Recent attention to home-school partnerships has been noted in the literature on Positive Behavior Intervention and Support, particularly as applied at the schoolwide level. One example of a successful application of Schoolwide Positive Behavior Supports and home-school partnerships is Positive Behavioral Interventions and Supports New Hampshire (PBIS-NH; Muscott et al., 2008). The PBIS-NH project identified family-friendly schools as incorporating the following values, which include the essential characteristics of home-school partnerships:

Families are informed of school activities in a variety of ways.

Families have access to information about how they can support their child's learning.

Families have access to information about how they can be involved in supporting learning in school through volunteering and assisting.

Families know what resources are available and how to access those resources. (p. 11)

The schools participating in the PBIS-NH program used Epstein's (2002) framework for developing home-school partnerships. The program developed the following activities that included key components of that framework.

- *Parenting and learning at home.* Parents were taught PBIS strategies so they could create a home environment conducive to studying and completing homework.

- *Two-way communication strategies.* Several schools created a monthly newsletter that featured a write-in parent advice section. Periodic surveys assessing parents' feelings of connectedness were distributed, and follow-up was done with nonresponders and non-English speakers.
- *Volunteering and shared decision making.* A variety of opportunities for volunteering were provided, and family members were encouraged to participate in leadership teams and other committees making decisions that affected schools, teachers, administrators, families, and students.

The PBIS-NH project has taken the concepts of effective home-school partnerships and applied it to an effective program for preventing behavioral problems. PBS easily lends itself to the concept of home-school partnerships. Lucyshyn, Horner, Dunlap, Albin, and Ben (2002) defined *family partnerships* in PBS as

> the establishment of a truly respectful, trusting, caring, and reciprocal relationship in which interventionists and family members believe in each other's ability to make important contributions to the support process; share their knowledge and expertise; and mutually influence the selection goals, the design of behavior support plans, and the quality of family-practitioner interactions. (p. 12)

This definition underscores the importance of the relationship to the success of PBS. Practicing adherence to this definition will encourage partnerships and increase the likelihood of full participation by families.

Families of children at risk for or exhibiting challenging behaviors are likely to present with difficulties that may inhibit establishing a home-school partnership. Friend (2008) described several issues that may pose barriers to these families. One key issue is the likelihood of multiple negative interactions between teachers and parents. The teacher's frustration with the child may lead to a negative perception of the family. The resulting interactions between parent and teacher may be negative. Continued requests for parents to participate in a behavior plan in whose development they had no input increases parental frustration. When parents are unable to comply with the plan or their efforts are unsuccessful, the frustration of both the parent and teacher escalates. Negative interactions may carry over into parent conferences. Parents who are anxious about hearing of yet another problem related to their child may seem combative. Negative opinions are again formed about the family and the student.

It is important to recognize that families of children with challenging behaviors want their child to behave appropriately and will do anything to they can to help that child (Hallahan et al., 2008). Blaming parents for their child's behavior is nonproductive. They need supportive resources, which are best provided in concert with the family. It is essential that teachers make every effort to form partnerships with these families and work collaboratively to help their children.

These problems may be avoided if schools actively promote strong home-school partnerships. School professionals who view partnerships as important will see families for their strengths and their knowledge of their children. Families who feel that they are welcomed, respected, and supported are more likely to be involved with their children's education and in their children's schools. As we've discussed, the benefits of this involvement to the child and the school are enormous and worth the efforts of school professionals to establish.

An Illustration From Practice

Ms. Sams, the behavior resource teacher at Larchmont Elementary, is preparing for a 3:00 PM meeting with Doug Johns, a fourth grader; his parents; and Ms. Graham, his classroom teacher. Doug has recently been struggling in the classroom academically and socially. He seems unable to complete his work in class or his homework, and his grades are suffering. Ms. Graham has noticed that he is spending more time alone and argues with the boys who have been his friends since kindergarten. Ms. Sams is concerned about Doug and is anxious for the meeting.

Mrs. Graham has arranged for the meeting in the conference room. She is prepared for the meeting with her observation notes and examples of Doug's work. She has also spoken with the music teacher and PE coach. When she spoke with Doug's parents, they preferred to come to school for the meeting, and due to Mr. Johns's work schedule, immediately after school was best. Mrs. Graham agreed, and the meeting was scheduled.

Mr. and Mrs. Johns are driving to a meeting with their son's classroom teacher and the school's behavior resource teacher. They had noticed a change in Doug's behavior lately and that his grades have fallen slightly. They weren't surprised to get the call from Mrs. Graham and are hopeful that the meeting will be helpful for Doug. In preparing for the meeting, Mrs. Johns has made her own notes about Doug's behavior and has prepared a list of her concerns.

The parent-teacher conference is an extremely important method for sharing information and working collaboratively with parents to solve problems and promote student success. Larchmont is a small rural elementary school with 535 preschool through fifth-grade students, 75 percent of who qualify for free or reduced lunch. For Larchmont Elementary, located in a sparsely populated rural community, these meetings may be the only chance for teachers to have meaningful conversations with parents. The faculty and administration realize this and during the past few years have worked to improve the tone and outcomes of meetings with family members. Their goal is to conduct meetings in which family members and teachers felt respected and valued as members of a team and participate meaningfully and that both be willing to follow up with plans. Meetings are scheduled to meet parent timelines and locations. Teachers are prepared for meetings with information on the child, including notes on strengths as well as concerns. The staff developed checklists for both teachers and parents to use to prepare for conferences. They also developed guidelines for conducting the conference.

The meeting with Mr. and Mrs. Johns, Ms. Sams, and Mrs. Graham resulted in a plan to address Doug's needs. Mrs. Graham conducted the meeting and began with introductions. She then asked Mr. and Mrs. Johns to address their concerns. By asking them to talk about their child, Mrs. Graham was letting them know that what they have to say is important and that they are a primary source of information. Both felt comfortable discussing their concerns and offered insights into the problem. As Mrs. Graham and then Ms. Sams discussed their observations, the Johns interjected their own comments. Ms. Sams offered several ideas for assisting Doug. Together, Ms. Sams, Mrs. Graham, and the Johns talked through a plan and agreed on actions that each could take. They will monitor his progress through a journal that will travel between school and home. They agreed to give the plan four weeks and set a follow-up meeting date.

This conference was designed to succeed. The parents were included in all decisions, beginning with setting the time and place, and they were encouraged to add important information about their child. The conference ended in agreement on a solution. When teachers recognize and value family input, parent-teacher conferences are more likely to end like this one. When parents feel they have input in designing an intervention, they are also more likely to follow through at home. These parents left with the idea that they are partners.

References

Chapter 1

Association for Supervision and Curriculum Development. (2002). *ASCD education update*. Alexandria, VA: Author.

Dailey, D., & Zantal-Wiener, K. (2000). *Reforming high school learning: The effect of the standards movement on secondary students with disabilities*. Alexandria, VA: Center for Policy Research.

Johnson, J. (2003, November). What does the public say about accountability? *Educational Leadership, 61*(3), 39.

Jolivette, K., Stichter, J., & McCormick, K. (2002, January 1). Making choices—improving behavior—engaging in learning. *Teaching Exceptional Children, 34*(3), 24–30.

Kleinert, H. L., Green, P., Hurte, M., Clayton, J., & Oetinger, C. (2002). Creating and using meaningful alternate assessments. *Teaching Exceptional Children, 34*(4), 40–47.

Lamorey, S. (2002). The effects of culture on special education services: Evil eyes, prayer meetings, and IEPs. *Teaching Exceptional Children, 34*(5), 67–71.

McLaughlin, M. (2000). *Reform for EVERY learner: Teachers' views on standards and students with disabilities*. Alexandria, VA: Center for Policy Research.

McLesky, J., & Waldron, N. (2002). Inclusion and school change: Teacher perceptions regarding curricular and instructional adaptations. *Teacher Education and Special Education, 25*(1), 53.

Tomlinson, C. (2001). Grading for success. *Teaching Exceptional Children, 58*, 12–15.

U.S. Department of Education. (1998). *Twentieth annual report to Congress on the implementation of the Individuals with Disabilities Education Act*. Washington, DC: Author (Writers of the modules included OSEP personnel and staff from OSEP-funded research and technical assistance projects.). Available at http://www.ed.gov/offices/OSERS/OSEP/Research/OSEP98 AnlRpt/index.html

Wissick, C., & Gardner, E. (2000). Multimedia or not to multimedia? That is the question for students with learning disabilities. *Teaching Exceptional Children, 32*(4), 34–43.

Chapter 2

Allen, L. (2001). Courage is the letting go. On *Women's work* [CD]. Bellingham, WA: October Rose Productions.

Banks, J. A. (2003a). Educating global citizens in a diverse world. *New horizons for learning*. Retrieved March 24, 2010, from http://www.newhorizons.org/strategies/multicultural/banks2.htm

Battistich, V., Schaps, E., & Wilson, N. (2004). Effects of an elementary school intervention on students' connectedness to school and social adjustment during middle school. *The Journal of Primary Prevention, 24*(3), 243–262.

Blue, B. (1990). Courage. *On Starting small.* Harrisonville, NH: Black Socks Press. Available from http://www.bobblue.org/pages/prod_descrip/StartingSmall1.html

Osterman, K. E. (2000). Students' need for belonging in the school community. *Review of Educational Research, 70,* 323–367.

Perry, W., & Smith, G. (1992). What part of no [Recorded by Lorrie Morgan]. On *Watch me* [CD]. Nashville, TN: BNA Records.

Sapon-Shevin, M. (2007). *Widening the circle: The power of inclusive classrooms.* Boston: Beacon Press.

Wade, R. (2007). *Social studies for social justice: Teaching strategies for the elementary classroom.* New York: Teachers College Press.

Chapter 3

Caron, E. A., & McLaughlin, M. J. (2003). Indicators of "Beacons of Excellence" schools: Collaborative practices. *Journal of Educational and Psychological Consultation, 13*(4), 285–313.

Friend, M., & Cook, L. (1996). *Interactions: Collaboration skills for school professionals.* New York: Longman.

Mager, R. F. (1997). *Preparing instructional objectives: A critical tool in the development of effective instruction.* Atlanta, GA: Center for Effective Performance.

Chapter 4

Adelman, H. S., & Taylor, L. (1990). Intrinsic motivation and school misbehavior: Some intervention implications. *Journal of Learning Disabilities, 23,* 541–550.

Barkin, B., Gardner, E., Kass, L., & Polo, M. (1981). *Activities, ideas, definition, strategies (AIDS). Learning disabilities: A book of resources for the classroom teacher.* New Rochelle, NY: City School District of New Rochelle. (ERIC Document Reproduction Service No. ED214358)

Bellgrove, M. A., & Mattingley, J. B. (2008). Molecular genetics of attention. *Annals of the New York Academy of Sciences, 1129,* 200–212. Retrieved July 1, 2009, from Academic Search Premier database. (AN 32659556)

Bergert, S. (2000). *The warning signs of learning disabilities* (ERIC Digest E603). (ERIC Document Reproduction Service No. ED449633)

Blabock, J. W. (1982). Persistent auditory language deficits in adults with learning disabilities. *Journal of Learning Disabilities, 15,* 604–609.

Bloom, B. S. (Ed.). (1956). *Taxonomy of educational objectives: The classification of educational goals. Handbook 1: Cognitive domain.* New York: McKay.

Boden, C., & Brodeur, D. A. (1999). Visual processing of verbal and nonverbal stimuli in adolescents with reading disabilities. *Journal of Learning Disabilities, 32,* 58–71.

Boudah, D. J., & Weiss, M. P. (2002). *Learning disabilities overview: Update 2002* (ERIC Digest E624). (ERIC Document Reproduction Service No. ED462808)

Brown, A. I. (1975). The development of memory: Knowing, knowing about knowing, and knowing how to know. In W. H. Reece (Ed.), *Advances in child development and behavior* (Vol. 10, pp. 103–152). New York: Academic Press.

Brown, A. I. (1978). Knowing when, where, and how to remember: A problem of metacognition. In R. Glaser (Ed.), *Advances in instructional psychology.* Hillsdale, NJ: Erlbaum.

Brown, A. I. (1979). Metacognitive development and reading. In R. J. Spiro, B. Bruce, & W. R. Brewer (Eds.), *Theoretical issues in reading comprehension*. Hillsdale, NJ: Erlbaum.

Brown, A. L., & Palincsar, A. S. (1982). Inducing strategic learning from texts by means of informed self-control training. *Topics in Learning and Learning Disabilities, 2*, 1–17.

Cherkes-Julkowski, M., & Stolzenberg, J. (1991, October). *Reading comprehension, extended processing and attention dysfunction*. Paper presented at the meeting of the National Council on Learning Disabilities, Minneapolis, MN. (ERIC Document Reproduction Service No. ED340194)

Chiu, M. M., Chow, B. W-Y., & Mcbride-Chang, C. (2007). Universals and specifics in learning strategies: Explaining adolescent mathematics, science, and reading achievement across 34 countries. *Learning & Individual Differences, 17*(4), 344–365.

Cohen, L., Spruill, J., & Herns, V. (1982, April). *The relationship between language disorders, learning disabilities, verbal and performance IQ discrepancies and measures of language abilities*. Paper presented at the annual international convention of the Council for Exceptional Children, Houston, TX. (ERIC Document Reproduction Service No. ED223011)

D'Amico, A., & Passolunghi, M. C. (2009). Naming speed and effortful and automatic inhibition in children with arithmetic learning disabilities. *Learning & Individual Differences, 19*(2), 170–180.

Dev, P. C. (1998). Intrinsic motivation and the student with learning disabilities. *Journal of Research and Development in Education, 31*(2), 98–108.

Flavell, J. H. (1971). What is memory development the development of? *Human Development, 14*, 272–278.

Flavell, J. H. (1979). Metacognitive and cognitive monitoring: A new area of cognitive-developmental inquiry. *American Psychologist, 34*, 906–911.

Flavell, J. H. (1999). Cognitive development: Children's knowledge about the mind. *Annual Review of Psychology, 50*, 21–45.

Fontana, J. L., Scruggs, T., & Mastropieri, M. A. (2007). Mnemonic strategy instruction in inclusive secondary social studies classes. *Remedial & Special Education, 28*(6), 345–355. Retrieved from Professional Development Collection database. (AN 27616050)

Foss, J. M. (2001). *Nonverbal learning disability: How to recognize it and minimize its effects* (ERIC Digest E619). (ERIC Document Reproduction Service No. ED461238)

Fulk, B. M., Brigham, F. J., & Lohman, D. A. (1998). Motivation and self-regulation: A comparison of students with learning and behavior problems. *Remedial and Special Education, 19*, 300–309.

García, J.-N. & Fidalgo, R. (2008). Orchestration of writing processes and writing products: A comparison of sixth-grade students with and without learning disabilities. *Learning Disabilities—A Contemporary Journal, 6*(2), 77–98.

Gizer, I. R., Waldman, I. D., Abramowitz, A., Barr, C. L., Yu, F., Wigg, K. G., et al. (2008). Relations between multi-informant assessments of ADHD symptoms, DAT1, and DRD4. *Journal of Abnormal Psychology, 117*(4), 869–880.

Graves, A., Semmel, M., & Gerber, M. L. (1994). The effects of story prompts on the narrative production of students with and without learning disabilities. *Learning Disability Quarterly, 17*, 154–164.

Guyton, G. (1968, February). *Individual programming for children with learning disabilities as determined by screening, identification, and differential diagnosis*. Paper presented at the Association for Children with Learning Disabilities, Boston, MA. (ERIC Document Reproduction Service No. ED029756)

Hurst, D., & Smerdon, B. (Eds.). (2000a). Postsecondary students with disabilities: Enrollment, services, and persistence. *Education Statistics Quarterly, 2*(3), 55–58.

Hurst, D., & Smerdon, B. (2000b). *Post secondary students with disabilities: Enrollment, services, and persistence: Stats in brief.* Washington DC: National Center for Education Statistics. (ERIC Document Reproduction Service No. ED 444329)

Itier, R. J., & Batty, M. (2009). Neural bases of eye and gaze processing: The core of social cognition. *Neuroscience & Biobehavioral Reviews, 33*(6), 843–863.

Johnson, D., & Myklebust, H. R. (1967). *Learning disabilities: Educational principles and practices.* New York: Grune and Stratton.

Jordan, D. R. (2000). *Understanding and managing learning disabilities in adults.* Professional Practices in Adult Education and Human Resource Development Series. Melbourne, FL: Krieger.

Kavale, K. A. (1982). Meta-analysis of the relationship between visual perceptual skills and reading achievement. *Journal of Learning Disabilities, 15*(1), 42–51.

Kidd, J. W. (1970). The discriminatory repertoire—the basis of all learning. *Journal of Learning Disabilities, 3,* 530–533.

Klorman, R. (1991). Cognitive event-related potentials in attention deficit disorder. *Journal of Learning Disabilities, 24*(3), 130–140.

Kronick, D. (1978). An examination of psychosocial aspects of learning disabled adolescents. *Learning Disability Quarterly, 1*(4), 86–93.

Kruger, R. J., Kruger, J. J., Hugo, R., & Campbell, N. G. (2001). Relationship patterns between central auditory processing disorders and language disorders, learning disabilities, and sensory integration dysfunction. *Communication Disorders Quarterly, 22*(2), 87–98.

Lancaster, S., Mellard, D., & Hoffman, L. (2001). *Experiences of students with disabilities in selected community and technical colleges. The individual accommodations model: Accommodating students with disabilities in post-secondary settings.* (ERIC Document Reproduction Service No. ED452617)

Larson, K. A., & Gerber, M. M. (1987). Effects of social metacognitive training for enhancing overt behavior in learning disabled and low achieving delinquents. *Exceptional Children, 54,* 201–211.

Määtt, S., Nurmi, J.-E., & Stattin, H. (2007). Achievement orientations, school adjustment, and well-being: A longitudinal study. *Journal of Research on Adolescence, 17*(4), 789–812.

Malcolm, C. B., Polatajko, H. J., & Simons, J. (1990). A descriptive study of adults with suspected learning disabilities. *Journal of Learning Disabilities, 23,* 518–520.

Marshall, R. M., & Hynd, G. W. (1997). Academic achievement in ADHD subtypes. *Journal of Learning Disabilities, 30,* 635.

Mays, F., & Imel, S. (1982). *Adult learning disabilities. Overview* (ERIC Fact Sheet No. 9). (ERIC Document Reproduction Service No. ED237797)

McGlaughlin, S. M., Knoop, A. J., & Holliday, G. A. (2005). Differentiating students with mathematics difficulty in college: Mathematics disorders versus no diagnosis. *Learning Disability Quarterly, 28*(3), 223–232.

McLeskey, J. (1977, December). *Learning set acquisition by reading disabled and normal children.* Paper presented at the 27th annual meeting of the National Reading Conference, New Orleans, LA. (ERIC Document Reproduction Service No. ED151754)

McMillen, M. M., Kaufman, P., & Klein, S. (1997). *Dropout rates in the United States: 1995.* Washington, DC: U.S. Government Printing Office. (ERIC Document Reproduction Service No. ED410370)

McNamara, J. K. (1999). *Social information processing in students with and without learning disabilities.* (ERIC Document Reproduction Service No. ED436867)

Moffatt, C. W., et al. (1995, March). Discrimination of emotion, affective perspective-taking and empathy in individuals with mental retardation. *Education and Training in Mental Retardation and Developmental Disabilities, 30*(1), 76–85.

Most, T., & Greenbank, A. (2000). Auditory, visual, and auditory-visual perception of emotions by adolescents with and without learning disabilities and their relationship to social skills. *Learning Disabilities: Research & Practice, 15*, 171–178.

Murray, J., & Whittenberger, D. (1983). The aggressively, severely behavior disordered child. *Journal of Learning Disabilities, 16*, 76–80.

Newport, R., & Howarth, S. (2009). Social gaze cueing to auditory locations. *Quarterly Journal of Experimental Psychology, 62*(4), 625–634.

Okolo, C. M., & Bahr, C. M. (1995). Increasing achievement motivation of elementary school students with mild disabilities. *Intervention in School and Clinic, 30*(5), 279–286, 312. Retrieved December 21, 2002, from Professional Development Collection database.

Richards, G. P., Samuels, J., Ternure, J. E., & Ysseldyke, J. E. (1990). Sustained and selective attention in children with learning disabilities. *Journal of Learning Disabilities, 23*,129–136. Retrieved January 14, 2003, from Academic Search Premier database.

Rosen, C. L. (1968). An investigation of perceptual training and reading achievement in first grade [Abstract]. *American Journal of Optometry, 45*, 322–332. (ERIC Document Reproduction Service No. ED025400)

Salend, S. J., & Gajria, M. (1995). Increasing the homework completion states of students with mild disabilities. *Remedial and Special Education, 16*, 271–278. Retrieved January 4, 2003, from Academic Search Premier database.

Schiff, M. M., Kaufman, A. S., & Kaufman, N. L. (1981). Scatter analysis of WISC-R profiles for learning disabled children with superior intelligence. *Journal of Learning Disabilities, 14*(7), 400–404. Retrieved January 1, 2003, from the Professional Development Collection database.

Schiff, R., Bauminger, N., & Toledo, I. (2009). Analogical problem solving in children with verbal and nonverbal learning disabilities. *Journal of Learning Disabilities, 42* (1), 3–13.

Schweitzer, K., Zimmermann, P., & Koch, W. (2000). Sustained attention, intelligence, and the crucial role of perceptual processes. *Learning and Individual Differences, 12*(3), 271–287. Retrieved February 13, 2003, from the Professional Development Collection database.

Scime, M., & Norvilitis, J. M. (2006). Task performance and response to frustration in children with attention deficit hyperactivity disorder. *Psychology in the Schools, 43*(3), 377–386.

Scott, T. M., & Nelson, C. M. (1998). Confusion and failure in facilitating generalized social responding in the school setting: Sometimes 2 + 2 = 5. *Behavioral Disorders, 23*, 264–275.

Scruggs, T. E., & Mastropieri, M. A. (2007). Science learning in special education: The case for constructed versus instructed learning. *Exceptionality, 15*(2), 57–74.

Seligman, M. E. P. (1975). *Helplessness: On depression, development, and death.* San Francisco: W. H. Freeman.

Smith, D. D. (1981). *Teaching the learning disabled.* Englewood Cliffs, NJ: Prentice Hall.

Smith, S. W. (1992). Effects of a metacognitive strategy on aggressive acts and anger behavior of elementary and secondary-aged students. *Florida Educational Research Council Research Bulletin, 24*, 1–2. (ERIC Document Reproduction Service No. ED355687)

Somers, C. L., Owens, D., & Piliawsky, M. (2008). Individual and social factors related to urban African American adolescents' school performance. *High School Journal, 91*(3), 1–11.

Stanovich, K. E. (1993). Dysrationalia: A new specific learning disability. *Journal of Learning Disabilities, 26,* 501–515.

Steele, M. M. (2007). Teaching social studies to high school students with learning problems. *Social Studies, 98*(2), 59–63. Retrieved from Academic Search Complete database. (AN 25127305)

Sternberg, R. J. (1993). Would you rather take orders from Kirk or Spock? The relation between rational thinking and intelligence. *Journal of Learning Disabilities, 26,* 516–519. Retrieved December 23, 2002, from Academic Search Premier database.

Sternberg, R. J. (1994). What if the construct of dysrationalia were an example of itself? *Educational Researcher, 23*(4), 22–23.

Swanson, H. L. (2001). Research on interventions for adolescents with learning disabilities: A meta-analysis of outcomes related to higher order processing. *Elementary School Journal, 101,* 331–349.

Swanson, H. L., Xinhua, Z., & Jerman, O. (2009).Working memory, short-term memory, and reading disabilities. *Journal of Learning Disabilities, 42*(3), 260–287.

Toro, P. A., Weissberg, R. P., Guare, J., & Libenstein, N. L. (1990). A comparison of children with and without learning disabilities on social problem-solving skill, school behavior, and family background. *Journal of Learning Disabilities, 23,* 115–120. Retrieved December 28, 2002, from Academic Search Premier database.

Utzinger, J. (1982). *Logic for everyone. Alternative techniques for teaching logic to learning disabled students in the university. A part of the HELDS Project (Higher Education for Learning Disabled Students).* (ERIC Document Reproduction Service No. ED234549)

Valas, H. (2001). Learned helplessness and psychological adjustment II: Effects of learning disabilities and low achievement. *Scandinavian Journal of Educational Research, 45*(2), 101–114. Retrieved December 23, 2002, from Professional Development Collection database.

Wang, M. C. (1987). Toward achieving educational excellence for all students: Program design and instructional outcomes. *Remedial and Special Education, 8*(3), 25–34.

Wang, M. C., Haertel, G. D., & Walberg, H. J. (1993/1994). What helps students learn? *Educational Leadership, 51*(4), 74–79.

Ward-Lonergan, J. M., Liles, B. Z., & Anderson, A. M. (1998). Listening comprehension and recall abilities in adolescents with language-learning disabilities and without disabilities for social studies lectures. *Journal of Communication Disorders, 31*(1), 1–32.

Watson, B. U. (1991). Some relationships between intelligence and auditory discrimination. *Journal of Speech and Hearing Research, 3,* 621–627.

Wong, B. Y. L. (1985). Metacognition and learning disabilities. In T. J. Waller, D. Forrest-Pressley, & E. MacKinnon (Eds.), *Metacognition, cognition, and human performance* (pp. 137–180). New York: Academic Press.

Wright, C. M., & Conlon, E. G. (2009). Auditory and visual processing in children with dyslexia. *Developmental Neuropsychology, 34*(3), 330–335.

Zera, D. A., & Lucian, D. G. (2001). Self-organization and learning disabilities: A theoretical perspective for the interpretation and understanding of dysfunction. *Learning Disability Quarterly, 24,*107–118.

Chapter 5

Burstein, N., Sears, S., Wilcoxen, A., Cabello, B., & Spagna, M. (2004). Moving toward inclusive practices. *Remedial and Special Education, 25*, 104–117.

Harriott, W. (2004). Inclusion inservice: Content and training procedures across the United States. *Journal of Special Education Leadership, 17*, 91–102.

Karten, T. (2005). *Inclusion strategies that work!* Thousand Oaks, CA: Corwin.

Kozleski, E., Mainzer, R., & Deshler, D. (2000). Bright futures for exceptional learners: An agenda to achieve. Reston, VA: Council for Exceptional Children. (ERIC Document Reproduction Service No. ED451668)

Odom, S., Brantlinger, E., Gersten, R., Horner, R., Thompson, B., & Harris, K. (2005). Research in special education: Scientific methods and evidence-based practices. *Exceptional Children, 71*(2), 137–148.

Tang, G. (2003). *Math appeal.* New York: Scholastic.

Ward, R. (2005). Using children's literature to inspire K–8 preservice teachers' future mathematics pedagogy. *The Reading Teacher, 59*(2), 132–143.

Chapter 6

Brandt, R. 1987. On cooperation in schools: A conversation with David and Roger Johnson. *Educational Leadership 45*(3): 14–19.

Fishbaugh, M. S. E. 1997. *Models of collaboration.* Needham Heights, MA: Allyn & Bacon.

Friend, M., and L. Cook. 2002. *Interactions: Collaboration skills for school professionals.* 4th ed. Needham Heights, MA: Allyn & Bacon.

Hourcade, J., and J. Bauwens. 2002. *Cooperative teaching: Re-building and sharing the schoolhouse.* Austin, TX: PRO-ED.

Idol, L., A. Nevin, and P. Paolucci-Whitcomb. 1999. *Collaborative consultation.* 3rd ed. Austin, TX: PRO-ED.

Johnson, D. W., and R. T. Johnson. 1999. *Learning together and alone: Cooperative, competitive, and individualistic learning.* 5th ed. Needham Heights, MA: Allyn & Bacon.

Skrtic, T. 1991. *Behind special education: A critical analysis of professional culture and school organization.* Denver, CO: Love.

Villa, R., and J. Thousand. 2004. *Creating an inclusive school.* 2nd ed. Alexandria, VA: Association for Supervision and Curriculum Development.

Chapter 7

Albin, R. W., & Horner, R. H. (1988). Generalization with precision. In R.H. Horner, G. Dunlap, & R. L. Koegel (Eds.), *Generalization and maintenance: Lifestyle changes in applied settings* (pp. 99–120). Baltimore: Paul H. Brookes.

Carter, E. W., Cushing, L.S., & Kennedy, C.H. (2009). *Peer support strategies for improving all students' social lives and learning.* Baltimore: Paul H. Brookes.

Clayton, J., Burdge, M., Denham, A., Kleinert, H. L., & Kearns, J. (2006). A four-step process for accessing the general curriculum for students with significant cognitive disabilities. *TEACHING Exceptional Children, 38*(5), 20–27.

Colozzi, G. A., Ward, L. W., & Crotty, K. E. (2008). Comparison of simultaneous prompting procedure in 1:1 and small group instruction to teach play skills to preschool students with pervasive disabilities. *Education and Training in Developmental Disabilities, 43,* 226–248.

Cummings, K., Atkins, T., Allison, R., & Cole, C. (2008). Response to intervention: Investigating the new role of special educators. *TEACHING Exceptional Children, 40*(4), 24–31.

Danzer, G. A., de Alva, J. J. K., Krieger, L. S., Wilson, L. E., & Woloch, N. (2007). *The Americans.* Geneva, IL: McDougal Littell.

Downing, J. E. (2003). Accommodating motor and sensory impairments in inclusive settings. In D. L. Ryndak & S. Alper (Eds.), *Curriculum and instruction for students with significant disabilities in inclusive settings* (2nd ed., pp. 411–431). Boston: Allyn and Bacon.

Downing, J. E., Spencer, S., & Cavallaro, C. (2004). The development of an inclusive charter elementary school: Lessons learned. *Research and Practice for Persons With Severe Disabilities, 29,* 11–24.

Dymond, S. K., Renzaglia, A., Rosenstein, A., Chun, E. J., Banks, R. A., Niswander, V., et al. (2006). Using a participatory action research approach to create a universally designed inclusive high school science course: A case study. *Research and Practice for Persons With Severe Disabilities, 31,* 293–308.

Falkenstine, K. J., Collins, B. C., Schuster, J. W., & Kleinert, H. (2009). Presenting chained and discrete tasks as non-targeted information when teaching discrete academic skills through small group instruction. *Education and Training in Developmental Disabilities, 44*(1), 127–142.

Frank, D. V., Little, J. G., & Miller, S. (2009). *Science explorers: Chemical interaction.* Upper Saddle River, NJ: Prentice Hall.

Fuchs, D., Mock, D., Morgan, P. L., & Young, C. L. (2003). Responsiveness-to-intervention: Definitions, evidence, and implications for the learning disabilities construct. *Learning Disabilities Research and Practice, 18,* 157–171.

Greenwood, C. R., Arreaga-Mayer, C., Utley, C. A., Gavin, K. M., & Terry, B. J. (2001). Classwide peer tutoring learning management system: Applications with elementary-level English language learners. *Remedial and Special Education, 22,* 34–47.

Gresham, F. M., Reschly, D. J., Tilly, W. D., Fletcher, J., Burns, M., Prasse, D., et al. (2005). A response to intervention perspective. *The School Psychologist, 59,* 26–33.

Harcourt. (2007). *Social studies. The United States: Making a new nation.* Orlando, FL: Harcourt School Publishers.

Janney, R., & Snell, M. E. (2004). *Modifying schoolwork* (2nd ed.). Baltimore: Paul H. Brookes.

Ohtake, Y. (2003). Increasing class membership of students with severe disabilities through contribution to classmates' learning. *Research and Practice for Persons With Severe Disabilities, 28,* 228–231.

Parrish, P. R., & Stodden, R. A. (2009). Aligning assessment and instruction with state standards for children with significant disabilities. *TEACHING Exceptional Children, 41*(4), 22–32, 46–57.

Riley, G. A. (1995). Guidelines for devising a hierarchy when fading response prompts. *Education and Training in Mental Retardation and Developmental Disabilities, 30,* 231–242.

Rose, D., & Meyer, A. (2002). *Teaching every student in the digital age: Universal design for learning*. Alexandria, VA: Association for Supervision and Curriculum Development.

Rose, D., & Meyer, A. (Eds.). (2006). *A practical reader in universal design for learning*. Cambridge, MA: Harvard Education Press.

Ryndak, D. L., & Ward, T. (2003). Adapting environments, materials, and instruction to facilitate inclusion. In D. L. Ryndak & S. Alper (Eds.), *Curriculum and instruction for students with significant disabilities in inclusive settings* (2nd ed., pp. 382–411). Boston: Pearson.

Salisbury, C., Palombaro, M. M., & Hollowood, T. M. (1993). On the nature and change of an inclusive elementary school. *Journal of the Association for Persons With Severe Handicaps, 18*, 75–84.

Shumaker, J. B., Deshler, D. D., Bulgren, J. A., Davis, B., Lenz, B. K., & Grossen, B. (2002). Access of adolescents with disabilities to general education curriculum: Myth or reality? *Focus on Exceptional Children, 35*(3), 1–16.

Soukup, J. H., Wehmeyer, M. L., Bashinski, S. M., & Bovaird, J. (2007). Classroom variables and access to the general education curriculum of students with intellectual and developmental disabilities. *Exceptional Children, 74*, 101–120.

Spooner, F., Baker, J. N., Harris, A. A., Ahlgrim-Delzell, L., & Browder, D. M. (2007). Effects of training in universal design for learning on lesson plan development. *Remedial and Special Education, 28*, 108–116.

Szczepanski, M. (2004). Physical management in the classroom: Handling and positioning. In F. P. Orelove, D. Sobsey, & R. K. Silberman (Eds.), *Educating children with multiple disabilities: A collaborative approach* (4th ed., pp. 249–310). Baltimore: Paul H. Brookes.

U.S. Department of Education. (2005). *Alternate achievement standards for students with the most significant cognitive disabilities: Nonregulatory guidance*. Washington, DC: Office of Elementary and Secondary Education.

Wehmeyer, M. L., Lattin, D. L., Lapp-Rincker, G., & Agran, M. (2003). Access to the general curriculum of middle school students with mental retardation: An observational study. *Remedial and Special Education, 24*, 262–272.

Westling, D. L., & Fox, L. (2009). *Teaching students with severe disabilities* (4th ed.). Upper Saddle River, NJ: Merrill/Prentice Hall.

Chapter 8

Albus, D., Thurlow, M., Liu, K., & Bielinski, J. (2005). Reading test performance of English language learners using an English dictionary. *The Journal of Educational Research, 98*, 245–253.

Bouck, E. C., & Bouck, M. K. (2008). Does it add up? Calculators as accommodations for sixth grade students with disabilities. *Journal of Special Education Technology, 23*(2), 17–32.

Brinckerhoff, L. C., & Banerjee, M. (2007). Misconceptions regarding accommodations on high-stakes tests: Recommendations for preparing disability documentation for test takers with learning disabilities. *Learning Disabilities Research and Practice, 22*, 246–255.

Brookhart, S. M., & Nitko, A. J. (2008). *Assessment and grading in classrooms*. Columbus, OH: Merrill/Prentice Hall.

Byrnes, M. A. (2008). Educators' interpretations of ambiguous accommodations. *Remedial and Special Education, 29*(3), 306–315.

Clapper, A. T., Morse, A. B., Thurlow, M. L., & Thompson, S. J. (2006). *How to develop state guidelines for access assistants: Scribes, readers, and sign language interpreters.* Minneapolis: University of Minnesota, National Center on Educational Outcomes.

Cohen, A. S., Gregg, N., & Deng, M. (2005). The role of extended time and item content on a high-stakes mathematics test. *Learning Disabilities Research and Practice, 20,* 225–233.

Cox, M. L., Herner, J. G., Demczyk, M. J., & Nieberding, J. J. (2006). Provision of testing accommodations for students with disabilities on statewide assessments: Statistical links with participation and discipline rates. *Remedial and Special Education, 27,* 346–354.

Edgemon, E. A., Jablonski, B. R., & Lloyd, J. W. (2006). Large-scale assessments: A teacher's guide to making decisions about accommodations. *Teaching Exceptional Children, 38*(3), 6–11.

Elbaum, B. (2007). Effects of an oral testing accommodation on the mathematics performance of secondary students with and without learning disabilities. *Journal of Special Education, 40,* 218–229.

Elliott, J. L., & Thurlow, M. L. (2006). *Improving test performance of students with disabilities . . . on district and state assessments* (2nd ed.). Thousand Oaks, CA: Corwin.

Elliott, S. N., Kratochwill, T. R., & Schulte, T. R. (1998). The assessment accommodation checklist. *Teaching Exceptional Children, 31*(2), 10–14.

Elliott, S. N., & Marquart, A. (2004). Extended time as a testing accommodation: Its effects and perceived consequences. *Exceptional Children, 70,* 349–367.

Fuchs, L. S., & Fuchs, D. (2001). Helping teachers formulate sound test accommodation decisions for students with learning disabilities. *Learning Disabilities Research & Practice, 16,* 174–181.

Gajria, M., Giek, K., Hemrick, M., & Salend, S. J. (1992, April). *Teacher acceptability of testing modifications for mainstreamed students.* Paper presented at the meeting of the Council for Exceptional Children, Baltimore, MD.

Herrera, S. G., Murry, K. G., & Cabral, R. M. (2007). *Assessment accommodations for classroom teachers of culturally and linguistically diverse students.* Boston: Allyn & Bacon.

Ketterlin-Geller, L. R., Alonzo, J., Braun-Monegan, J., & Tindal, G. (2007). Recommendations for accommodations: Implications of (in)consistency. *Remedial and Special Education, 28,* 194–206.

MacArthur, C. A., & Cavalier, A. R. (2004). Dictation and speech recognition technology as test accommodations. *Exceptional Children, 71,* 43–58.

Michaelson, L., & Sweet, M. (2008). Team-based learning. *NEA Higher Education Advocate, 25*(6), 5–8.

Pomplun, M. (1996). Cooperative groups: Alternate assessment for students with disabilities? *Journal of Special Education, 30*(1), 1–17.

Salend, S. J. (2008). *Creating inclusive classrooms: Effective and reflective practices* (6th ed.). Columbus, OH: Merrill/Prentice Hall.

Salend, S. J., & Garrick Duhaney, L. M. (2002). Grading students in inclusive settings. *Teaching Exceptional Children, 34*(3), 8–15.

Stern, J., & Avigliano, J. (2008, November). *Differentiated team teaching.* Presentation at the State University of New York at New Paltz.

Towles-Reeves, E., Kleinert, A., & Muhomba, M. (2009). Alternate assessment: Have we learned anything new? *Exceptional Children, 75*(2), 233–252.

Chapter 9

Allen, J. (2008). Family partnerships that count. *Educational Leadership, 66*(1), 22–27.

Baker, A. J. L. (2001). Improving parent involvement programs and practice: A qualitative study of parent perceptions. In S. Redding & L. G. Thomas (Eds.), *The community of the school* (pp. 127–154). Lincoln, IL: Academic Development Institute. (Originally published in 1997, *School Community Journal, 7*(1), 9–35.) Retrieved October 28, 2009, from http://www.adi.org/journal/cots/2001 SCJBook.pdf

Blue-Banning, M., Summers, J. A., Frankland, C., Nelson, L. G. & Beegle, G. (2004). Dimensions of family partnerships: Constructive guidelines for collaboration. *Exceptional Children, 70,* 167–184.

Boethel, M. (Ed.). (2003). *Diversity: School, family, & community connections* (Annual synthesis 2003). Austin, TX: National Center for Family & Community Connections with Schools. Southwest Educational Development Laboratory. Retrieved October 28, 2009, from http://www.sedl.org/connections/research -syntheses.html

Broussard, A. C. (2000). Preparing teachers to work with families: A national survey of teacher education programs. *Equity and Excellence in Education, 33,* 41–49.

Christenson, S. L. (2002). *Supporting home-school collaboration.* Retrieved October 28, 2009, from the Children, Youth, and Family Consortium website: http:// www.cyfc.umn.edu/schoolage/resources/supporting.html

Decker, L. E., & Decker, V. A. (2003). *Home, school, and community partnerships.* Lanham, MD: Scarecrow Press.

Education for All Handicapped Children Act of 1975 (Public Law 94-142), 20 U.S.C. § 1411–1420.

Epstein, J. L. (2001). *School, family, and community partnerships: Preparing educators and improving schools.* Boulder, CO: Westview Press.

Epstein, J. L. (2002). *School, family, and community partnerships: Your handbook for action.* Thousand Oaks, CA: Corwin.

Fan, X. T., & Chen, M. (2001). Parental involvement and students' academic achievement: A meta-analysis. *Educational Psychology Review, 13,* 1–22.

Friend, M. (2008). *Special education: Contemporary perspectives for school professionals.* Boston: Pearson.

Hall, T. E., Wolfe, P. S., & Bollig, A. A. (2003). The home-to-school notebook: An effective communication strategy for students with severe disabilities. *Teaching Exceptional Children, 36*(2), 68–73.

Hallahan, D. P., Kauffman, J. M., & Pullen, P. C. (2008). *Exceptional learners: An introduction to special education* (11th ed.). Boston: Allyn & Bacon.

Harry, B. (2008). Family-professional collaboration with culturally and linguistically diverse families: Ideal vs. reality. *Exceptional Children, 72*(3), 372–388.

Henderson, A., & Berla, N. (Eds.). (1994). *A new generation of evidence: The family is critical to student achievement.* Washington, DC: Center for Law and Education.

Henderson, A. T., & Mapp, K. I. (2002). *A new wave of evidence: The impact of school, family, and community connections on student achievement* [Key Findings Abstract]. Austin, TX: Southwest Educational Development Laboratory. Retrieved October 28, 2009, from http://www.sedl.org/connections/resources/Keyfindings-reference.pdf

Hoover-Dempsey, K. V., Walker, J. M., Jones, K. P., & Reed, R. P. (2002). Teachers Involving Parents (TIP): An in-service teacher education program for enhancing parental involvement. *Teaching and Teacher Education, 18*(7), 843–867

Hoy, W. K. (2002). Faculty trust: A key to student achievement. Journal of Public *School Relations, 23*, 88–103.

Individuals with Disabilities Education Act (IDEA) of 1997, 20 U.S.C. § 1400 *et seq.*

Jeynes, W. H. (2005). *Parental involvement and student achievement: A meta-analysis* (Family Involvement Research Digest). Cambridge, MA: Harvard Family Research Project. Retrieved October 28, 2009, from http://www.hfrp.org/family-involvement/publications-resources/parental-involvement-and-student-achievement-a-meta-analysis

Kagan, S. L. (1984). *Parent involvement research: A field in search of itself.* Boston: Institute for Responsive Education.

Lucyshyn, J. M., Horner, R. H., Dunlap, G., Albin, R.W., & Ben, K. R. (2002). Positive behavior support with families. In J. M. Lucyshyn, G. Dunlap, & R. W. Albin (Eds.), *Families and positive behavior support: Addressing problem behavior in family contexts* (pp. 3–43). Baltimore, MD: Brookes.

Muscott, H. S., Szczesiui, S., Berk, B., Staub, K., Hoover, J., & Perry-Chisholm, P. (2008). Creating home-school partnerships by engaging families in school-wide positive behavior supports. *Teaching Exceptional Children, 40*(6), 6–14.

No Child Left Behind Act of 2001 (NCLB), 20 U.S.C. § 6301 *et seq.*

Parette, H. P., & Petch-Hogan, B. (2000). Approaching families: Facilitating culturally/linguistically diverse family involvement. *Teaching Exceptional Children, 33*(2), 4–10.

Shaheen, J. A. C., & Spencer, C. C. (2001). *Take charge! Advocating for your child's education.* Albany, NY: Delmar.

Smith, T. E. G., Gartin, B. C., Murdick, N. L., & Hilton, A. (2006). *Families and children with special needs: Professional and family partnerships.* Upper Saddle River, NJ: Pearson Merrill.

Soodak, L. C., & Erwin, E. J. (2000). Valued member or tolerated participant: Parents' experiences in inclusive early childhood settings. *The Journal of the Association for Persons with Severe Handicaps, 25*, 29–44.

Trivette, C. M., Dunst, C. J., Boyd, K., & Hamby, D. W. (1995). Family-oriented program models, help giving practices and parental control appraisals. *Exceptional Children, 62*, 237–248.

Turnbull, A. P., Turnbull, R., Erwin, E., & Soodak, L. (2006). *Families, professionals, and exceptionality: Positive outcomes through partnerships and trust.* Upper Saddle River, NJ: Merrill/Prentice Hall.

Turnbull, A., Turnbull, R., & Wehmeyer, M. L. (2009). *Exceptional lives: Special education in today's schools* (6th ed.). Upper Saddle River, NJ: Merrill/Prentice Hall.

Whitbread, K. M., Bruder, M. B., Fleming, G., & Park, H. J. (2007). Collaboration in special education: Parent-professional training. *Teaching Exceptional Children, 35*, 6–14.

CORWIN
A SAGE Company

The Corwin logo—a raven striding across an open book—represents the union of courage and learning. Corwin is committed to improving education for all learners by publishing books and other professional development resources for those serving the field of PreK–12 education. By providing practical, hands-on materials, Corwin continues to carry out the promise of its motto: **"Helping Educators Do Their Work Better."**